THE
GARDENER'S
GUIDE
TO BRITAIN

THE GARDENER'S GUIDE

TO BRITAIN

PATRICK TAYLOR

A personal selection of the best gardens,
nurseries and specialist plant suppliers.

PAVILION

DEDICATION
For Laura, with much love

First published 1992 by
PAVILION BOOKS LIMITED
26 Upper Ground, London SE1 9PD

Reprinted 1993, 1994 and 1995

Text copyright © 1995 Patrick Taylor

Illustrations © Open Books Publishing Ltd

This book was devised and produced by
Open Books Publishing Ltd, Beaumont House,
Wells BA5 2LD, Somerset, UK

Designer: Andrew Barron

Maps: John Gilkes

Computer Consultant: Mike Mepham

A CIP catalogue record for this book is available from the
British Library

ISBN: 1-85793-509-8

Printed and Bound in Hong Kong by
Mandarin Offset

CONTENTS

INTRODUCTION & ACKNOWLEDGEMENTS

THIS is the fourth edition of *The Gardener's Guide to Britain*. All details of every place in the book have been checked and, where necessary, revised. This, of course, includes opening times, telephone numbers and other practicalities of this sort. In addition I have noted any major changes in the gardens and described shifts of direction in the nurseries. In the case of one or two places, a change of ownership or a radical alteration of opening policy was under way when we were in the process of checking entries. With the agreement of the owners I have included them in the *Guide* as open by appointment only.

I should like to spell out once again the principles that lie behind the book. It describes, region by region, places of special interest to gardeners that are open regularly to the public. Uniquely, it includes nurseries and shops for pots and ornaments, as well as gardens of every kind. It is a *personal* choice but occasionally I have included some historic garden, not much to my taste, because its renown has conferred upon it almost holy status and it cannot be ignored. My own taste is fairly wide-ranging but I do have a predilection for the wild and woolly (such as Hackfall Wood or Wolterton Park) and for such exquisite oddities as The Pineapple or The Gnome Reserve.

Opening times, and other practical details, have been checked to the very last moment. But these may change and it is always worth checking by phone before setting out on a long special journey. Dates shown are inclusive – Mar to Sept means from the 1st March to the 30th September. One or two places had not fixed their opening times when we went to press. I have left these in, giving the phone number so that visits can be made. Most gardens will not welcome you less than 45 minutes before closing time. I have indicated those places where the house is also open but I do not give opening times for it. While it is often possible, by prior appointment, to

Illustration opposite: Spring at Heligan

make visits at other times than those shown, it is absolutely essential to give plenty of notice. It is not wise to assume that you can just turn up – no garden welcomes last minute intrusions.

Many of the best nurseries are very small and the proprietor has from time to time to desert his or her post. For these, it is especially important to check by phone beforehand. Some of the nurseries produce catalogues, many of which are precious reference books. I have included the price of them where appropriate.

I should like to thank The National Trust, and The National Trust for Scotland, both of which gave me much vital help. Private owners have also been extremely helpful and I am truly grateful to them. My wife Caroline has become an even more essential contributor than before and I am very deeply in her debt. The designer, Andrew Barron of Andrew Barron and Collis Clements Associates, has continued to weave his magic spell over the appearance of the book, for which I thank him most warmly.

Colin Webb and his colleagues at Pavilion Books have been the ideal publishers – most grateful thanks to them for all their friendly advice and help.

Patrick Taylor
Wells, Somerset

SOUTH-EAST ENGLAND

Kent
London
Surrey
Sussex

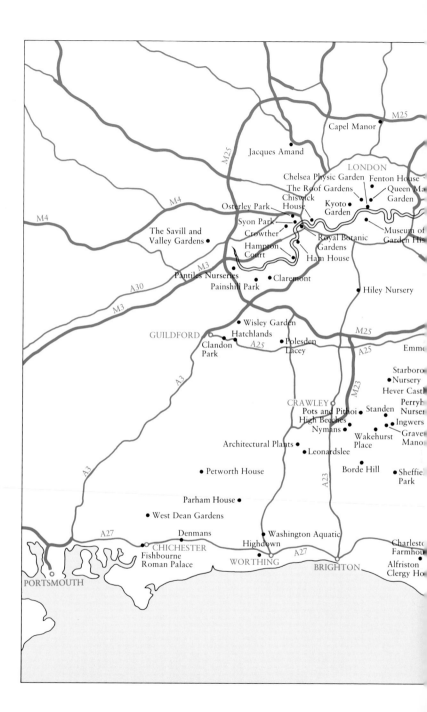

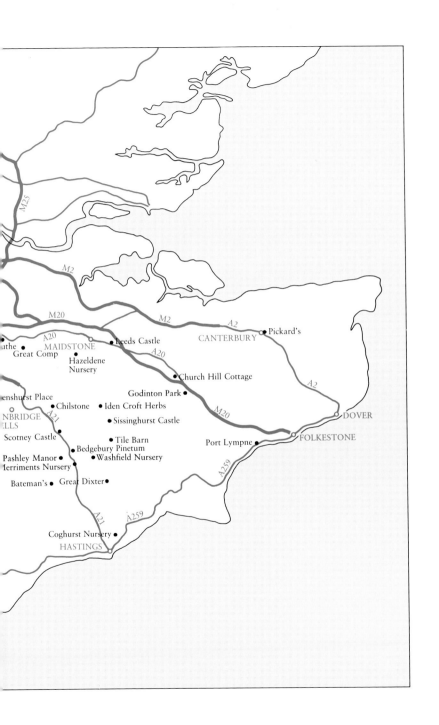

ALFRISTON CLERGY HOUSE

East Sussex

The Tye, Alfriston,
Polegate BN26 5TL
4m NE of Seaford by
B2108
Tel: 01323 870001

Owner:
The National Trust

Open: Apr to Oct, daily
10.30-5 or sunset if earlier.
1/2 acre. House open

ALTHOUGH THE garden surrounding this beautiful
medieval hall house is quite small it has all sorts
of virtues and many ideas for owners of gardens with
limited space. It has a wide range of different styles –
from brick-edged borders of cottage-garden
exuberance to a charmingly austere parterre of
standard box trees clipped into umbrellas and
underplanted with pinks. A herb garden has square
beds with low hedges of santolina and there is a
proper kitchen garden. A trickling stream runs along
one side of the garden and beyond there are views of
the countryside and the downs.

JACQUES AMAND LTD

Middlesex

The Nurseries, 146 Clamp
Hill, Stanmore HA7 3JS
NW of London off the
Uxbridge Road (A410)
Tel: 0181 954 8138

Open: Mon to Fri 9–5, Sat
9–4, Sun 9–1.30 (closed Sun
in Dec and Jan)

JACQUES AMAND specialises in bulbs of which he
sells one of the best selections in the country, and
regularly wins medals at RHS shows and elsewhere.
Although he also carries a few shrubs such as dwarf
rhododendrons and some herbaceous perennials,
especially those that are suitable for woodland
gardens, like *Jeffersonia diphylla* and *Mertensia
virginica*, it is the bulbs that are the great glory of the
place – very many alliums, fritillaries, lilies and
narcissi are stocked, and less usual plants such as
trilliums of which an exceptional range is listed. Well

illustrated complimentary catalogues, full of useful advice on cultivation, are produced in spring and autumn from which orders by post may be made. There is a special spring display area.

ARCHITECTURAL PLANTS
West Sussex

Cooks Farm, Nuthurst,
Horsham RH13 6LH
2m S of Horsham by A281
and minor roads
Tel: 01403 891772

Open: Mon to Sat 9–5

ARCHITECTURAL PLANTS has a completely distinctive house style. It sells plants that have strong architectural shapes and contribute to the structure of the garden. Angus White, the founder, described his garden in winter as being as fascinating to look at as 'a wet breeze block'; he wanted to find exotic, preferably evergreen plants to give winter liveliness. This nursery is his answer. His elegant list (free) is colour coded – green means that a plant is perfectly hardy, orange that a plant will survive in the right site in the southern counties, and red that a plant will survive only on the Atlantic coast or the privileged islands. The list is full of rarities – like *Neolitsia glauca* ('with bronze bunny's ears') or the Mexican strawberry tree (*Arbutus glandulosa*) – and packed with information. A mail order service is provided but it is much better to go to Cooks Farm and see the exotics in splendid action.

BATEMAN'S
East Sussex

Burwash,
Etchingham TN19 7DS
1/2 m S of Burwash by
A265
Tel: 01435 882302

Owner:
The National Trust

Open: Apr to Oct, daily
except Thur and Fri (open
Good Fri) 11–5.
10 acres. House open

RUDYARD KIPLING lived here, in the handsome early 17th-century house, from 1902 to 1936 and himself designed many of the existing features of the elegant garden. The site is flat but it is animated by attractive decorative ingredients and a strongly designed layout. Above the house a beautiful tunnel of pears and clematis trained over broad arches is underplanted with bergenias, spring bulbs, geraniums and Corsican hellebores. A path leads down one side of the house and occasional 'windows' cut in a yew hedge give glimpses of the country beyond. In the formal garden a curved seat in a bower of clipped yew overlooks a long rectangular pool. At the end of the pool there is a rose garden with flagged paths and beds of floribunda roses, and to one side of it a shady double pleached lime walk. The whole place has the air of the quintessential English garden of the Edwardian period; the sort of thing dreamed of by homesick men in Poona.

BEDGEBURY NATIONAL PINETUM
Kent

Illustration: The cones of Pinus koreana

nr Goudhurst, TN17 2SL
4 1/2 m S of Goudhurst by
B2079
Tel: 01580 211044

Owner:
The Forestry Commission

Open: Daily 10–dusk.
160 acres

Bedgebury Pinetum lies in a splendid site in a broad and deep valley. An ornamental lake at the bottom provides the right conditions for moisture-loving plants such as swamp cypresses, of which there are some handsome specimens, and on the slopes of the valley conifers are grouped either by kind – cypressess, junipers, spruces and so on – or by place of origin – the Chinese glade, the American glade or the Japanese glade. Conifers are obviously the main meal here but the menu is varied with some deciduous trees and many rhododendrons. The appearance of evergreens varies subtly through the growing year – the changing colour of foliage and fruit – and a visit is rewarding in any season. At the visitors' centre there is a marvellous display of different cones. Bedgebury holds National Collections of junipers, of Lawson cypress cultivars and of yews. In the autumn an added interest is the outstanding range of mushrooms that flourishes here.

BORDE HILL

West Sussex

Haywards Heath
RH16 1XP
1 1/2m N of Haywards
Heath by minor roads
Tel: 01444 450326

Owner:
Borde Hill Gardens Ltd

Open: Apr to Oct, daily
10–6. 40 acres

BORDE HILL is famous for trees and shrubs but near the house there are handsome flower gardens and formal planting: a pair of ebullient borders leads towards the house and, on the west terrace, a mysterious marble statue of a veiled lady emerges from clumps of euphorbia. That is all very decorative but the serious matter at Borde Hill is the splendid collection of ornamental woody plants. It was started in 1892 by Colonel Stephenson Clarke who was one of the sponsors of the great plant-hunting expeditions to the Chinese Himalayas between the wars. Thus, the garden is wonderfully rich in magnolias and rhododendrons (particularly species) which relish the light, slightly acid soil. But the collection is wide-ranging and there are also very good conifers in Warren Wood and rare deciduous trees, particularly American species, in Little Bentley Wood. The agreeably undulating site makes it a most attractive place in which to admire some marvellous plants.

CAPEL MANOR

Middlesex

DISPLAY GARDENS such as this can be both entertaining and instructive. On this substantial site surrounding the 18th-century manor house are many different thematic and demonstration gardens.

Bullsmoor Lane,
Enfield EN1 4RQ
14m N of Central London
by A10. Off M25 by
Jnct 25
Tel: 01992 763849

Owner: Capel Manor
Horticultural and
Environmental Centre

Open: Daily 10–5.30 (last
ticket 4.30, dusk in winter).
30 acres

A series of historical gardens includes a Tudor-style knot, a formal 17th-century garden and a recently planted prickly maze of holly taken from William Nesfield's design for the great exhibition in 1851. A garden for the physically disabled is full of ideas and a 'Sensory Garden' rich with the scent of herbs and the sounds of water is designed for the visually impaired. Demonstration gardens – woodland, water and courtyard – give ideas for design and planting. Recently opened are a beautifully laid out Japanese garden displaying all the essential features of that tradition of gardening; and a wildlife garden. Capel Manor is a satisfying mixture of both useful practical information and inspiration.

CHARLESTON FARMHOUSE
East Sussex

nr Firle, Lewes BN8 6LL
6m E of Lewes by A27
Tel: 01323 811265 (visitors)
01323 811626
(administration)

Owner:
The Charleston Trust

Open: Apr to Oct, Wed to
Sun and Bank Hol Mon
2–6 (12 Jul to 3 Sept 11–6);
last admission 5pm. 1 acre.
House open

CHARLESTON FARMHOUSE may fairly be described as the country seat of the Bloomsbury set. Vanessa and Clive Bell, and Duncan Grant, lived here, and the whole place, now most sympathetically restored, is redolent of Bloomsbury. In the walled garden, with gravel paths and narrow borders, the planting is cheerfully colourful – the horticultural equivalent of Omega workshop textiles. Old apple trees erupt from borders and a long box hedge has been clipped into undulating waves. Everywhere there are decorative touches – a pottery mask overlooking a little pool, mosaics of broken china (Bloomsbury and older) on a terrace, amusing busts dotted along a wall. Outside the walled garden, by a wild orchard, Ophelia floats on the edge of a pool and Venus lurks in a grove of cow parsley. All this gives a vivid picture of one of the most attractive aspects of Bloomsbury life.

CHELSEA PHYSIC GARDEN
London

Illustration opposite: Venus
among cow parsley at
Charleston Farmhouse

A 4-ACRE WALLED GARDEN – with full Secret Garden character – in the middle of London is a marvel. Founded as a garden of medicinal herbs in 1673 it became, especially under the directorship of Philip Miller in the 18th century, an important botanic

66 Royal Hospital Road,
SW3 4HS
Tube: Sloane Square
Tel: 0171 352 5646

Owner: Trustees of Chelsea
Physic Garden

Open: Apr to Oct, Sun 2–6
and Wed 2–5; also during
Chelsea Flower Show week
and Chelsea Festival week.
4 acres

garden. It still possesses a large collection of herbs,
a range of 'order' beds and a research area. But
there are magnificent trees – a superb *Koelreuteria
paniculata*, gnarled like an oak and probably the
oldest in Britain, a splendid olive tree (which in fine
years produces big crops) and all sorts of other
tender things relishing the protection of the old walls.
The garden holds the National Collection of cistus
and has some good plants for sale.

CHILSTONE GARDEN ORNAMENTS
Kent

Sprivers,
Lamberhurst Road,
Horsmonden TN12 8DR
On the southern edge of
Horsmonden village
Tel: 01892 723266

Open: Mon to Fri, 9–5,
Sun 10–4.30

CHILSTONE make high-quality composition stone
garden ornaments and architectural pieces, many
meticulous copies of fine originals. At Sprivers, an
elegant mid 18th-century house, urns, statues and
temples may be seen in the context of yew hedges,
distant vistas and herbaceous borders. In the display
garden is arranged a lovely profusion of the stock –
colonnades, sprinkling fountains, impassive sphinxes,
stately urns and the busts of emperors.

CHISWICK HOUSE
London

Burlington Lane,
Chiswick W4 2RP
4m SW of Central London
by A4 and A316
Tel: 0181 742 1225

Owner: London Borough
of Hounslow

Open: Daily 7.30–dusk.
62 acres. House open

LORD BURLINGTON built Chiswick House as a
pleasure dome in 1723-9 and surrounded it with
appropriate gardens. The house itself, domed and
portico'd, dominates the formal garden with its

avenue of cypresses interspersed with grand urns. To one side, slightly hidden, a circular sunken pool is surrounded by orange trees in pots and overlooked by a temple. At a little distance from the house a Victorian garden has a dazzling conservatory and a parterre of arabesques of clipped box, lush bedding schemes and an avenue of mop-headed acacias.

CHURCH HILL COTTAGE GARDENS

Kent

Charing Heath, Ashford
TN27 0BU
8m NW of Ashford by A20
Tel: 01233 712522

Open: Feb to Nov, Tue to Sun (and Bank Hol Mon) 10–5

AN ATTRACTIVE development in recent years is that of the small nursery alongside the owners' private garden where the plants can be seen in cultivation. The nursery here specialises in herbaceous perennials with excellent collections of penstemons, named varieties of pinks, herbaceous sages, unusual verbenas and violas. The garden next door to the nursery permits the distinctive virtues of these and other plants to be seen and savoured. A winding stream is edged with waterside plants, and herbaceous beds are given an occasional note of emphasis by some well-placed ornamental tree – a golden acacia or a variegated maple, for example. An immense number of plants is grown, some of them very unfamiliar.

CLANDON PARK
Surrey

West Clandon GU4 7RQ
3m E of Guildford off A25
Tel: 01483 222482

Owner:
The National Trust

Open: Apr to 29 Oct, daily
except Thur and Fri (open
Good Fri) 1.30–5.30; Bank
Hol Mon 11–5.30. 8 acres.

THE MANSION at Clandon Park, built of brick and
stone in about 1730, dominates the garden. Under
its south façade a neat parterre of box hedges,
topiary box cones and summer bedding is flanked by
raised hedges of clipped hornbeam. Across the lawn,
a damp and ferny flint grotto houses a cluster of
shivering nymphs, almost certainly dating from the
late 18th-century landscaping of the garden. To one
side of this, in the shade of an immense oak, there is
a charming oddity, a carved and painted Maori house
brought here in the 1890s by the 4th Earl of Onslow
who had served as Governor of New Zealand.
Half-way up the drive, rather tucked away and easy
to miss, is a Dutch garden enclosed in tall yew
hedges and laid out in a geometric pattern of hedges
of box, lavender and variegated euonymus, with
pyramids of white roses rising above.

CLAREMONT LANDSCAPE
GARDEN
Surrey

Portsmouth Road,
Esher KT10 9JG
14m SW of Central London
by A3
Tel: 01372 469421

Owner:
The National Trust

Open: Jan to Mar, daily
except Mon 10–5 (or sunset
if earlier); Apr to Oct,
Mon to Fri 10–6, Sat, Sun
and Bank Hol Mon 10–7
(12–16 Jul closes 4); Nov
to March, daily except
Mon 10–5 or sunset if
earlier (closed 25 Dec, 1
Jan). 49 acres

THE LANDSCAPE GARDEN at Claremont had virtually
disappeared from view, drowned in a sea of
rhododendrons and laurels, until the National Trust
took it in hand in 1975. Some of the greatest figures
in landscape design worked here from 1720 onwards
– Sir John Vanbrugh, Charles Bridgeman, William
Kent and 'Capability' Brown. What has now been

restored is chiefly the work of the first three and
what the visitor may see, never mind garden history,
is an enchanting garden of woodland, beech alleys
rising steeply uphill, a vast turf amphitheatre which
looks down on a lake with an island temple designed
by Kent, and beautiful stands of sweet chestnuts.
This is not a garden for those who love only flower
power. At summer weekends it fills with people
picnicking and savouring the delights of an Elysian
oasis threatened on all sides by suburbia.

COGHURST NURSERY
East Sussex

Ivy House Lane, nr Three
Oaks, Hastings TN35 4NP
3 1/2m NE of Hastings by
A259 and minor roads
Tel: 01424 756228

Open: Mon to Fri 12–4.30,
Sun 10–4.30

CAMELLIAS ARE the main thing at Coghurst and
they have one of the best collections in the
country, including many that are available
commercially nowhere else. They grow well over 300
varieties including a particularly choice range of
cultivars of the autumn-flowering *C. sasanqua* and
the tender *C. reticulata*. Coghurst also sell a good
range of rhododendrons – including many evergreen
azaleas – mostly cultivars but with a choice handful
of species. Catalogues are issued (two 2nd-class
stamps) and smaller specimens may be sent by post.

CROWTHER OF SYON LODGE
Middlesex

CROWTHER PIONEERED dealing in antique garden
ornaments and architectural fragments and their
premises at Syon Lodge are a treasure trove of
wonderful things. Here, displayed in a crowded
garden is a bewildering and constantly changing

Busch Corner, London
Road, Isleworth TW7 5BH
3 1/2m SW of central
London by A315
Tel: 0181 560 7978 and 7985

Open: Mon to Fri 9–5, Sat
to Sun 10.30–4.30 and at
other times by appointment

profusion of temples, seats, statues, urns and
fountains. All are decorative and some are
distinguished – and expensive – works of art. Many
of them have grand provenances and are the sort of
thing about which a new garden may be designed.
There are very few places anywhere in the world
where such a range of garden ornaments of this
quality may be found for sale.

DENMANS

West Sussex

Fontwell,
nr Arundel BN18 0SU
5m E of Chichester on A27
Tel: 01243 542808

Owner: Mrs J.H. Robinson
(with John Brookes)

Open: Daily 9–5 (closed 25
Dec and 1 Jan).
3 1/2 acres

THIS UNUSUAL GARDEN was started in 1946 by Mrs
J.H. Robinson and for the last thirteen years has
been run by the well-known garden designer and
writer, John Brookes. The entrance is through a huge
glasshouse, which houses a large collection of tender
plants. Gravel paths meander across a walled garden
in which profuse herbaceous planting is given
structure by huge clipped mounds of variegated box,
a handsome strawberry tree and the bold foliage of
rhus and rheum. Beyond, in the main garden,
sweeping beds have mixed plantings and there is
repeated use of yellow foliage, particularly of golden
yew and *Robinia pseudoacacia* 'Frisia'. There are
many unusual plants here, and an attractively bold
sense of design with the creative use of interesting
foliage. A small nursery sells some good plants,
mostly herbaceous but with a carefully chosen
selection of shrub roses. An excellent catalogue
(£2.50) is produced but there is no mail order. The
potential of most of the plants may be seen
handsomely displayed in the adjacent garden, so a
visit will be doubly rewarded.

EMMETTS GARDEN

Kent

Ide Hill,
Sevenoaks TN14 6AY
1 1/2m N of Ide Hill by
B2042
Tel: 01732 750367/750429

Owner:
The National Trust

Open: Apr to Oct, Wed to
Sun and Bank Hol Mon
1–6. 6 acres

THIS IS THE highest point in Kent and the garden has splendid views of the North Downs. Many of the best plants date from the sale of stock from Veitch's famous nursery in 1907 when Frederick Lubbock, a friend of William Robinson, lived here. He put into practice Robinson's idea of arranging hardy exotic plants in a naturalistic setting. A formal rose garden hedged in thuja, and a rock garden added by a later owner, are the only tamed parts of what is essentially an informal garden of wild character which merges almost imperceptibly with the surrounding woodland and scrub. The soil is acid and there are many azaleas, camellias, eucryphias rhododendrons, stewartias and other ericaceous plants. Excellent trees and shrubs are to be seen everywhere – *Kalmia latifolia*, magnolias, maples, dogwoods – and there are also real rarities, such as the charming American fringe tree, *Chionanthus virginicus*. The slopes of the densely wooded valley are carpeted with bluebells. The two best seasons are spring for the profusion of flowering shrubs and bulbs, and autumn when there is a wonderful display of colour from azaleas, cercidiphyllums, maples and other deciduous trees and shrubs. The fine undulating site and profusion of good plants make it a wonderful place to explore.

FENTON HOUSE

London

Windmill Hill,
Hampstead NW3 6RT
In Hampstead village.
Tube: Hampstead
Tel: 0171 435 3471

Owner:
The National Trust

Open: Mar, Sat and Sun
2–5; Apr to Oct, Sat, Sun
and Bank Hol Mon
11–5.30, Mon, Tue and
Wed 1–5.30. 1 acre. House
open

A COMPLETE COUNTRY garden in the middle of Hampstead village reminds the visitor of the former rural character of this part of London. Fenton House, a suave Georgian house of brick, looks out over a formal garden in which a gravel path is edged with standard-trained Portugal laurels in tubs, and borders are given formality with rhythmic plantings of clipped lavender or Irish yews. At the far end, yew hedges conceal hidden borders and elegant benches. At a lower level, parallel to this, an orchard bursts into life in spring, with fruit blossom and many bulbs naturalised in the long grass – anemones, narcissi and snake's head fritillaries.

FISHBOURNE ROMAN PALACE GARDEN

West Sussex

Salthill Road,
Fishbourne PO19 3QR
1 1/2m W of Chichester by
A259
Tel: 01243 785859

Owner: Sussex
Archaeological Society

Open: Mar, Apr, Oct, daily
10–5; May to Sept, daily
10–6; 14 to 28 Feb, Nov,
1 to 16 Dec, daily 10–4;
remainder of year, Sun
10–4. 2 acres

THIS IS an unusual attempt to show what an aristocratic Roman garden would have looked like, based on archaeological examination of the site, and Roman gardening practice. The garden was originally entirely surrounded by a verandah with a colonnade; in this area a low box hedge is shaped into a geometric pattern and some of the characteristic Roman plants (such as acanthus) are used. A new development is the planting of an ornamental kitchen garden containing period plants. In the adjoining museum are mosaics of exquisite beauty and a detailed model of the palace and the garden, showing how it appeared in its original state.

GODINTON PARK

Kent

Ashford TN23 3BW
1 1/2m W of Ashford at
Potter's Corner on A20
Tel: 01233 620773

Owner: The Godinton
House Preservation Trust

Open: Easter weekend, Jun
to Sept, Sun 2–5. 12 acres.
House open

NOTHING COULD BE a greater contrast to the creeping urbanism of Ashford than the exceptional park, dotted with wonderful oaks and Spanish chestnuts, through which one drives to Godinton. The gabled brick house is Jacobean and in 1902 Sir Reginal Blomfield added an appropriately gabled garden – superb yew hedges clipped into gables surround the forecourt – deploying the full, delightful repertoire of the architectural garden. A figure of Pan lies at the heart of an intricate box parterre, Venus stands among purple cotinus at the head of a canal, a wisteria-hung white marble colonnade decorated with fine statues leads to a little Italian garden with a formal pool and loggia.

GRAVETYE MANOR

West Sussex

*Illustration opposite: The
Italian Garden at Godinton*

THIS WAS the house and garden of William Robinson, the greatest and most influential of late-Victorian gardeners. Thanks to a brilliant restoration carried out by the present owner, visitors may now see a properly Robinsonian garden in all its

nr East Grinstead
RH19 4LJ
4m SW of East Grinstead
by B2110
Tel: 01342 810567

Owner: Peter Herbert

Open: Perimeter walk only,
Tue and Fri 10–5; private
gardens by house, for use
of hotel and restaurant
customers *only*. 30 acres

splendour. The gabled 17th-century manor house,
now an unashamedly comfortable hotel with one of
the best restaurants in England, looks south across a
valley. South and west of the house are formal
gardens with many of the plants that Robinson loved.
On the northern wooded slopes things become
wilder, with azaleas, camellias and magnolias planted
among the trees. South of the house, sweeping down
to a lake made by Robinson, is a meadow dazzling in
spring with naturalised bulbs where in summer the
grass is allowed to grow long. Although in a densely
populated part of England, Gravetye is at the heart of
a large Forestry Commission wood and has preserved
to a remarkable degree the authentically wild
atmosphere that Robinson cherished.

GREAT COMP

Kent

Comp Lane, St Mary's
Platt, nr Borough Green
TN15 8QS
7m E of Sevenoaks off A25;
signposted on B2016, off
A20/A25 between
Sevenoaks and Maidstone
Tel: 01732 882669 and
886154

Owner: Great Comp
Charitable Trust

Open: Apr to Oct, daily
11–6. 7 acres

THERE IS something enticing about the design of
the garden at Great Comp – paths lead the
visitor on, curving out of sight round bold plantings.
The atmosphere is essentially informal, an impression
which is only sharpened by the occasional straight
line and touch of formality. Against a background of
deciduous woodland a very wide range of ornamental
trees and shrubs relishes the acid loam. Spreading out
south of the house a generous apron of impeccable
lawn is fringed with tall conifers, oaks and willows
and, as it reaches the woodland, bordered with beds

of heathers. Paths lead off into the wilder woodland (and a temple lost in the woods) and thence back towards the house. Everywhere there are excellent trees and shrubs set off by well chosen underplanting – the larger campanulas, geraniums, hostas, lilies and violas. This is not a garden which depends on superficial fripperies – but capitalises on the very skilful use of carefully chosen ornaments and plants; and, although very densely planted, it has managed to preserve an air of spacious repose.

GREAT DIXTER

East Sussex

Northiam, Rye TN31 6PH
11m N of Hastings off A28
Tel: 01797 253107

Owner: Christopher Lloyd

Open: Apr to mid-Oct,
daily except Mon (but
open Bank Hol Mon) 2–5.
5 acres. House open

THE DISTINGUISHED gardener-writer Christopher Lloyd is the genius of this place, with its timbered 15th-century house restored by Edwin Lutyens who also planned the garden upon which Mr Lloyd has put his lively stamp. Billowing yew topiary and cunning vistas date from Lutyens's time but most of the planting is of more recent date. Here is Christopher Lloyd's virtuoso mixed border which he constantly improves; sheets of spring flowers in the orchard; a meadow garden; and, wherever you look, fastidiously chosen plants of all kinds planted with a crafty eye for colour. No gardener could visit Great Dixter without making discoveries and rekindling the zest for gardening. There are good plants for sale of which there is a catalogue (75p), and they are sold by mail order.

HAM HOUSE
Surrey

Ham, Richmond
TW10 7RS
Off A307 at Petersham,
SW of Central London
Tel: 0181 940 1950

Owner:
The National Trust

Open: Daily except Fri
(open Good Fri) 10.30–6 or
dusk if earlier, closed 25
and 26 Dec and 1 Jan.
18 acres. House open

THE EARLY 17th-century brick house was modernised in the smartest taste in the 1670s by the Duke and Duchess of Lauderdale who took as much interest in the garden as they did in the house. The garden decayed until in 1976 work was started by the National Trust on its restoration. This was helped by the survival of late 17th-century documentation – plans and plant lists – which enabled an authentic reconstruction. The formal walled garden south of the house is divided into spacious grass plats with a maze-like wilderness of hornbeam, winding paths and hidden pavilions. To one side a further walled garden has a large orangery (now a tea-room) with, sprawling in front of it, a vast *Paliurus spina-christi*, the thorned tree from which Christ's crown of thorns was supposed to have been made. In the east court on the other side of the house a parterre of gravel paths and box hedges is arranged in racy lozenges of lavender and santolina and overlooked by shady tunnels of yew and pleached hornbeam.

HAMPTON COURT

Surrey

East Molesey KT8 9AU
At Hampton Wick where
A308 and A309 meet,
6m SW of Central
London
Tel: 0181 781 9500

Owner:
Historic Royal Palaces

Open: Daily, dawn–dusk.
30 acres. Palace open

THIS IS ONE of the most famous places in England
and has much to interest the gardener. It was
started by Thomas Wolsey in the early 16th century
and became a royal palace, which it remains. In the
late 17th century Sir Christopher Wren added
grandiose extensions to the Tudor palace and was
involved in the design of a new garden of which part
of his 'wilderness' survives, a yew maze – the earliest
known hedge maze in England. South of the palace
the original royal privy garden, has been undergoing
an exciting restoration to be completed in 1995.
Views of the Thames are framed by Jean Tijou's
exquisite late 17th-century wrought-iron screen.
Nearer the palace there is a colourful sunken pond
garden and a reconstructed Tudor knot. In the vinery
is a 'Black Hamburgh' grape-vine planted in 1768 and
still productive. To the east of the palace old topiary
of yew and holly rise above spring and summer
bedding schemes, and three noble lime avenues
radiate from a semi-circle of clipped yew and holly.

HATCHLANDS

Surrey

East Clandon,
Guildford GU4 7RT
3m E of Guildford by A25
and A246
Tel: 01483 222482

Owner:
The National Trust

Open: 2 Apr to Oct, Tue,
Wed, Thur, Sun and Bank
Hol Mon 2–5.30; Aug, also
Fri 2–5.30. 12 acres. House
open

THE GARDEN at Hatchlands has in recent years been restored and it is now especially worth a visit to see how work of this sort is carried out. South of the brick 18th-century mansion a formal garden of geometric box-edged beds has been modified to take into account Gertrude Jekyll's suggestions, and to the west a fussy Victorian parterre has been changed to resemble Humphry Repton's early 19th-century design. The park, with its decorative pillared temple, also designed by Repton, is undergoing a long-term programme of restoration.

HAZELDENE NURSERY

Kent

Illustration: Viola *'Princesse
de Galles'*

Dean Street, East Farleigh,
Maidstone ME15 0PS
3m SW of Maidstone by
B2010
Tel: 01622 726248

Open: Mar to Sept, daily
except Sun and Mon 10–3;
other times by appointment

PANSIES AND VIOLAS are the speciality of this nursery which has won Gold Medals at Chelsea for its excellent plants. An immense range is sold of winter- and summer-flowering pansies, violas, violettas and species violets. Many varieties are propagated by cuttings to preserve their identity. An informative list is produced (s.a.e.), with valuable information on cultivation, and a mail order service is provided both for growing plants and for seeds of those varieties that come true from seed; the catalogue includes invaluable advice on germination.

HEVER CASTLE

Kent

nr Edenbridge TN8 7NG
3m SE of Edenbridge by
minor roads
Tel: 01732 865224

Owner:
Broadland Properties Ltd

Open: 14 Mar to 5 Nov,
daily 11–6. 50 acres. Castle
open

Hever has everything a castle should have – a romantic moat, whimsical topiary, an infuriating maze and an excellent garden. The setting of old woodland is very fine and in spring there are some excellent rhododendrons and azaleas. The enormous Italian garden was designed chiefly to show off the collection of classical statuary collected by William Waldorf Astor who bought the estate in 1903. Much of the statuary is artfully arranged in enclosures running along the Pompeian Wall which is planted to great decorative effect. Facing it, on the shady north-facing side, is an immense pergola draped with vines, clematis and roses, and behind which there is a series of grotto-like niches, dripping with water, where ferns, hostas and other moisture-loving plants thrive. Much of the garden is flamboyantly grand – a swashbuckling Italianate loggia with fountains and naked nymphs, for example – but there are more intimate moments and much attractive planting.

THE HIGH BEECHES

West Sussex

After walking round this exquisite woodland garden it is hard to believe that it is only 20 acres in area. Winding paths, shifting views and the subtle lie of the gently undulating land give such a rich diversity of scenery. The High Beeches formerly

Handcross RH17 6HQ
1m E of Handcross off
B2110
Tel: 01444 400589

Owner: High Beeches
Gardens Conservation
Trust

Open: Easter Mon to Jun,
3 Sept to Oct, daily except
Wed 1–5. 20 acres

belonged to the Loder family of Leonardslee and
Wakehurst; the Hon. Edward and Mrs Boscawen
came here in 1966 and have added immensely to it.
The emphasis is as much on the quality of the
landscape as on the distinction of the planting. There
are marvellous camellias, magnolias, maples and
rhododendrons and many other groups of woody
plants, including a National Collection of stewartias.
But there are many herbaceous plants – drifts of
naturalised willow gentian, irises and primulas – and
a 4-acre meadow, unploughed in living memory, with
15 species of grass, many cowslips and orchids.

HIGHDOWN

West Sussex

SIR FREDERICK STERN, who died in 1967, was a
banker whose passionate hobby was gardening. He
lived at Highdown and the making of the garden here
is vividly described in his book *A Chalk Garden*, a
20th-century gardening classic. On his death it was
left to Worthing Borough Council and there is still

Littlehampton Road,
Goring-by-Sea BN12 6NY
3m W of Worthing by A259
Tel: 01903 501054

Owner:
Worthing Borough Council

Open: Apr to Sept, Mon to
Fri 10–6; Sat, Sun and
Bank Hol Mon 10–8. Oct
to Mar, Mon to Fri 10–4.
9 1/2 acres

much to admire; the site is a steep, south-facing slope and the layout is informal with occasional formality such as the avenue of *Prunus serrula*, with its glistening, peeling bark, at the entrance. The garden is of particular interest to gardeners who want to know more about the splendours and miseries of gardening on chalk. Stern was able to discover here exactly what flourished in chalk; for example, maples from China and Europe did very well but those from Japan and the U.S.A. did not. Although the garden is particularly rich in woody plants there are marvellous groups of herbaceous perennials and bulbs – agapanthus, anemones, hellebores, irises, narcissi and peonies – which provide floriferous underplanting.

HILEY NURSERY
Surrey

Illustration: Bidens
ferulifolia

25 Little Woodcote Estate,
Wallington SM5 4AU
Off Woodmansterne Lane
Tel: 0181 647 9679

Open: Wed to Sat 9–5

BRIAN HILEY SPECIALISES in rare perennials and tender plants and has an excellent eye for a good plant. Some groups are very deeply represented; he has a particularly good collection of penstemons – species and cultivars – and an exceptional list of sages, woody and herbaceous. But throughout his list there are unusual and well chosen things, not all of them herbaceous. He sells the tender yellow *Bidens ferulifolia*, felicias, the mysterious *Hieracium candidum*, a creeping loosestrife *Lysimachia henryi*, several kinds of phygelius and of polemonium. A catalogue is issued (three 1st-class stamps) and there is a mail order but plants are often propagated in numbers too small to allow them to be listed. Brian Hiley's own 1-acre garden next door, stuffed with excellent plants, is open on Wednesday and Saturday and by appointment.

IDEN CROFT HERBS

Kent

Frittenden Road,
Staplehurst TN12 0DH
In the village of Staplehurst
8m S of Maidstone by
A229
Tel: 01580 891432

Open: Feb to Sept, Mon to
Sat 9–5, Sun and Bank Hol
Mon 11–5; Oct to Jan,
daily except Sun 9–5

IDEN CROFT supplies culinary herbs on a massive scale to the catering trade, and this is a full-scale working herb farm. There are also well planted herbaceous beds, a garden designed for the blind, partially sighted or disabled – with plenty to feel and smell – and a walled garden. Iden Croft holds National Collections of mint and origanums, and has large collections of lavender, sedums and thymes. Many other culinary herbs are sold as well as a selection of other herbaceous perennials. There is a mail order service (catalogue £2.50; plant list, s.a.e.).

W . E . Th . INGWERSEN LTD

West Sussex

Birch Farm Nursery,
Gravetye,
East Grinstead RH19 4LE
2 1/2m SW of East
Grinstead by B2110 and
minor roads
Tel: 01342 810236

Open: Mar to Sept, daily
9–1, 1.30–4; Nov to Feb,
Mon to Fri 9–1, 1.30–4

ANYONE WHO HAS not heard of Ingwersen has probably not heard of alpine plants either. Will Ingwersen, who died in 1990, was one of the great plantsmen and nurserymen of his time. His half brother Paul carries on the business and offers 1,800 different types of plants for sale, grown to exemplary standards and often rare. The elegantly produced list (£1 stamps) has wonderful groups of alliums, campanulas, dianthus, primulas, dwarf rhododendrons, saxifrages and violas. Among bulbs are excellent colchicums, crocuses, fritillaries, narcissi, and species tulips. Not everything available is in the catalogue, so although there is a mail order service, a visit is essential. The nursery presents a mouth-watering sight, with endless neat rows of plants. It is on sacred ground, too, for this was formerly part of William Robinson's Gravetye estate.

KYOTO GARDEN

London

Holland Park W14
W of the centre of London
in the middle of Holland
Park
Tube: Holland Park

Owner: The Royal
Borough of Kensington and
Chelsea

Open: Daily 8–sunset.
1 acre

INTO THE SEDATE and splendid setting of Holland Park the Kyoto Garden made an exotic arrival in 1991. Largely financed by Japanese firms, and designed by Japanese garden designers, it is of the type known as a 'tour garden', with all the ingredients one expects – a pool fed by a rocky cascade, stepping stones, Japanese maples, raked gravel, snow lanterns and an atmosphere pregnant with meaning even if one cannot understand it. At all events, on its sloping site and backed by fine old trees, it is a welcome and exhilarating presence.

LEEDS CASTLE

Kent

DISTANT VIEWS of Leeds Castle are enchanting – the silvery 12th-century castle wildly romantic, apparently floating on its vast moat. The gardens are modern and there are two features of special interest. The Culpeper Garden, designed by Russell Page, is a series of box-edged beds overflowing with herbaceous

nr Maidstone ME17 1PL
4m E of Maidstone by A20
and B2163. Jnct 8 of M20
Tel: 01622 765400

Owner:
Leeds Castle Foundation

Open: Daily: Mar to Oct,
10–5; Nov to Feb, 10–3.
500 acres. Castle open

plants underplanted among shrub roses. Farther from
the castle a yew maze, finished in 1988, was designed
by Randall Coate and Adrian Fisher, its shape
echoing the medieval architecture of the castle. The
elusive goal at its centre is the entrance to an
extraordinary grotto lined with tufa embellished by
Diana Rennell and Simon Verity with statues, rare
stones and shells, the cave-like gloom occasionally
pierced by circular skylights.

LEONARDSLEE GARDENS
West Sussex

Lower Beeding,
nr Horsham RH13 6PP
4m SW of Handcross
(bottom of M23) by A279
Tel: 01403 891212

Owner: The Loder Family

Open: Apr to Oct, daily
10–6 (closes at 8 in May).
200 acres

SIR EDMUND LODER bought the estate of Leonardslee
in 1889 and started to make his great woodland
garden. The spectacular site – a shallow valley with a
series of linked lakes running along the bottom –
makes a superb place to grow ornamental trees and
shrubs. The soil is a slightly acid moisture-retentive
silt; the densely clothed sides of the valley give
protection from the wind, and there is excellent frost
drainage. Rhododendrons were Sir Edmund's first

love and he raised the hybrid *R*. 'Loderi' which has produced some of the best garden varieties. But there are also especially choice collections of camellias and magnolias, including some of the largest specimens in the country. Large numbers of evergreens – wellingtonias, Douglas firs, deodars and spruce – make a fine background for spring flowering and the explosion of autumn colour. A bonsai display and alpine house have recently been added, and a summer wildflower walk opens this year.

MERRIMENTS NURSERY AND GARDENS

East Sussex

Illustration: Gaura
lindheimeri

Hawkhurst Road, Hurst
Green TN19 7RA
12m SE of Tunbridge Wells
by A21
Tel: 01580 860 666

Open: Daily 10–5.30

THIS FAMILY NURSERY was started in 1988 and a splendid garden alongside was subsequently added to display its wares. It carries a general stock of shrubs, trees and climbers but of special interest to gardeners, is the wide range of herbaceous perennials: named cultivars of dianthus, euphorbias, geraniums, excellent lobelias, many penstemons, poppies, sages and violas. These are very well chosen and, in addition, there is a choice selection of ferns. A useful catalogue is published (75p) but there is no mail order. The well planned and richly planted garden is beginning to show its paces, and forms an attractive display ground for the wide range of plants that the nursery sells.

MUSEUM OF GARDEN HISTORY

London

Lambeth Palace Road,
SE1 7LB
Immediately S of Lambeth
Bridge. *Tube*: Victoria or
Waterloo
Tel: 0171 261 1891

Owner:
The Tradescant Trust

Open: Mon to Fri 11–3,
Sun 10.30–5

JOHN TRADESCANT, father and son, immensely
influential gardeners and collectors of exotic plants
in the 17th century, lived and died in Lambeth where
they are buried in a magnificent tomb. In the disused
church an excellent museum of garden history has
been formed, containing a permanent collection and a
small gallery devoted to Gertrude Jekyll, and
presenting temporary exhibitions, courses and
lectures. In the old churchyard a charming replica
17th-century garden has been made, with a knot of
box hedges designed by the Marchioness of Salisbury
and containing plants of a Tradescantian flavour.

NYMANS GARDEN

West Sussex

THERE ARE FEW gardens anywhere in England
where rare and beautiful plants are grown in
such an attractive setting, in which formality and
informality are subtly interwoven. Nymans was
acquired by Leonard Messel in 1890 when he began
introducing a wide range of plants. He made a
woodland garden in which magnificent trees and
flowering shrubs – particularly camellias, eucryphias,
magnolias and rhododendrons – are seen to great
advantage. One of the best hybrid eucryphias, *E.* ×
nymansensis, had its origins here. In an irregularly

Handcross, nr Haywards
Heath RH17 6EB
7m NW of Haywards
Heath by A272 and B2114
Tel: 01444 400321/400002

Owner:
The National Trust

Open: Mar to Oct, daily
except Mon and Tue (open
Bank Hol Mon) 11–6 (Sat
and Sun 11–7 or sunset if
earlier). 30 acres

shaped walled garden Messel laid out a pair of
spectacular herbaceous borders, whose design was
influenced by William Robinson. These are
wonderful today, and in late summer their flowering
season is prolonged by the subtle use of annuals.
Surrounding the borders are choice ornamental trees,
such as dogwoods, *Koelreuteria paniculata* and
styrax. There is much topiary of yew and box –
geometric shapes and plump birds – and romantic
ruins. A great number of trees were lost in the great
storm of October 1987 but the rose garden containing
many old roses – in whose use Mrs Messel was a
pioneer – has been restored.

OSTERLEY PARK

Middlesex

Isleworth TW7 4RB
5m W of Central London
by A4
Tube: Osterley
Tel: 0181 560 3918

Owner:
The National Trust

Open: Daily 9–7.30 or
sunset if earlier. 140 acres.
House open

THE PARK AT Osterley survives only in part, but
there are some good remaining garden buildings
and some marvellous trees decorate the landscape.
Block your ears to the roar of the Great West Road
and something of the Elysian atmosphere of the past
can be brought to life. The late Elizabethan mansion
was rebuilt after 1761 by Robert Adam who also
designed the semi-circular conservatory against the
old kitchen garden wall. A series of lakes to the
south and east of the house glitter among splendid
trees – old cedars of Lebanon, oaks, limes and
London planes. The lake nearest the house has an
octagonal Chinese pavilion on an island.

PAINSHILL PARK
Surrey

Portsmouth Road,
Cobham KT11 1JE
1m W of Cobham by
A245
Tel: 01932 868113

Owner:
Painshill Park Trust

Open: Mid Apr to mid
Oct, Sun 11–6. Further
openings in 1995 are
possible; telephone 01932
864674 for details.
158 acres

T HIS EXTRAORDINARY landscape garden is being
restored by a private trust and it is one of the
most worthwhile of all recent garden restorations.
The garden was made by the Hon. Charles Hamilton
between 1738 and 1773, when he ran out of money.
It is an intensely original example of the large-scale
creation of ornamental landscape. At the heart of the
garden a long curvaceous lake with islands is
overlooked by decorative buildings – an airy
ten-sided gothic pavilion, a fake ruined abbey and a
ruined Roman arch. One of the islands has the
remains of a dazzling grotto and is linked to the
mainland by an elegant Chinese bridge. Paths wind
through woods and across meadows about the shores
of the lake. In the westernmost part of the park a
huge water wheel is revealed, and on the wooded
slopes high above, a castellated gothic tower
commanding immense views over the landscape and
the country beyond. A visit to Painshill is a great
adventure, with its exotic and picturesque ingredients
giving constant surprises. Everywhere the landscape
composes itself into delicious views and the place has
an unforgettable exhilaration.

PANTILES NURSERIES LTD
Surrey

Illustration: Acer griseum

Almners Road, Lyne,
Chertsey KT16 0BJ
1 1/2m W of Chertsey, Jnct
11 of M25
Tel: 01932 872195

Open: Daily 9–5.30
(Sun 9–5)

M ANY PEOPLE WILLINGLY spend thousands of
pounds on a new kitchen but might never think
of buying expensive large trees and shrubs which will
give instant character to a new garden. At Pantiles
there is a wide selection of woody plants in
whopping sizes: a 20ft high *Magnolia grandiflora*
'Galissonière' (not the commonest tree in the world)
will cost over £3,000, but it will last your lifetime,
getting lovelier all the time, which is more than you
can say of a new kitchen. A new line of Tasmanian
tree ferns, *Dicksonia antarctica*, which withstand up
to –13°C in their native habitat, will make this lovely
plant available to a much wider range of gardeners.
A catalogue is produced, and delivery and planting –
a tricky business with a very large tree – can be
arranged by the nursery.

PARHAM HOUSE
West Sussex

P ARHAM IS a grand Elizabethan house and is
splendidly situated in an atmospheric old deer
park dotted with ancient oaks. The chief ornamental
part of the garden lies in the walled former kitchen
garden, divided by gravel paths. Here are some very
effective herbaceous borders with carefully controlled
colour schemes: a pair of blue borders enlivened with
dashes of magenta, pink diascias and purple

Pulborough RH20 4HS
4m S of Pulborough by
A283
Tel: 01903 744888

Owner: Parham Park Ltd

Open: Easter Sun to 1st
Sun in Oct, Sun, Wed,
Thur and Bank Hol Mon
1–6. 11 acres. House open

penstemons; a gold border, given structure by repeated plantings of yellow potentilla, golden elder and juniper, yellow loosestrife and achilleas; and a long border, facing west, of hot, bright colours. It is very much a working kitchen garden, providing cut flowers, fruit and vegetables for the house. To the west, a lake is overlooked by a pavilion and, to one side, a fiendish new turf maze with infuriatingly complicated rules.

PASHLEY MANOR

East Sussex

nr Ticehurst TN5 7HE
1 1/2m SE of Ticehurst by
B2099
Tel: 01580 200692

Owner:
Mr and Mrs James Sellick

Open: mid Apr to mid Oct,
Tue, Wed, Thur and Sat
and Bank Hol Mon 11–5.
8 acres

THE APPROACH TO Pashley manor lies through beautiful parkland and the house, mid 16th-century half-timbered on one façade and Queen Anne on another, sits well in its setting. The gardens have recently been revived with the help of the garden designer Anthony du Gard Pasley who has contrived elegant formal plantings near the house, with carefully judged colour associations, and a wilder garden of woodland character behind it. All this is impeccably well maintained. The Sellicks have by no means completed their ambitious garden schemes and this will be a place to watch keenly in the future.

PENSHURST PLACE
Kent

Penshurst,
nr Tonbridge TN11 8DG
In Penshurst village
Tel: 01892 870307

Owner: The Rt Hon.
Viscount De L'Isle

Open: 26 Mar to 2 Oct,
daily 11–6. 10 acres.
House open

THE SIDNEY FAMILY have been here since the 16th century but the house is much older and magnificently dominates the huge walled gardens that surround it. Although the planting is modern in this enclosure, with its lovely Tudor bricks, the present pattern of beds, pools and walks closely resembles that shown in Kip's engraving of around 1700. Very few gardens preserve their essential layout from such an early time as Penshurst does. The entrance leads past a border planted as a dazzling Union Jack, with the colours picked out in spring and summer bedding. Beyond it all sorts of ornamental schemes spread out: a charming orchard of apples and Kentish cobs; a garden of magnolias and golden Irish yews; a pair of herbaceous borders; a rose garden; a spring garden; and a pair of handsome borders designed by Lanning Roper.

PERRYHILL NURSERIES
East Sussex

Illustration:
Rosa *'Gertrude Jekyll'*

Hartfield TN7 4JP
8m W of Tunbridge Wells
by A264 and B2026, 1m N
of Hartfield
Tel: 01892 770377

Open: Daily 9–5 (closes
4.30 in winter)

A MARVELLOUS GARDEN could be made using Perryhill as your only source of plants. They have well chosen representatives of the most valuable ornamental plants, both woody and herbaceous, and there is a small selection of fruit. With some plants, such as roses, they have an exceptional choice of the best kinds. In other groups – species peonies, for example – you will find things which you would not see in the average garden centre. A useful catalogue is produced (£1.60), but there is no mail order.

PETWORTH HOUSE
West Sussex

Petworth GU28 0AE
In Petworth village
Tel: 01798 42207 and
Answerphone 01798 42207

Owner:
The National Trust

Open: Pleasure grounds: 19
and 26 Mar 2–5; Apr to
Oct, daily except Mon and
Fri (open Good Fri and
Bank Hol Mon, closed Tue
following) 12.30–6. *Park:*
Daily 8–sunset. 700 acres.
House open

PETWORTH HAS an ancient gardening history:
Elizabethan gardens had a fountain and roses, and
in the late 17th century formal gardens were made
for the newly built house. Today the park is the
thing at Petworth and it is best appreciated by taking
a long walk in it (for this, go to the Park, rather than
the House, car park). It was laid out from 1752 for
the 2nd Earl of Egremont by 'Capability' Brown and
is one of the best of all his surviving landscapes. It is
big enough to reduce the very large mansion, seen
from a distance framed in trees, to the stature of a
garden ornament. Brown placed a Doric temple to
the north of the house and an Ionic rotunda beyond
it on an eminence. Marvellous limes, oaks, sweet
chestnuts and planes survive from Brown's time.

PICKARD'S MAGNOLIA
GARDENS
Kent

IT IS QUITE clear what the speciality of this unusual
establishment is. Unique hybrids of magnolia are
bred by the Pickards which include various *Magnolia*
× *soulangeana* hybrids, rare forms of *M. stellata* and
other interesting kinds. In addition to these there are

Stodmarsh Road,
Canterbury CT3 4AG
E of the city centre by
A257, near golf course
Tel: 01227 463951

Open: Feb to Christmas
Eve, daily except Mon:
Wed, Fri 12–dusk, other
days 10–dusk (5 in winter)

collections of yakushimanum rhododendrons, camellias, deciduous azaleas and various cultivars of pieris. Almost all the plants are raised from cuttings and grown on their own roots. Plants are sold on a cash and carry basis only. The fact that several are unique to Pickards is another reason for visiting – a visit at magnolia time would reveal some unexpected, possibly unique, treasures.

POLESDEN LACEY

Surrey

nr Dorking RH5 6BD
5m NW of Dorking by
A246
Tel: 01372 458203/452048

Owner:
The National Trust

Open: Daily 11–6 or sunset
if earlier. 30 acres. House
open

THE DAPPER early 19th-century house was owned by the great Edwardian political hostess, the Hon. Mrs Ronald Greville, and the garden has much of the blowsy charm of the age. A beech avenue leads up the hill and wonderful views of the valley are revealed from the house at the top. Beyond the house a very large formal rose garden, with such distinctive Edwardian varieties as 'Dorothy Perkins' and 'American Pillar', has at its centre a white marble well-head. Although there are about 2,000 plants only a relatively small number of rose varieties is used in a colour scheme of pink and white with occasional sharper tones of red. South of the rose garden a magnificent herbaceous border, backed by a wall festooned with climbing plants, is an object lesson in bold but disciplined planting.

PORT LYMPNE GARDENS
Kent

Lympne, Hythe CT21 4PD
3m W of Hythe by A20
and B2067; Jnct 11 of M20
Tel: 01303 26464/7

Owner: John Aspinall

Open: Daily 10–5 (or 1
hour before dusk in
winter). 15 acres

HIGH ABOVE Romney Marsh the gabled brick house was built by Sir Philip Sassoon to designs by Sir Herbert Baker before World War I, and completed after the war by Philip Tilden who, in collaboration with his patron, laid out the garden. Sassoon died in 1939 and subsequently the place deteriorated until John Aspinall bought it in 1973 and commissioned a complete restoration with advice from Russell Page. The garden is formal in spirit and decorative in execution, making full use of the lovely position. Compartments are hedged in yew or Leyland cypress and the chess-board garden and the striped garden present dazzling geometric patterns in bedding schemes. Beautiful herbaceous borders, a fig garden, vineyard, and terraces of roses and dahlias decorate the slopes. Within its carefully designed architectural setting the garden at Port Lympne has a brilliantly festive air.

POTS AND PITHOI
West Sussex

MOST GARDEN POTS are mass produced to fairly commonplace designs but Pots and Pithoi sell a unique range of hand-made Cretan pots in many different designs and sizes. They are fired at a very high temperature and are therefore resistant to frost. The great attraction is their beautiful patina and the

The Barns, East Street,
Turners Hill RH10 4QQ
E of Turners Hill on
B2110, 5m E of Crawley by
A264 and B2028
Tel: 01342 714793

Open: Daily 10–4 including
Bank Hol Mon (closed 24
Dec–2 Jan and Sat and Sun
in Jan)

liveliness of their design and decoration, with
patterns that are either incised or applied in delicate
ribbons of clay. These are the kind of pots that,
without being in the slightest pretentious, can have
tremendous presence in a garden. A well illustrated
catalogue is produced and delivery can be arranged.
But a visit is really essential to appreciate the beauty
of these rare pots.

QUEEN MARY'S GARDEN
London

Inner Circle,
Regents Park NW1
In S part of Regents Park.
Tube: Regents Park
Tel: 0171 486 7905

Owner: Department of the
Environment

Open: Daily, dawn–dusk

THIS CHARMING PIECE of miniature picturesque
landscaping has much to offer. There are
ramparts of roses in season, and a famous rosy
rondel with swags of flowers trained on ropes. To
one side there is a little lake with weeping willows
and a fern-bedecked rocky waterfall. A bridge leads
to an island with winding paths, ornamental shrubs
and a rock garden. Handsome trees – oaks, acacias
and purple beeches – mute the roar of London traffic.

G. REUTHE LTD
Kent

Illustration: Rhododendron
campylocarpum

REUTHE IS FAMOUS for rhododendrons. Here is an
exceptionally wide range of species and hybrids
and a choice collection of evergreen and deciduous
azaleas. The nursery sells other things, particularly

Crown Point Nursery,
Sevenoaks Road, Ightham,
nr Sevenoaks TN15 0HB
4m E of Sevenoaks by A25
Tel: 01732 865614

Open: Mon to Sat 9.30–4.30

woody plants, but its real distinction lies in its
rhododendrons of which it publishes an especially
good list (£1.50); mail order is available. The nursery
is now part of Starborough Nursery (see p. 54) to
whom all correspondence should be sent.

THE ROOF GARDENS
London

99 Kensington High Street,
W8 5ED
Central London.
Tube: High Street,
Kensington
Tel: 0171 937 7994

Open: Daily 9–5 but
telephone beforehand as
sometimes closed for
private functions.
1 1/2 acres

THESE ARE THE largest roof gardens open to the
public in London. On the top of the old Derry &
Toms department store, they are one of the most
unexpected horticultural sights that the capital has to
offer. This extraordinary place, complete with pink
flamingoes, is delightful. It has well tended borders
with substantial shrubs, secluded sitting places,
thoughtfully planted pots, attractive paths of old
York stone and herring-bone laid brick, and a
knock-out Moorish extravanganza with more than a
whiff of the Alhambra – old coloured tiles, and a
scalloped canal with fountains and palm trees.

ROYAL BOTANIC GARDENS, KEW
Surrey

*Illustration opposite: The
Chinese pagoda at Kew*

IT IS NOT THE PURPOSE of Kew to be interesting to
gardeners but this, despite itself, it effortlessly is.
The landscape park with its great Chinoiserie pagoda
(designed by Sir William Chambers in 1751) and
many specimen trees going back to the 18th century

Kew, Richmond TW9 3AB
7m SW of Central London.
Tube: Kew Gardens
Tel: 0181 940 1171

Owner: Trustees of the
Royal Botanic Gardens

Open: Daily 9.30–4 (6.30
on summer weekdays; 7.30
on Sun and Bank Hol Mon
in high summer). 300 acres

is exquisite; its setting on the Thames wonderful.
Most of the plants are wild species rather than
garden varieties but it is a perfect place to come on
any day of the year and discover new plants,
impeccably labelled and well grown. The various
glasshouses are immensely rich in non-hardy plants:
the Palm House designed by Richard Turner and
Decimus Burton; the Temperate House; and the
Princess of Wales Conservatory with tender plants of
different climates arranged in naturalistic settings.
Among the hardy plants there are several reference
collections of great interest to gardeners – they
include heathers, bulbs, bamboos and grasses, and
several others.

THE SAVILL AND VALLEY GARDENS

Surrey

The Great Park, Windsor
SL4 2HT
3m W of Egham by A30
and Wick Road
Tel: 01753 860222

Owner: Crown Property

Open: Savill Garden: daily
10–6 (closed for Christmas
period). 35 acres. *Valley
Garden:* daily sunrise–
sunset. 400 acres

SOME GARDENS set a style and affect the future style
of gardening. The Savill Garden has had a strong
influence on the tradition of woodland gardening. It
was started in 1932 by E.H. (later Sir Eric) Savill who
was Deputy Ranger of Windsor Great Park. He
invented a natural style of woodland gardening which
gave the plants appropriate habitats and made
something that was beautiful. The well-watered site
with many old trees – especially marvellous beeches
and oaks – was an excellent place for such a garden.
He planted large numbers of ornamental trees and
shrubs – azaleas, camellias, dogwoods, magnolias,
rhododendrons – and about the streams
moisture-loving plants such as ferns, lysichiton,
primulas and rheums. In addition to this there are
handsome formal gardens – herbaceous borders, a
dry garden and rose gardens – which are maintained
to wonderful old-fashioned standards. In 1947 Sir
Eric turned his attention to the nearby Valley
Garden, on a wonderful undulating site on the north
bank of Virginia Water. Here the planting is of a
similar style but, on an immensely larger site, the
variety is much greater. You'll find here National
Collections of dwarf conifers, hollies, magnolias,
mahonias, pernettyas, pieris and species
rhododendrons. It is a rare feast of woody plants in a
memorably attractive setting.

SCOTNEY CASTLE

Kent

Lamberhurst, Tunbridge
Wells TN3 8JN
1m S of Lamberhurst by
A21
Tel: 01892 890651

Owner:
The National Trust

Open: Apr to Oct, Wed to
Fri 11–6 or sunset if earlier
(closed Good Fri), Sat and
Sun 2–6 or sunset if earlier,
Bank Hol Mon 12–6. 19
acres

THE GARDENS AT Scotney Castle are a piece of
irresistibly romantic picturesque landscape
gardening made in the middle of the 19th century by
Edward Hussey, with advice from William Sawrey
Gilpin. At the same time Hussey built a new house
high on a hill, benefitting from wonderful views
down towards the moated medieval castle which
became an exotic eye-catcher for his landscaping
schemes. Walks descend the precipitous and rocky
hill with superb trees and shrubs; the flowers of
azaleas and rhododendrons, and the new foliage of
maples, are dazzling in spring. In the castle forecourt
there is a pretty herb garden designed by Lanning
Roper and, nearby on an island, a bronze by Henry
Moore seems strangely at home in the wild planting.

SHEFFIELD PARK

East Sussex

THERE IS SOMETHING dream-like about Sheffield
Park and it is certainly one of the most
memorable of all gardens. Both 'Capability' Brown
and Humphry Repton had a hand in the design but
the present appearance of the gardens is due chiefly
to Arthur Soames who bought the estate in 1905. The
house, a gothic palace designed by James Wyatt in
1775–8, sits on an eminence at the head of a broad
valley, with a series of four descending lakes

Uckfield TN22 3QX
Midway between East
Grinstead and Lewes off
A275
Tel: 01825 790655

Owner:
The National Trust

Open: Mar, Sat and Sun
11–4; Apr to 5 Nov, Tue to
Sun and Bank Hol Mon
11–6 or sunset if earlier; 8
Nov to 16 Dec, Wed to Sat
11–4. 100 acres.

extending far into the distance. On the banks of these lakes trees and shrubs are arranged in bold groups with subtle contrast of shape and foliage colour; here conifers and deciduous trees are artfully mingled. Many visitors see only the first two lakes and their immediate banks; this is a pity because acres of woods in the hinterland surrounding the lakes are laced with paths and full of marvellous trees and shrubs, with the occasional dazzling piece of herbaceous planting such as a path fringed with gentians. The garden is exquisitely laid out and a slow walk at any time during the long opening season offers some of the most beautiful garden scenes the visitor may ever see.

SISSINGHURST CASTLE GARDEN
Kent

Sissinghurst,
nr Cranbrook TN17 2AB
2m NE of Cranbrook off
A262
Tel: 01580 712850

Owner:
The National Trust

Open: Apr to 14 Oct, Tue
to Fri 1–6.30, Sat, Sun and
Good Fri 10–5.30. 10 acres.
House open

THE HISTORY OF this garden is quickly told – it was made by Vita Sackville-West and Harold Nicolson from 1930 onwards, and became the most admired English garden of its time. Few great gardens live up to their reputation so effortlessly as this. Whatever superlatives have been heaped on it, Sissinghurst never disappoints and each visit will reveal new pleasures. The National Trust was fortunate to inherit two gardeners, Pamela Schwerdt and Sibylle Kreutzberger, who had worked with Vita Sackville-West before her death in 1963. They maintained the garden to perfectionist standards until their recent retirement and their successor seems every bit as good. Within the disciplined enclosures of old brick walls, cool hedges of yew, and linking paths and vistas, here is a profusion of fastidiously chosen plants in which an immense collection of old roses provides a recurring theme. One of the many refreshing things about Sissinghurst is the way in which virtuoso changes in mood are effortlessly achieved – from the hot oranges and reds of the Cottage Garden, for example, to the austere yew alley that separates the formal gardens from the orchard. Despite Vita Sackville-West's aristocratic spirit, it would be wrong to think of Sissinghurst as far from the interests of everyday gardeners. In terms of practical gardening – the pruning, training and

Illustration opposite:
Sissinghurst Castle Garden

feeding of plants, for example – the highest standards were maintained and are still a delight to observe. Certainly Sissinghurst has the power to enchant but it is also an unending source of practical inspiration for all gardeners.

STANDEN

West Sussex

East Grinstead RH19 4NE
2m S of East Grinstead off
B2110
Tel: 01342 323029

Owner:
The National Trust

Open: 18, 19, 25, 26 Mar,
1.30–4.30; Apr to Oct, Wed
to Sun and Bank Hol Mon
12.30–6. 10 acres. House
open

STANDEN HAS a most marvellous position, high on an eminence with views across the Medway Valley to Crowborough Beacon. Below the house, which was designed by Philip Webb, the land falls away on south-facing slopes. An enclosed formal garden is hedged in beech and yew and has square beds edged in catmint with an Irish juniper at each corner and a crab apple at each centre, surrounded by rugosa roses. The rest of the garden consists of terraced lawns and paths that amble through groups of shrubs and trees – azaleas and rhododendrons with maples rising above. A wonderful tulip tree and a very large Scots pine at the foot of a sloping lawn frame distant views of cornfields surrounded by woodland.

STARBOROUGH NURSERY

Kent

Illustration: Styrax japonica

Marsh Green,
Edenbridge TN8 5RB
Tel: 01732 865614

Open: Daily except Tue
and Wed 10–4; closed all
Jan and Jul

STARBOROUGH SPECIALISES in acid-loving woody plants – many of them rarely seen in nurseries. There are also good selections of acers, camellias, daphnes, magnolias, pieris, rhododendrons, stewartias, styrax, viburnums and a choice selection of climbing plants; among all these are many rare and lovely things. A catalogue is published (£1.50) and mail orders are fulfilled. The nursery is in the same ownership as G. Reuthe (see p. 47).

SYON PARK AND GARDENS
Middlesex

Brentford TW8 8JF
On the N bank of the
Thames between Brentford
and Isleworth
Tel: 0181 560 0881

Owner: The Duke of
Northumberland

Open: Mar to Oct, daily
10–6; Nov to Feb, daily
10–sunset. 55 acres. House
open

IT IS SURPRISING to find a complete great country estate so near to the centre of London. The approach to the house, which was rebuilt by Robert Adam, runs through classic parkland. The chief pleasure gardens lie on one side of the house and are dominated by one of the finest conservatories you will see anywhere, built by Charles Fowler in 1827 in beautiful golden stone. There is an excellent collection of trees – acacias, catalpas, holm oaks and sweet chestnuts, and rarer things such as sweet buckeye (*Aesculus flava*). A long narrow lake is edged with trees including some good swamp cypresses. A very large garden centre has a good stock in all departments, and a fine selection of garden pots.

TILE BARN NURSERY
Kent

Illustration:
Cyclamen repandum

Standen Street, Iden Green,
Benenden TN17 4LB
In the hamlet of Standen
Street 1/2m S of Benenden
Tel: 01580 240221

Open: Wed to Sat 9–5

THIS IS THE kind of nursery that makes converts of even the most unyielding. It specialises in cyclamen and stocks all the most garden-worthy species and varieties of these charmingly seductive plants, several of which are very hard to come by. An excellent list is produced (s.a.e.), giving valuable information on their cultivation. Plants are sold by mail order but visitors are welcomed and a few additional bulbous plants are available to callers only.

WAKEHURST PLACE GARDEN
West Sussex

nr Ardingly, Haywards
Heath RH17 6TN
1 1/2m NW of Ardingly on
B2028
Tel: 01444 892701

Owner:
The National Trust

Open: Daily except 25 Dec
and 1 Jan; Nov to Jan
10–4; Feb, Oct 10–5; Mar
10–6; Apr to Sept 10–7.
170 acres

ALTHOUGH THERE IS an attractively planted walled garden and some good borders (albeit with a botanical slant – one is devoted to monocotyledons) Wakehurst Place is really about trees and shrubs. It is the country department of the Royal Botanic Gardens at Kew and it is full of wonderful things. By the house the site is relatively flat and the house looks out onto pools and a water garden fringed with maples and moisture-loving plants. Farther from the house the ground sweeps down into the Himalayan Glade and the precipitous ravine of Westwood Valley and its lake, and beyond that, to more woodland. There are wonderful collections of azaleas, magnolias and rhododendrons in the Himalayan Glade and the Westwood Valley, and particularly fine groups of conifers in the Pinetum. The lie of the land adds immensely to the beauty of the trees and this is a wonderful place in which to spend a few hours walking, looking and learning.

WASHFIELD NURSERY
Kent

Illustration:
Helleborus orientalis

Hawkhurst TN18 4QU
1m SW of Hawkhurst by
A229
Tel: 01580 752522

Open: Wed to Sat 10–5

WONDERFUL HERBACEOUS PERENNIALS are the strongest point of this exceptional nursery. The presiding genius behind it, Elizabeth Strangman, is an authority on hellebores and has bred some exquisite hybrids of *Helleborus orientalis* in which she aims for 'purity of colour and full rounded flower'. But throughout the list there are great treasures – epimediums, hardy geraniums, kniphofias, pulmonarias – all chosen in the very best species and cultivars. Some of these are from seed collected in the wild by the nursery's botanist friends, and thus the true, unadulterated form. A very good catalogue is produced but there is no mail order.

WASHINGTON GARDEN CENTRE
West Sussex

London Road,
Washington RH20 3BL
6m N of Worthing by A24
Tel: 01903 892006

Open: Daily 9–5.30

THIS NURSERY describes itself as 'a real garden centre for plantsmen' which may certainly be true but does not do justice to this extraordinary place. Its speciality is everything to do with water gardens – plants, ponds and equipment, of which it has one of the very best stocks in the country, an inspiration for the aquatic gardener. It is also remarkable for its mature trees of many kinds, at prices that may take your breath away. Not everything is in stock but the nursery can often track down a mature specimen to order. There is a list of plants from which orders may be sent by mail.

WEST DEAN GARDENS
West Sussex

West Dean,
Chichester PO18 0QZ
6m N of Chichester by
A286
Tel: 01243 811303

Owner: The Edward James
Foundation

Open: Mar to Oct, daily
11–6. 90 acres

THE FLINT AND STONE early 19th-century gothic house by James Wyatt belonged to Edward James, patron of surrealism, though there is nothing surrealistic about his garden. It is set in a beautiful valley and at its heart is an immense pergola designed by Harold Peto, draped in clematis, roses and wisteria and underplanted with agapanthus, daylilies, ferns, geraniums and lamium. Marking one end of it is a pretty gothic flint summer house whose floor is curiously paved in horse's teeth, and at the other end a sunken garden has a pool, ornamental grasses, a sea of *Alchemilla mollis*, ferns and roses. Half way down the pergola the tunnel of foliage is interrupted by a long rectangular lily pond. The fine old walled kitchen garden, with Edwardian glasshouses, has recently been restored. Beyond the garden, handsome

parkland with some outstanding old trees, especially conifers, in St. Roche's Arboretum, spreads across folds in the South Downs, of which there are fine views from the circuit walk.

WISLEY GARDEN
Surrey

nr Ripley, Woking
GU23 6QB
6m NE of Guildford by
A3; S of Jnct 10 of the M25
Tel: 01483 224234

Owner: The Royal
Horticultural Society

Open: Daily 10–7 (Sun for
RHS Members only).
250 acres

W ISLEY IS WHERE the Royal Horticultural Society shows the gardening public how it should be done. Here are the highest standards of practical horticulture deployed over an immense range of different kinds of gardening, in the setting of a splendid old site rich in fine trees and a very large number of other plants all impeccably labelled. There is a pinetum, an alpine house, a vast and beautifully kept rock garden, trial grounds of various kinds, and practical display areas giving examples of different styles of gardening. A huge shop contains the biggest selection of new gardening books in Britain, and a large nursery sells plants of high quality, many unusual. There is no catalogue and no mail order.

SOUTH-CENTRAL ENGLAND

Berkshire
Buckinghamshire
Hampshire
Oxfordshire
Wiltshire

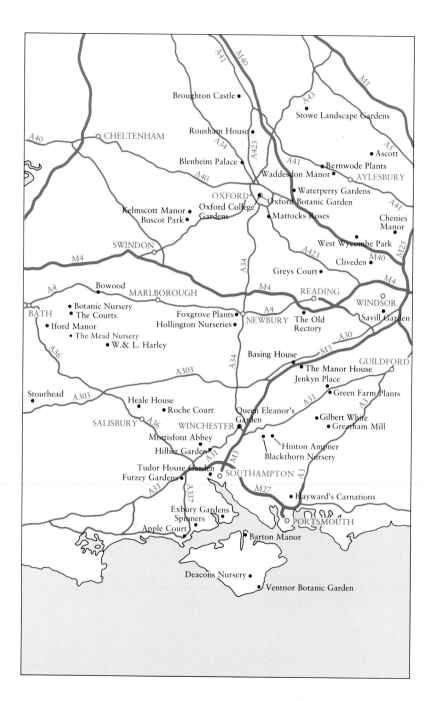

APPLE COURT
Hampshire

Hordle Lane, Lymington
SO41 0HU
3 1/2m W of Lymington by
A337
Tel: 01590 642130

Open: Feb to Nov, daily
except Tue and Wed
9.30–1, 2–5; closed last
week in Aug

THIS VERY attractive nursery and garden have some outstandingly good plants – hostas (over 80 varieties), daylilies, ferns and ornamental grasses. In the charming, recently completed garden, which is now really beginning to show its paces, there is a splendid hosta walk where many different kinds may be seen performing. Many of the other specialities of the nursery are displayed in excellent borders. A catalogue is produced (three 1st-class stamps) and a mail order service is provided but a visit to the garden where many of the plants sold are displayed so handsomely is particularly worthwhile.

ASCOTT
Buckinghamshire

Wing, nr Leighton Buzzard
LU7 0PS
2m SW of Leighton
Buzzard by A418
Tel: 01296 688242

Owner:
The National Trust

Open: 5 Apr to 7 May and
Sept, Tue to Sun 2–6; 10
May to 30 Aug, every Wed
and last Sun in each month
2–6. 39 acres. House open

THIS IS a rare garden, in which the distinctive late Victorian character is cherished and made into something special. The house was a hunting box on the Rothschilds' Mentmore estate, and the gardens were made at the end of the 19th century. Behind the house, lawns are terraced down towards a long double herbaceous border hedged with variegated holly and golden yew. From the middle of these borders a path leads to rose beds and a splashing fountain of Venus designed by Ralph Waldo Story. To the east there are great topiary pieces in golden and common yew, and a unique topiary sundial. From the terraces marvellous views of the Vale of Aylesbury are seen in the distance.

BARTON MANOR
Isle of Wight

Whippingham, East Cowes
PO32 6LB
1m SE of Cowes by A3021
next to Osborne House
Tel: 01983 292835

Owner:
Mr Robert Stigwood

Open: Apr to second Sun
in Oct, daily 10.30–5.30. 20
acres

FORMERLY PART of the Osborne House estate, the
Barton estate, with its gabled stone manor house,
was a particular interest of Prince Albert who laid
out the gardens and planted the splendid grove of
cork oaks (*Quercus suber*) at the entrance. Today a
large part of it is run as a commercial vineyard but
since 1976 the gardens have been very well restored
to preserve their Victorian character. By the house
there are herbaceous borders and a secret garden of
roses and winding paths. An avenue of bushes of St
John's Wort leads down to a lake with a romantic
19th-century thatched boat house. Here are many
good trees (especially willows relishing the moist
ground) and the banks are brilliant with daffodils in
spring. In summer a National Collection (over 100
species and cultivars) of red hot pokers (*Kniphofia*)
may be seen doing its dazzling stuff. A new rose
hedge maze was added in 1993.

BASING HOUSE
Hampshire

2m E of Basingstoke in the
centre of the village of Old
Basing, 2m from Jnct 6 on
M3
Tel: 01256 467294

Owner: Hampshire County
Council

Open: Apr to Sept, Wed to
Sun and Bank Hol Mon
2–6. 10 acres

BASING HOUSE WAS one of the great palaces of
16th-century England, the home of the Paulet
family who became Marquesses of Winchester.
Despite Inigo Jones's defensive architecture the house
fell to Cromwell but the ruins remain and have been
conserved by Hampshire County Council. They have
tremendous atmosphere and a formal garden, based
on the evidence of an archaeological dig, was

reconstructed in 1991 in a great walled enclosure. It is Jacobean in spirit, a parterre planted of box, germander, sage and santolina with, spelled out in clipped box, the family motto 'Aymez Loyautei'.

BERNWODE PLANTS
Buckinghamshire

Wotton Road, Ludgershall, nr Aylesbury HP18 9NZ 1m SE of Ludgershall on Wotton Road; 11m W of Aylesbury by A41
Tel: 01844 237415 (evenings only); 0860 798115 (daytime)

Open: Mar to Oct, Wed to Sun and Bank Hol Mon 10–6

BERNWODE PLANTS used to be called 'Plants from a Country Garden' and the lovely plants sold by Derek and Judy Tolman remain 'rare, old-fashioned and desirable'. The emphasis is on herbaceous plants, and the selections of many groups of plants are among the best you will find. There are several achilleas, aquilegias, campanulas, euphorbias (probably the largest collection for sale in the country) hardy geraniums, a marvellous range of Michaelmas daisies, mints, an irresistible selection of pinks (including some of the oldest cultivars), a wide range of primulas, very many violas and several perennial wall-flowers. It would be hard to imagine any gardener visiting this nursery and coming away empty-handed. An excellent catalogue (£1.50) is available and orders are fulfilled by cheap courier.

BLACKTHORN NURSERY
Hampshire

Kilmeston, nr Alresford SO24 0NL 6 1/2m SE of Winchester by A272
Tel: 01962 771796

Open: Mar to 15 Oct, Fri and Sat 9–5

Illustration:
Helleborus × ericsmithii

THERE ARE SOME very rare and desirable plants at the Blackthorn Nursery, which you will not often see offered for sale. The nursery specialises in herbaceous perennials but among a short list of woody plants is an excellent selection of daphnes.

Among the herbaceous plants are many epimediums, an exceptional range of hellebores, ferns, and a wide range of alpines. There is no mail order but a good catalogue is produced (three 1st-class stamps).

BLENHEIM PALACE
Oxfordshire

Woodstock OX20 1PX
In Woodstock, 8m N of
Oxford by A44
Tel: 01993 811091

Owner: The Duke of
Marlborough

Open: Park daily 9–4.45
(closed Christmas Day);
formal gardens at palace,
mid Mar to Oct, daily
10.30–4.45. 2,000 acres
(including parkland). Palace
open

THE PARK AT Blenheim has an immensely long history: in the 12th century it was the site of Henry II's Rosamond's Bower – and her well still exists; the gardens were originally laid out by Henry Wise in the early 18th century, and Sir John Vanbrugh who designed the immense palace also had a hand in them; in the 1760s the park was landscaped by 'Capability' Brown; and in the early 20th century new parterres by the palace were laid out by the French designer Achille Duchêne – fortissimo exercises in the grand formal manner. The water parterre has arabesques of box outlining pools and classical statuary; the Italian parterre has a magnificent central fountain, topiary of golden yew and pots of oranges and agapanthus. Everywhere ingredients from different periods are harmoniously interwoven with, at their heart, the palace and its vista leading north across Vanbrugh's bridge to the immense Column of Victory surmounted by a statue of the Duke of Marlborough clasping a winged victory 'as an ordinary man might hold a bird'. Brown's park, disposed on gently undulating land about the vast serpentine lake that he made by damming the River Glyme, is one of his masterpieces – a subtle and satisfyingly rural contrast to the extravagant architecture of the palace.

THE BOTANIC NURSERY
Wiltshire

Atworth,
nr Melksham SN12 8NU
9m E of Bath by A4 and
A365
Tel: 0850 328756

Open: Daily except Tue
10–1, 2–5

TERENCE AND MARY Baker's nursery specialises in lime tolerant plants of which it has an excellently chosen range. Those who garden on alkaline soil will find a wide selection that will flourish in their gardens. The nursery concentrates on no particular groups of plants but what it has is carefully selected – for example a list of species foxgloves of which it

holds the National Collection. Although their catalogue (£1.50) is full of good, and unusual, plants the Bakers are always on the look out for something new, and many items are available in numbers too small to be listed. In addition, many plants are considered too large or too fragile to be posted, so a visit is essential.

BOWOOD
Wiltshire

Calne SN11 0LZ
2 1/2m W of Calne by A4
Tel: 01249 812102

Owner: Earl and Countess of Shelburne

Open: Apr to Oct, daily 11–6. Garden centre: daily 10–5. 100 acres. House open

THE HOUSE – partly designed by Robert Adam – is a splendid 18th-century confection and very much in keeping with the park which is chiefly of the same period. The park, with its great serpentine lake, spreads out below the house and is enlivened by a wonderfully picturesque cascade concealed in the woods, a hermit's cave and an elegant pillared temple; all this is at some distance from the house but there is no point in going to Bowood if you cannot be bothered to walk as far as this. This is the work partly of 'Capability' Brown and, later, of Humphry Repton, and it is one of the very best of its kind. There are marvellous trees at Bowood and the mid 19th-century pinetum is exceptionally good, with some of the finest specimens of conifers in the country – magnificent cedars of Lebanon, pines, firs and giant redwoods. Immediately alongside the house there are 19th-century formal gardens with beds of roses, balustrades, vases and clipped Irish yews. The particularly good garden centre concentrates on woody plants and also has Haddonstone ornaments and terracotta pots. A mail order service is available.

BROUGHTON CASTLE
Oxfordshire

Broughton Castle, nr
Banbury OX15 5EB
2m SW of Banbury by
B4035
Tel: 01295 262624/720041

Owner: Lord Saye and Sele

Open: 18 May to 14 Sept,
Wed and Sun 2–5; Jul and
Aug, also Thur 2–5; also
Bank Hol Mon and
preceding Sun 2–5. 3 acres.
Castle open

THIS SPECTACULAR castle is really a 14th-century
moated and fortified manor house, set in
exquisite parkland, and occupying a beautiful site
next to the church. Within the castle walls there are
very distinguished borders showing a fastidious sense
of colour harmony. Running along a wall
overlooking the moat a mixed border is planted in
yellow, cream and blue with much grey and
variegated foliage. The Ladies' Garden has a pattern
of *fleur de lis* clipped in box and a Victorian
centrepiece well planted with trailing *Convolvulus
sabatius*, pelargoniums and ivy. Disposed around the
walls, overflowing mixed borders are planted with
many shrub roses in a colour scheme of pink, mauve
and white. They look superb against the grey stone
and are an object lesson in charming, and
appropriate, design and planting – generous
abundance softening the stern castle walls. Visitors to
the castle may go out onto the roof, from which
there is a bird's eye view of this garden and the
surrounding parkland; it is one of loveliest views you
will ever see and should certainly not be missed –
unforgettable in June but marvellous in any season.

BUSCOT PARK
Oxfordshire

Faringdon SN7 8BU
3m NW of Faringdon on
A417
Tel: 01367 242094 (not
weekends)

Owner:
The National Trust

Open: Apr to Sept, Wed,
Thur, Fri and every 2nd
and 4th Sat and Sun
(including Easter) 2–6.
20 acres. House open

EAST OF THE HOUSE, running through woodland
towards a lake, is a water garden you will never
forget. Designed by Harold Peto before World War I
it is in the form of a canal that drops down the
incline in gentle steps, dips under occasional little
bridges, widens and contracts, and from time to time
bursts forth in exuberant fountains. The water garden
is edged with stately clipped hedges of box, and the
flanking path is punctuated by Irish yews, statues and
urns. Approaching the lake the visitor sees on its far
bank a gleaming temple and an ornamental bridge.
To one side of the water garden a pattern of
exhilarating avenues is punctuated by handsome
eyecatchers. On the far side of the house, by the
kitchen garden, there is a recent development of
strongly designed borders in yellow and blue by the
late Peter Coats; and, within the walls, Tim Rees has
made tunnels of pleached hop hornbeam and Judas
trees underplanted with spring bulbs followed by
waves of many different daylilies – an admirable and
instructive piece of modern design.

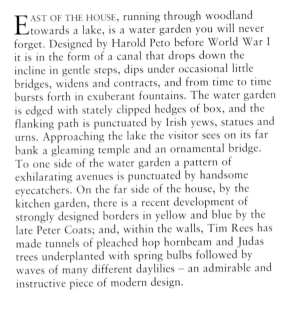

CHENIES MANOR
Buckinghamshire

Chenies WD3 6ER
4m E of Amersham on
A404
Tel: 0149476 2888

Owner: Lt. Col. and Mrs
MacLeod Matthews

Open: Apr to Oct, Wed,
Thur 2–5, also Bank Hol
Mon 2–6. 3 acres. House
open

THE MANOR is an early Tudor brick house of
tremendous character, and the recently made
garden is an excellent setting for it. The formal
gardens are chiefly behind the house, with a white
garden in which a figure of Cupid takes pot shots at
plump topiary birds of yew, a cool tunnel of pleached
lime, and a virtuoso little sunken garden, intricately
planted, in which spring tulips are followed by an
elaborate summer bedding scheme. Beyond this, a
physic garden has beds of medicinal and culinary
herbs laid out round a decorative old octagonal
well-house. To one side of the house an ornamental
kitchen garden has gravel paths edged with catmint
or box, currants and gooseberries grown in cordons,
beautifully tended vegetables and a turf maze in an
orchard. The whole garden is impeccably well kept
and gives the impression of bursting with
horticultural endeavour.

CLIVEDEN
Buckinghamshire

Taplow, Maidenhead
SL6 0JA
2m N of Taplow on B476,
near Jnct 7 of M4 and Jnct
4 of M40
Tel: 01628 605069

Owner:
The National Trust

Open: Daily: Mar to Oct
11–6; Nov and Dec 11–4.
375 acres. House open

THE MANSION at Cliveden, built in the 17th century
and rebuilt twice in the 19th century, commands
a spectacular site on a bluff overlooking the snaking
Thames. A giant balustraded terrace looks south to a
vast parterre of box and santolina, first laid out for
the Duke of Sutherland in the 1850s. At its far end
the land falls away in wooded slopes that run down
to the river below. The pleasure gardens lie chiefly to
the north of the house. In the forecourt are excellent
herbaceous borders and, beyond the walls, a hidden
rose garden designed by Geoffrey Jellicoe. A lime
avenue leads to the eye-stopping Fountain of Love
commissioned by Lord Astor from the American
Ralph Waldo Story at the turn of the century. To one
side is the magical Long Garden with serpentine box
hedges, whimsical topiary and mysterious stone
figures from the Commedia dell'Arte. Farther up the
drive, the water garden has a pagoda overlooking a
lake fringed with maples and Japanese cherries. In
the woods that surround the house, and by the house
itself, there are many exceptional garden ornaments –
exquisite statues, urns and garden buildings.

THE COURTS
Wiltshire

Holt, nr Trowbridge
BA14 6RR
In Holt village, 3m SW of
Melksham by B3107
Tel: 01225 782340

Owner:
The National Trust

Open: 2 Apr to 29 Oct,
daily except Sat 2–5. Also
by appointment out of
season. 7 acres

CONCEALED BEHIND village walls a pleached lime alley leads up to an ornate Bath stone 18th-century house at the heart of a highly decorative garden in which yew topiary and Irish yews give firm structure. Good shrubs and ornamental trees half conceal an ornamental pool smothered in season with water-lilies, and a billowing hedge of two varieties of holly forms the eastern boundary to a meadow garden. This is a vision of a cottage garden seen through aristocratic eyes. The whole garden has recently been given a good wash and brush-up.

DEACONS NURSERY
Isle of Wight

Godshill, Isle of Wight,
PO38 3HW
In village of Godshill 9m
S of Cowes by A3020
Tel: 01983 840750/522243

Open: Daily except Sun 8–4

DEACONS NURSERY specialises in fruit trees and bushes, of which it has an immense collection – around 250 varieties of apples alone, for example, which may be ordered on a choice of five rootstocks. There is virtually no fruit that is hardy in Britain which is not stocked, and many of the varieties, especially the old kinds, are very difficult to find elsewhere. Although visitors are welcome, virtually all the business of this nursery is conducted by mail order, and an exceptionally informative catalogue is produced (29p stamp).

EXBURY GARDENS
Hampshire

nr Southampton SO4 1AZ
From Totton (W of
Southhampton) 14m to
Exbury village by A326 and
B3054
Tel: 01703 891203

Owner: E.L. de Rothschild

Open: Mar to Oct 10–5.30
or sunset if earlier.
250 acres

Illustration opposite: The Courts

THE CLIMATE is particularly mild at Exbury. Lionel de Rothschild came here in 1919 and started to build up the collection of rhododendrons, many bred by him, which was to make the garden famous. His son has continued the tradition and has added many new varieties which may be seen growing in this huge garden. But even for those not interested in rhododendrons there is much to see throughout the season, especially superb old specimens of ornamental trees. There is an excellent plant centre; a catalogue is available (s.a.e.) and a mail order service.

FOXGROVE PLANTS
Berkshire

Foxgrove Farm, Enborne,
nr Newbury RG14 6RE
1m W of Newbury
Tel: 01635 40554

Open: Wed to Sun and
Bank Hol Mon 10–5;
closed throughout Aug

THIS LITTLE NURSERY has won several medals at RHS shows and elsewhere. Its speciality is smaller herbaceous plants and, although the stock is small, the plants are particularly well chosen. There are large selections of campanulas, geraniums, primulas (including some pretty auriculas), saxifrages, snowdrops (of which a special list is published) and violas. Louise Vockins has an eye for a good plant and the visitor is likely to find something unfamiliar and worth buying.

FURZEY GARDENS
Hampshire

THIS GARDEN was started in 1922 on rough grazing land which benefited from some good old trees and a rich natural vegetation which in many parts of the garden has been preserved. The site is sloping, the soil is acid, and the garden is full of excellent

Minstead,
nr Lyndhurst SO4 37GL
9m W of Southampton by
A336
Tel: 01703 812464

Owner: Furzey Gardens
Charitable Trust

Open: Daily except 25 and
26 Dec 10–5 or earlier in
winter. 8 acres

plants, many of them unusual. The layout is
informal, with grassy walks descending the hill and
winding between groups of shrubs. Herbaceous
plantings fringe the paths. In spring an immense
number of bulbs – narcissi, dog's tooth violets and
fritillaries – is followed by azaleas and
rhododendrons, many of them rare and tender. The
garden is outstanding in autumn with brilliant foliage
colours from such shrubs as enkianthus and witch
hazels and large specimens of *Liquidambar styraciflua*
and the scarlet oak, *Quercus coccinea*.

GREATHAM MILL

Hampshire

Greatham, nr Liss
GU33 6HH
7m SE of Alton by B3006
Tel: 01420 538 245

Owner:
Mrs E. Groves

Open: Apr to Oct, Sat, Sun
and Bank Hol Mon 2–6; by
appointment at other times

M RS PUMPHREY came to this mill house in 1949
and made a large and seductive garden on a
particularly attractive site – it is now run by her
granddaughter and grandson. Cottage-garden
profusion reigns at the front – an old plum tree
sprawls over richly planted beds of shrubs
underplanted with herbaceous plants. The plants have
been fastidiously chosen and there are substantial
groups of irises, geraniums and hostas. Mrs
Pumphrey also had an excellent eye for what goes
with what: a group of intense blue irises associating
with glaucous-leafed hostas, a wig-wam of golden
hop cooled down by a creamy flowered Scotch rose.
This gives the garden harmony rather than jumble.
Behind the house are old trees, a beautifully planted
bog garden, garlands of old roses and the occasional
well placed aristocratic shrub. Across a footbridge is
a nursery area with some good plants for sale.

GREEN FARM PLANTS
Hampshire

Illustration: Cistus creticus

Bentley, nr Farnham
GU10 5JX
In the village of Bentley 3m
SW of Farnham by A31
Tel: 01420 23202

Open: Mid Mar to mid
Oct, Wed to Sat 10–6;
other times by appointment

JOHN COKE AND MARINA CHRISTOPHER'S beautifully
kept nursery is well worth seeking out because
they have a connoisseur's eye for a good plant and
there are many things here that you will not easily
find elsewhere. Their specialities are smaller
decorative shrubs and hardy herbaceous plants.
Everything they choose has something distinguished
about it, which gives their range the feeling of a
house style. They do not have immense numbers of
any particular genus but there are discerningly chosen
groups of plants such as cistus, sages, mahonias and
toad lilies (*Tricyrtis* spp). There is no mail order but
a catalogue is produced (three 1st-class stamps).

GREYS COURT
Oxfordshire

Rotherfield Greys,
Henley-on-Thames
RG9 4PG
3m W of
Henley-on-Thames by A423
Tel: 01491 628529

Owner:
The National Trust

Open: Apr to Sept, daily
except Thur and Sun
(closed Good Fri) 2–6.
9 acres. House open

THE HOUSE, partly Tudor and partly Georgian,
built of red brick banded with silvery flint,
commands unforgettable views over the valley of
beech woods and downland. Passing through a white
garden and a garden of old roses underplanted with
pinks, a path leads under a great canopy of *Wisteria
sinensis*. In the former kitchen garden, paths are
edged with *Rosa mundi* or espaliered fruit trees. Here
a pergola veiled with vine and honeysuckle leads to
the Archbishop's Maze, an ornamental turf maze
designed in 1981 by Adrian Fisher and Randall

Coate. Turning back towards the house, by the Cromwellian Stables, is a brilliant little enclosed garden with knots of box hedges and topiary, London pride edging the paths of brick and cobble, beds burgeoning with herbaceous plants, screened by walls of pleached laburnum.

W. & L. HARLEY
Wiltshire

Parham Nursery, The Sands, Market Lavington, Devizes SN10 4QA
5m S of Devizes by A360
Tel: 01380 813712

Open: Mar to Nov, Sat 9.30–5 (closed throughout August); other times by appointment only

WILL AND LYNN Harley specialise in hardy perennials and alpine plants. Their list is not large but it is exceptionally well chosen, with many things (such as *Acanthus hirsutus*) that are very hard to find elsewhere. Among perennials they sell good ferns, geraniums, violas and many perennial wallflowers, and in the alpine department they are especially strong on phlox, saxifrages and sedums. A list is published, with seasonal supplements, and a mail order service is provided.

HAYWARD'S CARNATIONS
Hampshire

Illustration: Dianthus '*Queen of Sheba*'

The Chace Gardens, Stakes Road, Purbrook, Portsmouth PO7 5PL
4m NE of Portsmouth by A3
Tel: 01705 263047

Open: Mon to Fri 10–12, 2–4; closed first fortnight Aug, last fortnight Dec and first week Jan

CARNATIONS AND PINKS are very attractive and versatile garden plants and this is one of the best places in Britain to buy them. Haywards sells many cultivars which are nowhere else commercially available. A visit to the nursery in May or June is a heady experience, with the clove-scented ('true old-fashioned') pinks going full blast in the mild south Hampshire climate. A good list is produced, and a mail order service is provided.

HEALE GARDEN
Wiltshire

Middle Woodford,
nr Salisbury SP4 6NT
4m N of Salisbury in the
Woodford Valley by minor
roads
Tel: 01722 73504

Owner: Mr Guy Rasch

Open: Daily 10–5. 8 acres

Ο N LOW-LYING LAND on the banks of the Avon Heale House is an irresistibly decorative confection of rosy brick and stone dressings. The garden has a character all of its own and there are few places in England where a gardener is likely to have more fun. The 'landing stage' by the house and the scalloped fish ponds and rose terraces west of the house were designed by Harold Peto in 1910 for the Hon. Louis Greville who installed a Japanese garden with scarlet bridge and fragile tea-house after a tour of diplomatic duty in Japan before World War I. Nearby is a walled vegetable garden which the present owners have transformed with broad tunnels of espaliered apples, clipped mounds of box surrounding a pool and a beguiling mixture of fruit, vegetables and masterly ornamental planting. Everywhere in the garden there are roses – particularly old shrub roses – and the place is an unforgettable sight in late June; but there is always something to admire at other times. There is an excellent nursery, expanding all the time, which sells exceptionally good plants including the beautiful 'Terrace' roses, apparently unique to Heale, which have so far resisted identification. A catalogue is produced but there is no mail order.

Illustration opposite:
Heale Garden

THE SIR HAROLD HILLIER GARDENS AND ARBORETUM
Hampshire

Jermyns Lane, Ampfield,
nr Romsey SO51 0QA
3m NE of Romsey by
A31
Tel: 01794 368787

Owner: Hampshire
County Council

Open: Apr to Oct, daily
10.30–6; Nov to Mar,
daily 10.30–5. 160 acres

Τ HIS IS ONE of the greatest collections of woody plants in the country, and had its origin as the private arboretum of Sir Harold Hillier. The arboretum holds the National Collection of oaks but its riches are so extensive and various that there is little point in beginning to list them; one can say, however, that the soil is acid, and therefore the arboretum is especially good on acid-loving plants. A visit at any time of the year will be splendidly rewarded and this is a marvellous place for even expert gardeners to learn more; for beginners it is an essential part of gardening education.

HILLIER'S NURSERIES LTD
Hampshire

Ampfield House, Ampfield,
nr Romsey SO51 9PA
Tel: 01794 68733

Open: All branches: Mon
to Sat 9–5.30, Sun 10–5.30;
closed Christmas and New
Year

THIS IS THE headquarters of the Hillier empire from which mail orders are serviced. This nursery has the largest single collection of woody plants commercially available in the country (and quite possibly in the world) and its catalogue is a standard reference book. Herbaceous plants are also sold but there is nothing like the same range and depth. There are several garden centres in Hampshire, which include those at Jermyn's Lane, nr Romsey (01794 68407); in Romsey Road, west of Winchester (01962 842288); and at Botley Road, Romsey (01794 513459). These carry a good general stock – but it is only a pale reflection of the treasures available to order by mail or for collection from the headquarters.

HINTON AMPNER
Hampshire

Bramdean, nr Alresford
SO24 0LA
1m W of Bramdean village
by A272
Tel: 01962 771305

Owner:
The National Trust

Open: Apr to Sept, Sat,
Sun, Tue, Wed, Bank Hol
Mon (but closed Easter
Bank Hol) 1.30–5.30. 8
acres. House open

THIS IS AN exciting place to visit – an excellent old garden, redesigned in the 20th century and now being restored. The estate formerly belonged to Ralph Dutton, Lord Sherborne, who rebuilt the house, an 18th-century brick mansion, and laid out a new garden incorporating older features such as a superb lime avenue planted in 1720. It is a marvellous site and Dutton opened views into the exquisite surrounding parkland. Within the garden he laid out all sorts of decorative schemes – a cherry garden with formal hedges of box and yew, a yew walk backed with shrub roses, a leafy and mysterious dell, a sunken garden, yew topiary and much else. Everywhere there is a brilliant use of ornaments – statues and urns – which direct the gaze and emphasise a vista.

HOLLINGTON NURSERIES
Berkshire

ALTHOUGH THIS marvellous place certainly sells herbs it is misleading to call it a herb garden because it is of much wider interest that that. Simon and Judith Hopkinson have laid out a series of borders, knots, parterres and raised beds to show

Woolton Hill,
Newbury RG15 9XT
5m SW of Newbury by
A343
Tel: 01635 253908

Open: Mid Mar to Sept,
Mon to Sat 10–5.30, Sun
and Bank Hol Mon 11–5;
Oct to Mar, Mon to Fri
10–dusk

their plants in action. All this – beautifully designed and executed – is bursting with ideas for gardeners. In the nursery itself, apart from the very wide range of herbs there are also shrubs and trees with scented foliage, a small selection of conservatory plants and an interesting collection of ready-made topiary in cypress, box, yew and holly. A very good catalogue is produced (s.a.e.) but seeds only are sold by post and a separate list is available (s.a.e.).

IFORD MANOR
Wiltshire

Iford, nr Bradford-on-Avon
BA15 2BA
7m SE of Bath by A36
Tel: 01225 863146

Owner: Mrs
Cartwright-Hignett

Open: Apr and Oct, Sun
2–5; May to Sept, daily
except Mon and Fri 2–5.
2 1/2 acres

THE ARCHITECT and garden-designer Harold Peto came here in 1899 and remained until his death in 1933. On the steep wooded slopes of the Frome valley, above an 18th-century manor house, he laid out a terraced garden embellished everywhere by the collection of classical statuary and architectural fragments that he amassed over the years. Steep flights of steps ascend the slope, linking terraces with pools, fountains, loggias, colonnades, urns and figures. Cypresses add to the Italian atmosphere and many trees and shrubs flower among the statues. Peto was fully aware of the contrasts of his formal garden with its rural surrounds, and idyllic views open out everywhere over old woodland, and cattle grazing in meadows. In the woods above the garden a Japanese garden is being recreated by the present owners who have done a huge amount of restoration.

JENKYN PLACE
Hampshire

Bentley, nr Farnham
GU10 5LU
In Bentley village, 4m
SW of Farnham on A31
Tel: 01420 23118

Owner: Mrs G.E. Coke

Open: 14 Apr to 11 Sept,
Thur to Sun and Bank Hol
Mon 2–6. 6 acres

JENKYN PLACE is in the distinguished 20th-century tradition of gardens of compartments embellished with beautifully chosen, sometimes rare, plants. Laid out on a gentle slope, hedged in yew, beech or hawthorn, the garden has some very grand ingredients – a pair of large-scale true herbaceous borders, for example. But many of the most memorable features are of a simpler kind – waves of crinums planted under old apple trees, an avenue of pairs of different species of rowans, a single statue of a crouching lion at the end of a long, plain enclosure of beech hedging, and a long, refreshing grassy vista through old trees. Everywhere the visitor may see, as Gertrude Jekyll recommended, 'the best plants in the best places'.

KELMSCOTT MANOR
Oxfordshire

THE GABLED MANOR is 16th-century, handsomely set on the edge of the village by the wooded banks of the infant Thames. It is famous as the country house of William Morris and the garden

Kelmscott GL7 3HJ
In the village of Kelmscott,
6 1/2m NW of Faringdon by
A417, B4449 and minor road
Tel: 01367 252486

Owner: The Society of
Antiquaries

Open: Apr to Sept, Wed
11–1, 2–5. 1 1/2 acres

preserves an atmosphere of simple rural charm.
Recently, the custodians have been turning their
attention to the garden. Their careful plantings, with
well-chosen colours, now embellish this intensely
atmospheric place which is still so redolent of Morris
and his times. Rossetti found Kelmscott boring –
'The doziest dump of old grey beehives.' Other
visitors may disagree.

THE MANOR HOUSE
Hampshire

Upton Grey, nr Basingstoke
RG25 2RD
In the centre of Upton
Grey village, 6m SE of
Basingstoke by minor
roads; Jnct 5 of M3
Tel: 01256 862827

Owner: Mr and Mrs J.
Wallinger

Open: May to Jul, Wed
2–4.30; also by appointment

THE NAME OF Gertrude Jekyll seems to be on
almost every gardener's lips these days but very
few of her gardens survive and fewer still have been
restored with such care and affection as this. The
Wallingers came in 1984, long after the Jekyll garden
had disappeared, and have now reinstated her
original scheme with meticulous care. To one side of
the entrance drive the wild garden has sinuous mown
paths in long grass, rambling roses, thickets of
bamboo and a flag-fringed pool. Behind the house
the formal garden has a virtuoso Jekyll plat – two
squares of triangular beds edged with grey stachys
and brimming with swoony double pink peonies and
the double pink rose 'Caroline Testout'. Terraces
overlook it and the supporting dry-stone walls are
rich with aquilegia, corydalis, hart's tongue ferns and
valerian. Steps lead down to terraced bowling and
tennis lawns hedged in yew. This is one of the very
best Jekyll gardens from which to learn her essential
ideas which may be put into practice in any garden.

MATTOCKS ROSES
Oxfordshire

The Rose Nurseries,
Nuneham Courtenay
OX44 9PY
6m SE of Oxford by A4074
Tel: 01865 343265

Open: Mon to Sat 9–5.30
(5 in winter), Sun
10.30–5.30

Mattocks, which means roses to many gardeners, was established in 1875 and still has one of the best stocks of roses in the country. The emphasis is on modern cultivars, with regular new varieties introduced by Mattocks itself, but there are worthwhile collections of older types of shrub roses and of species. All these are of high quality and most may be seen growing at the nursery. A good catalogue is produced, with much background information including the names of breeders and dates of introduction. A mail order service is provided but nothing beats sniffing them in blooming fragrance in June or July.

THE MEAD NURSERY
Wiltshire

Illustration: Malva
moschata '*Alba*'

Brokerswood, nr Westbury
BA13 4EG
3 m NW of Westbury
between Woodland Park
and Rudge
Tel: 01373 859990

Open: Feb to Oct, Wed to
Sat and Bank Hol Mon
9–5, Sun 12–5

Stephen and Emma Lewis-Dale started their nursery only a couple of years ago and already it is showing its paces. The heart of their stock is herbaceous perennials with several of the smaller shrubs like artemisias, *Gaura lindheimeri*, lavender, sages and thymes that make such valuable companion plants. You would have to possess the best-stocked garden in the world, or be impossible to please, to come away empty-handed. Some attractive and well-planned display areas show the plants performing. There is no mail order but a very good catalogue is issued (five 1st-class stamps).

MOTTISFONT ABBEY GARDEN
Hampshire

Mottisfont,
nr Romsey SO51 0LJ
4 1/2m NW of Romsey by
A3057
Tel: 01794 341220/340757

Owner:
The National Trust

Open: 19 and 26 Mar, Apr
to Oct, Sat to Wed 12–6 or
dusk if earlier (in Jun
12–8.30, also Thur).
21 acres. House open

MOTTISFONT IS known for its Rose Garden in which an immense collection of shrub roses, with an emphasis on the older varieties, is arranged in the old walled kitchen garden. Here is housed the National Collection of pre-1900 shrub roses. Unlike many rose gardens, however, this is beautifully designed in box-edged beds divided by lawns and gravel paths, and the beds are enriched by all kinds of herbaceous plants which maintain interest when the roses are not performing. Visiting gardeners will not only meet many unfamiliar roses but they will discover an immense amount about their ornamental use in the garden. All this is a tribute to Graham Stuart Thomas who rediscovered so many old roses and supervised the making of this garden. Nearer the house, partly medieval stone and partly Georgian brick, there are other things worth seeing: a pleached lime alley designed by Sir Geoffrey Jellicoe with carpets of chionodoxa in the spring; a dashing box parterre with summer bedding; and, down by the River Test which flows through the grounds, a stupendous London plane tree, one of the most memorable trees you will ever see.

THE OLD RECTORY

Berkshire

Burghfield, Reading
RG3 3TH
In Burghfield village 5m
SW of Reading

Owner:
Mr and Mrs R.R. Merton

Open: Feb to Oct, last
Wed in month 11–4
(parties by appointment in
writing). 4 1/2 acres

THIS WONDERFUL GARDEN gets in only by the skin of its teeth because it is open so rarely, but it is so good that it would be worth planning a visit to these parts to coincide with its opening. Immediately behind the handsome brick house a marvellous cedar of Lebanon, the supreme garden ornament, is given full breathing space on a lawn. A pair of brilliant borders, separated by a crisp turf path and backed by yew hedges, leads towards a pool with a statue of Antinous, fringed with maples, bold foliage planting and flowering shrubs. All about the house are beautifully judged plantings (including some excellent troughs) and there is a splendid kitchen garden. On open days a plant *souk* appears in the yard and many good plants are sold.

OXFORD BOTANIC GARDEN

Oxfordshire

THIS WALLED GARDEN, with its lovely early 17th-century entrance gate, was founded in 1621, the first botanic garden in England. It still preserves its character of a 'repository of curious plants' but it is extremely attractively laid out and very well maintained. There are rectangular 'order' beds – with plants grouped according to botanical families – and there are also many ornamental trees and shrubs, some of them unusual (like the beautiful Himalayan

High Street,
Oxford OX1 4AX
In the centre of Oxford,
near Magdalen Bridge
Tel: 01865 276920

Owner: University of
Oxford

Open: Daily except Good
Fri and Christmas Day 9–5
(4.30 in winter);
greenhouses 2–4

birch, *Betula utilis jacquemontii*). Although much of the planting is severely botanical the ornamental aspects of horticulture are certainly not neglected: there are excellent borders and fine trees are well placed. Everything is impeccably labelled so it is an admirable place to learn about plants. To one side of the entrance, running along the High Street, is the 'Penicillin Garden', a pretty parterre of roses and hedges of box and yew, designed by Dame Sylvia Crowe both to celebrate Oxford's greatest medical discovery and to make the connection with the ancient physic garden.

OXFORD COLLEGE GARDENS
Oxfordshire

*Illustration: The entrance to
St John's College garden*

A LL OXFORD COLLEGES have some sort of garden, presenting to outsiders enticing green views glimpsed through iron railings or gates. A few of these are well worth visiting – hidden gardens of sometimes surprising size. **Magdalen College** (High St; *Open:* 2–6) has a deer park which gives the adjacent early 18th-century New Building something of the air of a rural seat; in front of it is an immense and beautiful London plane. Behind it, Addison's Walk, a shady tree-lined path loved by the 18th-century philosopher, skirts Magdalen Meadow, a lovely pasture which in spring is alive with snake's head fritillaries. **New College** (Holywell Street; *Open:* 11–5) in its Garden Quad, screened by handsome iron gates and railings, has bold borders with a jolly gallimaufry of colours against the sombre stone, given structure by crafty repeated plantings. In other parts of the college there are further signs of imaginative and skilful gardening; for example, bold pairs of distinguished shrubs such as *Carpenteria californica* flanking the entrance to a quad; all this, no doubt, the doing of Robin Lane Fox, the excellent gardener-writer who is a New College don. **St John's College** (St Giles; *Open:* 1–5) has an especially attractive view of the garden through the gate from Canterbury Quad; here is a grand lawn, with substantial trees, fringed with borders. A path to one side leads to a rock garden. **Wadham College** (Parks Road; *Open:* 1.30–4.30) has a long, curving mixed border and an exceptional old purple beech.

QUEEN ELEANOR'S GARDEN
Hampshire

Winchester Castle,
Winchester
In the centre of Winchester
Tel: 01962 840222

Owner: Winchester City
Council

Open: Daily 10–5

THIS LITTLE recreated 13th-century garden in the authentic medieval setting of Henry III's Great Hall was designed by Dr Sylvia Landsberg at the instigation of the Hampshire Gardens Trust. The planting consists only of plants known in gardens before 1300, and an ornamental fountain and stone seats are based on period survivals found at Winchester. A turf seat, a tunnel arbour of twining honeysuckle and vines, and the old walls of the Great Hall vividly evoke enclosed gardens of the period. No true medieval gardens survive in England and this gives a charming and historically accurate idea of what they looked like.

ROCHE COURT SCULPTURE
GARDEN
Wiltshire

THERE IS a renaissance of the use of ornaments in the garden and this is a splendid place to see them in action. The late Georgian house is in a wonderful position with wide views down a wooded

Winterslow,
nr Salisbury SP5 1BG
5m E of Salisbury by A30
Tel: 01980 862244

Owner:
The Earl and Countess of
Bessborough

Open: May to Oct, Sat and
Sun 11–5; also by
appointment at other times

valley, and the garden itself is rich in excellent old trees, yew hedges and old walls which make a very good setting in which to display ornaments. Roche Court is partly a private garden and partly a gallery in which sculptures and pots are displayed for sale; some by well known artists such as Barbara Hepworth, others by the new and little known. The exhibits, which change constantly, benefit immensely from their open air display, and the ensemble of house, garden, views and works of art make it a memorable place to visit.

ROUSHAM HOUSE
Oxfordshire

Steeple Aston OX6 3QX
12m N of Oxford by
A4260 and B4030
Tel: 01869 47110

Owner: C. Cottrell-Dormer

Open: Daily 10–4.30.
30 acres. House open

THERE ARE FEW 18th-century landscape gardens surviving in England where it is still possible to see exactly what the designer intended. Rousham was designed between 1737 and 1741 by William Kent who devised a virtuoso arrangement of statues, buildings, water, a serpentine woodland rill and, above all, made a framework from which to admire the views over the River Cherwell towards the rural landscape beyond. Some of the individual garden buildings are exceptionally beautiful: Praeneste, a wonderful arcaded curve of golden stone, giving viewpoints of subtly changing aspect; Kent's little covered seat of trellis and boards; a solemn gothic temple half-shaded by the woods. The statues are of fine quality and almost all of them turn their backs on the garden and gaze out to the countryside. All this is done with the effortless ease of a conjuror pulling rabbits out of a hat. Nearer the house, in the old kitchen garden with its decorative dovecote, there is a charming arrangement of mixed borders and a box-edged rose parterre.

SPINNERS
Hampshire

Boldre, Lymington
SO41 5QE
1m NE of Lymington by
A337
Tel: 01590 673347

Open: 14 Apr to 14 Sept,
Wed to Sat 10–5 (also Suns
in May); other times by
appointment

ON ACID SOIL and surrounded by woodland, Spinners is both a splendid and developing garden and a nursery garden selling a diverse selection of woody and herbaceous plants, many rare. The drive that winds downhill is well planted with ornamental trees and shrubs, and nearer the house there are excellent borders. Most of the plants displayed in the garden may be bought at the nursery. There are, for example, many different species and varieties of magnolia, several maples and rhododendrons, many dogwoods, rare oaks and witch hazels – and that is only in the woody department. There are also choice riches in herbaceous plants – 10 kinds of hardy cyclamen, ferns, excellent grasses, dozens of geraniums and a host of hostas. No catalogue is produced and there is no mail order, so you will have to visit – and discover its riches.

STOURHEAD
Wiltshire

Illustration opposite: The Temple of Flora at Stourhead

ALTHOUGH THIS IS probably the most photographed and certainly the best-known landscape garden in England the experience of visiting it, in different seasons of the year, always provides some new pleasure. It was started in 1741 by the banker Henry Hoare who dammed the River

Stourton, Warminster
BA12 6QH
In Stourton village, 3m
NW of Mere by A303 and
B3092
Tel: 01747 840348

Owner:
The National Trust

Open: Daily 9–7 or sunset
if earlier (except 19–22 Jul
when garden closes at 5).
40 acres. House open

Stour to make a sinuous lake about whose shores he
disposed paths, temples, urns, a shivery grotto and,
clothing the hillsides, a vast wealth of trees. Although
there has been much subsequent planting, continuing
in present times, the character of the original layout
is unimpaired. Even at rhododendron time it is
possible to escape the crush of visitors, ascend the
precipitous paths that wind up away from the lake,
and experience the authentic feeling of thrilling
solitude such gardens inspired in the 18th century.

STOWE LANDSCAPE GARDENS
Buckinghamshire

Buckingham MK18 5EH
3m NW of Buckingham of
A422
Tel: 01280 822850

Owner:
The National Trust

Open: Sun 10–6 and other
days during school holidays
and certain days during
term time. Please phone for
details. 250 acres. House
open

STOWE MAKES all other gardens seem like light
snacks – this is the full banquet. It is a giant
18th-century landscape garden in which the greatest
garden designers of the day worked – Charles
Bridgeman, William Kent and 'Capability' Brown,
who was head gardener in 1741. In this vast
landscape grass, trees, water, ornaments, buildings
and huge vistas form a series of exquisite pictures.
The monuments and buildings have all sorts of
meanings – many of them political – and are often

decorated with literary inscriptions. Even without unravelling their significance, any visitor can revel in the marvellous shifting scenes – the contrast of immense views and corners of pastoral intimacy, of grazing cattle and classical temples. To walk about Stowe is one of the greatest of all garden experiences.

TUDOR HOUSE GARDEN
Hampshire

Tudor House, Bugle Street, Southampton SO1 OA8
Centre of Southampton; follow signs to old town and docks
Tel: 01703 332513

Owner: Southampton County Council

Open: Tue to Fri 10–12, 1–5, Sat 10–12, 1–4, Sun 2–5

THIS IS a very attractive idea – a dashing recreation of a Tudor period garden, designed by Dr Sylvia Landsberg in 1982 as the annexe to an excellent museum in the old city of Southampton. A knot of box, plants of the period, characteristic columns painted in chevrons and surmounted by heraldic beasts, hives with honey bees, a rose arbour and a tunnel of vines give something of the true character of a garden of the period.

VENTNOR BOTANIC GARDEN
Isle of Wight

ON THE SOUTH coast of the Isle of Wight Ventnor has an exceptional microclimate and one of the chief interests of this botanic garden is the large collection of plants from the southern hemisphere

The Undercliff Drive,
Ventnor, Isle of Wight
PO38 1UL
Tel: 01983 855397

Owner: South Wight
Borough Council

Open: Daily dawn–dusk

and from the Mediterranean countries. These are displayed in sweeping beds and fine old holm oaks (*Quercus ilex*) and strawberry trees (*Arbutus unedo*) provide a handsome evergreen background. A large temperate house protects more tender subjects, where there are well arranged collections from South Africa and Australia and also from less familiar regions like the island of St Helena which has a fascinating flora.

WADDESDON MANOR
Buckinghamshire

Waddesdon,
nr Aylesbury HP18 0JH
6m NW of Aylesbury by
A41
Tel: 01296 651211

Owner:
The National Trust

Open: Mar to 22 Dec, Wed
to Sat 11–5; Sun, Bank Hol
Mon and Good Fri
10.30–5. 160 acres.

THIS IS a Rothschild garden and a splendid one. The house is a fantasy pastiche of a Loire château, finished in 1889 for Baron Ferdinand de Rothschild and built on a wonderful site – the top of a hill commanding views over the Vale of Aylesbury. The slopes of the hill are encircled with walks and clothed in splendid trees, and a marvellous collection of statues animates the scene. To the south of the house are terraced gardens which have recently been restored with elaborate bedding schemes to their original high Victorian splendour. Further work is in progress to restore other parts of the gardens which were laid out by the French landscape architect Lainé who also worked on the estates of the French Rothschilds. To one side of the house a superb aviary of delicate wrought-iron tracery and rococo curlicues houses a splendid collection of exotic birds. The house, after a long period of restoration, is now looking more beautiful than ever.

WATERPERRY GARDENS
Oxfordshire

nr Wheatley OX33 1JZ
9m E of Oxford by A40.
Near Jnct 8 of M40
Tel: 01844 339254/226

Owner: School of
Economic Science

Open: Mar to Oct, daily
10–5.30 (6 at weekends);
Nov to Feb 10–5. Closed
Christmas and New Year
hols and four days in July.
83 acres

WATERPERRY WAS started in 1932 as a pioneer
horticultural college for women by the
extraordinary Miss Beatrix Havergal. Although still
providing courses for amateurs, it is today chiefly a
nursery garden and a very attractive pleasure garden.
The nursery has an excellent range of all the essential
garden plants – including a comprehensive collection
of fruit trees, bushes and canes. Alpine plants are a
particular speciality and the garden holds the
National Collection of porophyllum saxifrages (over
300 species and cultivars). The ornamental gardens
have herbaceous borders, an alpine garden, fine trees
and the beautifully tended stock beds for the nursery.

WEST WYCOMBE PARK
Buckinghamshire

West Wycombe HP14 3AJ
2m W of High Wycombe
by A40
Tel: 01494 524411

Owner:
The National Trust

Open: Apr to May, Sun
and Wed 2–6; Easter, May
and Spring Bank Hol Mon
2–6; Jun to Aug, Sun to
Thur 2–6. 46 acres. House
open

THE PARK at West Wycombe, made for the
Dashwoods in the 18th century, is among the
smaller English landscape gardens and is an excellent
place to understand the particular charms of that
style. The 18th-century pillared and portico'd house
stands on a wooded eminence overlooking a lake
with an island on which is an airy Music Temple
and, nearby on the shore, a gothic boathouse. The
lake feeds a cascade guarded by two recumbent
nymphs and a stream winds across meadow land. In
the woods about the lake an exotic Temple of the
Winds marks the meeting point of two vistas. All the
ingredients are harmoniously interrelated and form a
series of shifting and seductive views giving the
impression of a much larger area.

GILBERT WHITE'S HOUSE
Hampshire

Selborne,
nr Alton GU34 3JH
In the village of Selborne,
5m SE of Alton by B3006
Tel: 01420 511275

Owner:
Oates Memorial Trust

Open: End Mar to end Oct
daily 11–5; Nov to Dec, Sat
and Sun 11–5 (closed 24
Dec)

GILBERT WHITE was as passionately observant about gardening as he was about natural history and his writings on the subject, contained in his *Garden Kalendar*, are still well worth reading. This place – his former house and garden – is sacred ground. Behind the house, which is in the village high street, the garden has wonderful views across to the wooded ridge known as the Hanger. A rose garden, yew hedges and topiary, a laburnum tunnel and herbaceous borders are well cared for. These are relatively modern features but there still remains much from White's time – the ha-ha he made in 1761, his fruit wall and a decorative sun-dial.

WROXTON ABBEY
Oxfordshire

Wroxton, Banbury OX15
6PX
In the village of Wroxton,
2 1/2 miles W of Banbury
by A422
Tel: 01295 730551

Owner: Fairleigh
Dickinson University

Open: Daily, dawn to
dusk. 56 acres

SOME HISTORIC GARDENS are of interest only to garden historians. The mansion is Jacobean with medieval origins and the garden at Wroxton is full of history – a splendid and complicated past with a 17th-century formal garden followed by an 18th-century landscape park with buildings by Sanderson Miller. It preserves considerable atmosphere, with a serpentine lake, a gentle cascade, a sinuous rill with bridges, all partly concealed in a wood. Now belonging to an American university, the park reveals its charms gradually as the visitor explores it and learns the lie of the land.

SOUTH-WEST ENGLAND

Avon
Cornwall
Devon
Dorset
Somerset

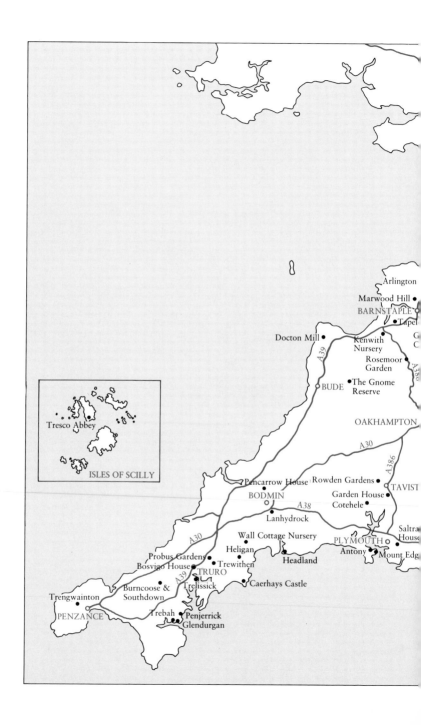

Arlington

Marwood Hill ●

BARNSTAPLE ○

● Tapel

Docton Mill ●

Kenwith
Nursery

Rosemoor ●
Garden

BUDE ○

● The Gnome
Reserve

OAKHAMPTON

A39

A30

A386

Tresco Abbey

ISLES OF SCILLY

● Pencarrow House

Rowden Gardens ●

TAVIST

BODMIN ○

Garden House ●

Cotehele ●

A38

Lanhydrock

Saltra
House

Wall Cottage Nursery

PLYMOUTH ○

Heligan ●

Headland

Antony ● ● Mount Edg

Probus Gardens ●

Bosvigo House ●

Trewithen ●

A30

TRURO ●

Burncoose & ● Trelissick ●

Southdown

● Caerhays Castle

Trengwainton
●

PENZANCE

Trebah ● Penjerrick

Glendurgan

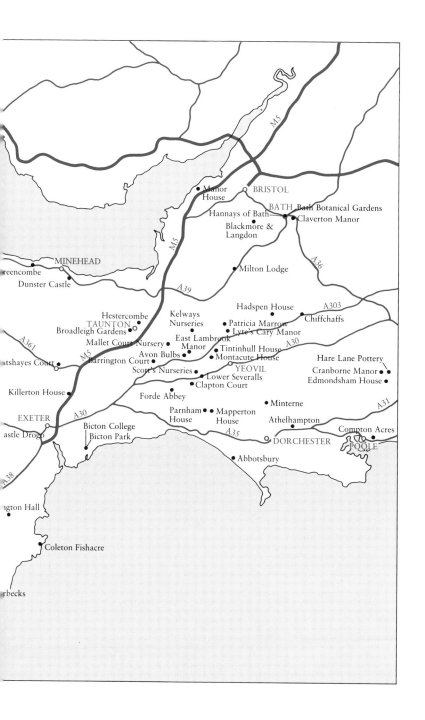

ABBOTSBURY SUB-TROPICAL GARDENS

Dorset

Abbotsbury,
nr Weymouth DT3 4LA
1/2m W of Abbotsbury
village, 9m NW of
Weymouth by B3157
Tel: 01305 871412/871344

Owner: Ilchester Estates

Open: Daily 10–5 (dusk in
winter); closed 25 Dec.
20 acres

B ENEFITING FROM a remarkably mild microclimate, Abbotsbury Gardens have an immense range of plants. The garden was started in the 1760s but the 4th Earl of Ilchester introduced many new plants in the 19th century. From the original walled garden with its beautiful wingnut (*Pterocarya fraxinifolia*), paths lead to the valley garden, a gentle combe with camellias, magnolias and rhododendrons in old woodland. Asiatic primulas enliven the banks of the stream in spring, followed by gunnera, petasites, rodgersias and rheums. It is a garden worth visiting at any time of the year; in winter, for example, it is full of interest. Everywhere there is something to catch the eye in the jungle-like luxuriance. A plant centre has some good plants for sale.

ANTONY HOUSE

Cornwall

Torpoint PL11 2QA
5m W of Plymouth by
Torpoint car ferry and A374
Tel: 01752 812191

Owner:
The National Trust

Open: Apr to Oct, Tue,
Wed, Thur and Bank Hol
Mon 1.30–5.30; Jun to
Aug, also Sun 1.30–5.30. 25
acres. House open

W HEN A HOUSE is as beautiful as Antony there is always a danger that any garden will be outfaced. As it is, helped by the genius of Humphry Repton, the two go together in perfect harmony. The house – an early 18th-century dream of silver Pentewan stone – presents its north façade to land which slopes gently towards the distant Tamar estuary. The view from the house, over shallow rose-planted terraces, is towards an immense lawn broken in the middle ground only by a superb old black walnut (*Juglans nigra*). Far beyond this, Repton pierced an opening through a deep belt of woodland to give glimpses of the shimmering water in the distance. In the woods there are marvellous trees, including some ancient holm oaks which Repton admired and was careful to preserve. A flower garden, and a recently made knot of box and germander, are enclosed in yew, and in the old vegetable garden there is an immense collection of daylilies of which Antony holds a National Collection. South of all this is a giant cork oak (*Quercus suber*), a wonder to see.

ANTONY WOODLAND GARDEN AND WOODS
Cornwall

Torpoint PL11 2QA
5m W of Plymouth by
Torpoint car ferry and
A374

Owner: Carew Pole Garden
Trust

Open: 15 Mar to 31 Oct,
Mon to Sat 11–5.30; Sun
2–5.30. 100 acres

ADJOINING THE HOUSE and garden at Antony, and still owned by the family that built it, is an atmospheric woodland garden. Sir John Carew Pole started to plant it before World War II but was interrupted by active service. Since then he has added an immense number of magnolias and rhododendrons which flourish in the naturalistic setting of a wooded combe protected to the west by windbreaks. The woods fringe the estuary of the River Lynher and an idyllic walk gives glimpses of the mainland and the castellated silhouette of Ince Castle.

ARLINGTON COURT
Devon

Arlington, nr Barnstaple
EX31 4LP
7m NE of Barnstaple by
A39
Tel: 01271 850629

Owner:
The National Trust

Open: Apr to Oct, daily
except Sat (open Sat Bank
Hol weekends) 11–5.30.
25 acres. House open

THE PLEASURES of Arlington are not dramatic but they are distinctive. The best thing here is a little Victorian garden with, as its central ornament, a handsome gabled glasshouse crowned with a decorative metal heron, the crest of the Chichester family who owned the estate for many centuries. The garden is backed by a high wall and the ground descends in bold turfed terraces to the entrance steps which are flanked by a pair of cast-iron herons holding wriggling worms in their beaks. On either side of a central pool and fountain, arbours are festooned with roses in summer. The Victorian garden is some distance from the house which is set in lawns with fine specimen trees, including the recent addition of a collection of species of ash. The lake was made at about the same time as the Victorian garden and a classical urn on a plinth to its north-east is in memory of Miss Rosalie Chichester who gave the estate to the National Trust.

ATHELHAMPTON HOUSE
Dorset

Athelhampton, Dorchester
DT2 7LG
5 1/2m NE of Dorchester
by A35(T)
Tel: 01305 848363

Owner: Patrick Cooke

Open: Easter to end Oct,
Tue, Wed, Thur and Sun
12–5; Jul and Aug, also
Mon and Fri.
15 acres. House open

THE GREAT THING about the garden at Athelhampton is the beauty of its design. This is a late medieval manor house of rare character and the garden, which was designed in the 1890s by F. Inigo Thomas, fits it to perfection. A balustraded terrace ornamented with two elegant summer houses overlooks a narrow canal and beyond, disposed on a sunken lawn with a pool, are twelve giant pyramids of clipped yew. On the far side a gate leads through to a series of enclosed gardens – cunningly connected to the house by penetrating vistas – which are richly ornamented with statues, fountains, obelisks, beautifully detailed walls and gate piers in golden Ham stone. The whole place is a virtuoso performance, a garden that is harmoniously related to house and site.

AVON BULBS
Somerset

Burnt House Farm, Mid Lambrook, South Petherton TA13 5HE
10m W of Yeovil by A3088 and A303 to South Petherton
Tel: 01460 242177

Open: Mid Feb to mid Apr; end Sept to mid Nov, Thur to Sat 9–4.30 (check by telephone; also by appointment)

BECAUSE OF the restricted opening times this wonderful place only just qualifies for inclusion. Avon Bulbs wins Gold Medals at Chelsea regularly and its list is stuffed with good things. There is an emphasis on species or natural forms and many genera are represented in quantity (e.g. 15 species and forms of fritillary and over 20 snowdrops). There is an excellent range of cyclamen, camassias, many fritillaries, irises and narcissi. The nursery's business is chiefly bulbs but it strays into other desirable areas such as hellebores, of which a choice selection is offered, and, increasingly, beautiful species peonies. The list (four 2nd-class stamps) is exceptionally good, beautifully illustrated and full of advice on cultivation. A mail order service is provided.

BARRINGTON COURT
Somerset

nr Ilminster TA19 0NQ
5m NE of Ilminster off A303
Tel: 01985 847777

Owner:
The National Trust

Open: Apr to Sept, daily except Fri 11–5.30.
9 acres. House open

THE BEAUTIFUL gabled manor house, of golden Ham stone, was built in 1514. The gardens have a pronounced Arts and Crafts atmosphere with marvellous basket-weave brick paths and fine masonry in walls and outhouses. Much of this is the work of the architects Forbes and Tate who restored the buildings in the 1920s and for whose intricately planned enclosures Gertrude Jekyll designed the planting, one of her very last commissions. The chief surviving part with something of her touch is the lily garden to one side of the stable block, with central pool and raised beds of azaleas and bold clumps of crinums. East of it there is a charming new white garden, designed by Christine Middleton, the present head gardener, in segmental beds radiating from the centre. A gate leads through to the iris garden of

Jekyllesque flavour, with a colour scheme of pink and lavender. One of the best parts of the garden is a beautifully kept walled kitchen garden from which produce is sold in season.

BATH BOTANICAL GARDENS
Avon

Royal Victoria Park, Upper Bristol Road, Bath BA1 2NQ
W of city centre by Upper Bristol Road

Owner: City of Bath

Open: Daily 9–sunset

As BOTANIC GARDENS go this is on a modest scale but it is very attractively laid out on a fine sloping site and is rich in good plants. Here, it is the trees and larger shrubs that are of special distinction. There are excellent specimens, many mature, of the golden *Catalpa bignonioïdes*, Japanese cherries, an exceptional dogwood, *Cornus kousa chinensis*, superb magnolias and Japanese maples. An atmospheric dell, across the road to the north of the gardens, has a monument to Shakespeare and lovely drifts of anemones and bluebells in season. The whole is excellently cared for by the city parks department.

BICTON COLLEGE OF AGRICULTURE
Devon

PART OF THE SAME ESTATE as Bicton Park, Bicton College now opens its doors to members of the public, who will find much to interest them. An avenue of monkey-puzzles leads towards the house, beyond which are several collections of trees and

East Budleigh, Budleigh
Salterton EX9 7DP
6m NE of Exmouth by
A376
Tel: 01395 568353

Owner: Bicton College

Open: Daily 10.30–5.
19 acres

shrubs – among them camellias, cherries, eucalyptus,
magnolias maples. The college holds the National
Collections of agapanthus and pittosporum; the
former is a real eye-opener (especially the lovely, and
rarely seen, species). In a 2-acre walled garden a
nursery has many excellent plants for sale, including
several tender rarities.

BICTON PARK GARDENS
Devon

East Budleigh, Budleigh
Salterton EX9 7DP
6m NE of Exmouth by
B3178
Tel: 01395 568465

Owner: Bicton Park Trust

Open: Mar to Oct, daily
10–6 (4 in Mar and Oct).
50 acres

THINGS ARE CHANGING at Bicton Park, which is
being restored to its true character as a pleasure
garden. At the heart of it is a formal arrangement,
the Italian Garden, which in essence dates from the
early 18th century but now has a jolly Victorian
character with bedded-out parterres, fountains, urns
and palm trees. To the north is a range of
glasshouses with collections of fuchsias and
pelargoniums and, to the west, a stunning
curvaceous palm house, like a ship's prow seen from
below. Recently restored, this very early building
dates from 1820, and has been planted with a
splendid range of conservatory plants. To one side of
the Italian Garden there is an ornamental shell-house
set in a ferny rock garden and, another relic of the
early 19th century, an American garden in which
plants from North America were grown. A woodland
railway through the grounds gives views of a fine
arboretum and the brick mansion. There is much to
see and admire here, not least the high standards of
maintenance.

BLACKMORE & LANGDON
Avon

Stanton Nurseries,
Pensford, Bristol BS18 4JL
6 1/2m S of Bristol by A37
Tel: 01275 332300

Open: Daily 9–5

OLD-ESTABLISHED FAMILY firms such as this are
becoming very rare. Blackmore & Langdon was
founded in 1901, and has won over 60 Gold Medals
at the Chelsea Flower Show and countless others
elsewhere. It is best known for delphiniums, border
phlox and begonias, and many varieties of these are
available only from Blackmore & Langdon whose
catalogue every year advertises interesting new
cultivars. It also sells gloxinias and polyanthus. The

catalogue (s.a.e.) is particularly informative, and excellent specialist pamphlets on growing some of these plants are issued. A mail order service is provided and various sundries, including special wire supports for begonias, are available. A visit at delphinium time is a wonderful treat.

BOSVIGO HOUSE
Cornwall

Bosvigo Lane, Truro
TR1 3NH
In the western suburbs of Truro by A390; at Highertown turn down Dobbs Lane (beside Shell garage). Bosvigo House is on the left after 500 yards
Tel: 01872 75774 (after dark)

Owner: Michael and Wendy Perry

Open: Mar to Sept, Wed to Sat 11–6. 3 acres

BOSVIGO HOUSE is a surprising and very attractive place to find on the edge of Truro with bungaloid growth gnawing all about. In the garden, however, all that seems far away. The Perrys are perfectionists, and although the garden is still being developed, they seem to be doing all the right things. To one side of the handsome 18th-century house is a new woodland garden, at its best in spring. About the house are several beautifully planted enclosures full of fastidiously chosen herbaceous plants which provide interest throughout the season. The Perrys also sell excellent plants, some very rare. There is a very good catalogue (four 2nd-class stamps) but no mail order.

BROADLEIGH GARDENS

Somerset

Illustration: Crown imperials (Fritillaria imperialis '*Maxima Lutea*')

Bishops Hull, Taunton TA4 1AE
3m SW of Taunton by A38
Tel: 01823 286231

Open: Mon to Fri 9–4 to view only. Mail order and pre-booked sales only

THIS IS AN outstandingly good nursery specialising in bulbs. Although the business is mail order only, you may visit the garden and view the plants on the spot. Spring is, of course, a good time but Lady Skelmersdale has all sorts of bulbous treats up her sleeve throughout the year – a rare selection of colchicums and autumn-flowering crocuses, for example. This is not a place for instant gardeners but you can go round, notebook in hand, making a list to order from the excellent catalogues (two 1st-class stamps) which are issued twice a year.

BURNCOOSE & SOUTH DOWN NURSERIES

Cornwall

Gwennap, Redruth TR16 6BJ
3m SE of Redruth by A393
Tel: 01209 861112

Open: Mon to Sat 8.30–5, Sun 11–5. Garden: 30 acres

THE NURSERY is in the ownership of the Williams family, famous plant collectors who also own Caerhays Castle. It carries a varied stock, of over 2,000 kinds, but there are specialities for which it is outstanding, some of which would be considered hopelessly tender anywhere outside the privileged south-west (for example, *Metrosideros*). The emphasis is on woody plants with some major groups, such as camellias, magnolias and rhododendrons, of which it has especially good selections. Several rarities are stocked (for example *Pittosporum tenuifolium* 'Silver Magic') which are scarcely to be found anywhere else. A very good catalogue (£1.00) is published, from which mail orders may be placed. Alongside the nursery is a fine old woodland garden in which camellias, magnolias and, above all, magnificent rhododendrons are attractively displayed among handsome trees.

CAERHAYS CASTLE
Cornwall

nr Gorran FA1 7DE
In the village of Caerhays
10m S of St Austell by
minor roads
Tel: 01872 501310

Owner: F.J. Williams

Open: 20 Mar to 5 May,
Mon to Fri 11–4.30; also
Suns 26 Mar and 16 Apr
and 8 May Bank Hol
11–4.30. 100 acres

THIS IS a special place for the three greatest groups of ornamental Asiatic shrubs: camellias, magnolias and rhododendrons. The Williams family, who own it, sponsored some of the great plant hunters – such as George Forrest and Frank Kingdon-Ward – and their discoveries found a marvellous home in this wild coastal setting. North of the early 19th-century castle designed by John Nash, woodland sweeps up the hill. It is a place for the observant visitor because the garden's chief glories may lie hidden in the jungle and the excitement of discovery is one of the exceptional pleasures here. Apart from the great trio of shrubs there are many others, some of them exceptionally rare and first planted here – such as the exotically scented *Michelia doltsopa* with its flowers of creamy yellow. The lavish feast of spring blossom, in this wildly romantic place, is a marvellous sight.

CASTLE DROGO
Devon

Drewsteignton EX6 6PB
21m W of Exeter by A30
Tel: 01647 433306

Owner:
The National Trust

Open: Apr to Oct, daily
10.30–5.30. 12 acres.
Castle open

CASTLE DROGO, the last castle to be built in Britain, was designed by Edwin Lutyens and started before World War I. It has a dramatic position on a rocky bluff near Dartmoor, commanding wide views with the River Teign in the distance. The garden, to the north of the drive, is concealed behind ramparts of yew strongly echoing the bold forms of the castle. Granite steps and a path lead to a rectangular sunken garden of subtly varying levels. Here, in each corner, is a shady arbour of *Parrotia persica* trained over a framework, and around two central lawns are lavishly planted mixed borders, among which scalloped paths of Mughal influence thread their way. In late spring an immense

old wisteria snakes along the terrace walls, its flowers dripping to the beds below. Granite steps rise to a path lined with flowering trees and shrubs, leading to a huge circular croquet lawn (which visitors may use) hedged in yew, devoid of ornament but with powerful atmosphere.

CHIFFCHAFFS

Dorset

Chaffeymoor, Bourton, Gillingham SP8 5BY
At W end of Bourton village, 3m E of Wincanton by A303; leave A303 (Bourton bypass) at sign to Bourton
Tel: 01747 840841

Owner:
Mr and Mrs K.R. Potts

Open: Garden: 26 Mar to 24 Sept, Sun, Wed and Thur (closed 1st Sun in month except Apr and May, closed 2nd Sun) and Bank Hol weekend 2–5.30; Nursery: Tue to Sat 10–1, 2– 5, and whenever garden is open. At other times by appointment. 11 acres

THIS GARDEN, in a surprisingly secluded valley just off the A303, was started from nothing fourteen years ago, and the owners recently incorporated within it their nursery garden, Abbey Plants. The sloping site has been skilfully terraced and linked with stone paths and steps. The soil is acid and a very wide range of plants is grown in beds separated by curving lawns. The different levels, and secluded nooks and crannies, provide a variety of sites in an attractively informal setting. Across a field is a woodland garden threaded with streams where moisture-loving plants such as primulas, gunnera and rheums thrive in the shade of rhododendrons and many ornamental trees. All this is an exceptional example of what can be achieved by skilled gardeners in a remarkably short time. The nursery has an excellent general range of plants at modest prices and a visit is essential as no mail order service is provided.

CLAPTON COURT GARDENS
Somerset

Clapton, nr Crewkerne
TA18 8PT
In the village of Clapton
3m S of Crewkerne by
B3165
Tel: 01460 73220

Owner: Captain S.J. Loder

Open: Mar to Oct, Mon to
Fri 10.30–5, Sun 2–5; also
open Easter Sat 2–5.
10 acres

THERE IS PLENTY to see at Clapton Court – two gardens of different character and a good nursery. The formal part has lively terraced garden rooms walled with yew, hornbeam and cotoneaster. Beyond the house, following a stream with some finely judged planting, there is a woodland garden with outstanding trees underplanted with rhododendrons and other ornamental shrubs. The nursery has an especially good range of clematis, and a wide general stock. A catalogue is produced (£1.35) but there is no mail order.

CLAVERTON MANOR
Avon

CLAVERTON MANOR, with its wonderful views across the Avon valley, is an elegant Bath stone mansion designed by Sir Jeffry Wyatville. The position of the garden, on south-facing slopes, is beautiful, with excellent old trees – evergreen oaks, limes and beeches – providing a backdrop for the gardens made here since the American Museum came in 1961. Under the walls of the house the American garden designer Lanning Roper laid out an effective mixed border punctuated by Irish yews. A further transatlantic flavour is given by a collection of herbs

Claverton, nr Bath
BA2 7BD
4m SE of Bath by A36
Tel: 01225 460503

Owner: The American
Museum in Britain

Open: end Mar to
beginning Nov, daily
except Mon 1–6 (Sat and
Sun 12–6; Bank Hol Sun
and Mon 11–6). 10 acres.
House open

used in colonial times, disposed in box-edged beds
with a bee-skep at the centre. To the west of the
house, overlooked by terraces, is a George
Washington garden, influenced by Washington's
Virginian estate of Mount Vernon. Here are sweeping
beds edged in brick or box, gravel paths and an
elegant octagonal pepper-pot gazebo. Farther down
the slopes an arboretum planted with American trees
and shrubs vividly reminds the visitor of the debt
owed by British gardens to American flora. All this is
impeccably maintained. A small selection of well
grown herbs is offered for sale.

COLETON FISHACRE GARDEN
Devon

Coleton, Kingswear,
Dartmouth TQ6 0EQ
4m S of Brixham off B3205
Tel: 0180 425 466

Owner:
The National Trust

Open: Mar, Sun 2–5; Apr
to Oct, Wed to Sun (except
Sat), also Bank Hol Mon
10.30–5.30 or dusk if
earlier. 20 acres

THIS IS a remote corner of south Devon and to
find a garden here at all seems pretty unlikely;
to find one of such special charm as this is amazing
good fortune. The house, built by Oswald Milne, a
follower of Edwin Lutyens, for the D'Oyly Carte
family, looks down a narrow valley that descends to
the sea. The garden has a very warm microclimate
and the sea adds to the humidity. Plants flourish here
and many tender things, tricky if not impossible to

grow elsewhere in Britain, seem luxuriantly at home. A stream runs the whole length of the garden, occasionally breaking out into little pools whose banks are finely planted with moisture-loving herbaceous perennials. The sides of the valley, threaded with winding paths, are densely planted with trees and shrubs. There are many camellias and rhododendrons but also far more exciting things – tender exotics such as the crape myrtle (*Lagerstroemia indica*), *Mandevilla suaveolens* and great thickets of mimosa (*Acacia dealbata*).

COMPTON ACRES

Dorset

Canford Cliffs Road, Poole
BH13 7ES
1 1/2m W of Bournemouth
by A35 and B3065
Tel: 01202 700778

Owner:
Pamlion Properties Ltd

Open: Mar to Oct, daily
10.30–6.30. 10 acres

IN SPITE of Compton Acres' popularity, garden snobs should not turn their backs on it for it has an immense amount to offer. The precipitous site, with old pine woods close to the sea, reveals occasional splendid views to the Isle of Purbeck. The garden is arranged in a series of thematic episodes, each of which is beautifully arranged to give surprise: an Italian garden with a long pool, splashing fountains, clipped hedges and statues; a palm court with a Moorish flavour; an elaborate water garden with conifers and paths winding over rocks; and an immense Japanese garden of great character, shady, richly ornamented and dramatic. There are many excellent plants – in particular rhododendrons in a valley garden and many conifers and heathers in the heather dell. All this is done with panache and maintained to exemplary standards.

COTEHELE
Cornwall

St Dominick, nr Saltash
PL12 6TA
8m SW of Tavistock off
A390
Tel: 01579 50434

Owner:
The National Trust

Open: Apr to Oct, daily
11–5.30 or dusk if earlier.
10 acres. House open

THE GABLED and towered courtyard house, built in late Tudor times of moody grey granite by the Edgcumbe family, is at the centre of a garden that has many different faces. The house itself and its splendid outhouses and courtyards provide sheltered corners for all sorts of tender things such as the yellow-flowered *Jasminum mesnyi*. North-west of the house is a meadow which in spring is bright with daffodils. From here a gate leads through to a garden of more formal atmosphere, with a pool at the centre and a good border running along the northern wall. East of the house a series of terraces is planted with wallflowers in spring, followed in summer by roses, and there are some superb magnolias on the lower lawn. From the bottom terrace a secret passage leads through to a complete change of atmosphere. Here is a woodland garden in a steep valley, with a pool and ancient dovecote shaped like a giant beehive. In the woods paths amble among many camellias, magnolias and rhododendrons richly underplanted with ferns and moisture-loving plants; hostas, primulas and the bold foliage of *Gunnera manicata* relish the banks of a rushing stream.

CRANBORNE MANOR GARDENS

Dorset

Cranborne, nr Wimborne
BH21 5PP
In the village of Cranborne
16 1/2m SW of Salisbury
by A354 and B3081
Tel: 01725 517248

Owner: Viscount and
Viscountess Cranborne

Open: Garden: Mar to
Sept, Wed 9–5; Garden
Centre: All the year, Tue
to Sat, 9–5 (Sun 10–5). 10
acres

THE MANOR house, once a medieval hunting lodge, has been in the Cecil family since the 17th century. There are excellent borders, an enclosed herb garden, walks of espaliered apple trees, a 17th-century mount and the exceptional charm of an ancient place embosomed in even more ancient woods. The garden centre next door to the manor is in fact a nursery garden and a particularly good one. It carries a wide general stock but with especially good collections of old and shrub roses and clematises. It also sells ornaments, furniture, trellis-work and some very good pots. A mail order service is provided for roses only, a speciality, and a catalogue (£1.00) of them is issued.

DARTINGTON HALL

Devon

THE HOUSE is one of the most spectacular medieval mansions in Devon and the garden which lies chiefly to the south-west of it is designed on a heroic scale. The natural combe has been sculpted into great grassy terraces looking down onto

Dartington, nr Totnes
TQ9 6EL
2m NW of Totnes by A384
Tel: 01803 862271

Owner: Dartington Hall
Trust

Open: Daily, dawn–dusk.
30 acres

an expanse of turf – according to legend, a medieval jousting lawn. The formal arrangement to the north of the terraces was designed by the American garden designer Beatrix Farrand, her only work in England. On the highest terrace, in the shade of immense old sweet chestnuts, a splendid stone carving by Henry Moore of a reclining woman turns her back on the terraces below. Nearby, a vertiginous flight of steps sweeps down the hill and giant magnolias ornament each side. At the far end of the terraces more steps lead up to an ornamental pond with a fountain of carved swans in the shade of a very large *Elaeagnus umbellata* 'Parvifolia', and farther to the west glades open out in old woodland. This powerful shaping of the land and sensitive planting is entirely worthy of the great house.

DOCTYN MILL

Devon

THIS GARDEN has been made since 1980 and is a model of sensitive planting and design in an exceptionally beautiful site. Less than a mile from the coast, it is set in a secluded valley and possesses a

Spekes Valley,
nr Hartland EX39 6EA
3m S of Hartland follow
signs to Elmscott and
Lymebridge Cross; the
garden is between
Lymebridge Cross and
Milford
Tel: 01237 441369

Owner:
Mr and Mrs G.G. Bourcier

Open: Mar to Oct, daily
10–5. 8 acres

favourable microclimate well protected from the coastal winds. In spring the garden explodes into life with an immense collection of daffodils and the upper slopes of the valley sparkle with the young foliage of many shrubs and ornamental trees. There is an excellent bog garden and the banks of streams are planted with moisture-loving plants – lysichitons, ligularias, candelabra primulas and hostas, with bold contrasts of foliage shape and colour. The intricate planting near the house contrasts well with a woodland garden that merges with the surrounding rural landscape.

DUNSTER CASTLE

Somerset

THE CASTLE OCCUPIES a marvellous position on its great wooded tor. It is partly 13th-century but much added to, especially in the 19th century by Anthony Salvin. The microclimate here is very privileged and the spectacular rocky crag on which

Dunster, nr Minehead
TA24 6SL
3m SE of Minehead by
A396
Tel: 01643 821314

Owner:
The National Trust

Open: Feb, Mar, Oct to
Dec, daily 11–4; Apr to
Sept, daily 11–5.
17 acres. Castle open

the castle is built provides shelter to tender plants.
The garden, which is informally arranged to spiral up
the wooded slopes to a secluded plateau at the
summit, has many plants from Australasia – such as
pittosporums, mimosas, olearias and the lovely white
banksian rose. A large lemon tree on a sunny terrace,
over 150 years old, with winter protection fruits
handsomely. The National Trust has been restoring
and adding to this garden in recent years – planting
an unusual grove of strawberry trees, for example.

EAST LAMBROOK MANOR

Somerset

East Lambrook, South
Petherton TA13 5HL
3m N of the A 303 to
South Petherton
Tel: 01460 240328

Owner: Mr and Mrs
Andrew Norton

Open: Garden: Mar to Oct,
daily except Sun (open
May Bank Hol weekend)
10–5; *Nursery:* daily except
Sun 10–5. 1 1/2 acres

THE GARDEN was made by Margery Fish from
1938 and, publicised by her excellent books,
became one of the best known gardens in England.
Mrs Fish invented a style of inspired cottage
gardening, often using carefully chosen forms of wild
plants. The design is informal and, although it is
given structure by clipped evergreens and pollarded
willows, there is scarcely a straight line in the place.
Her garden, superbly restored since 1985 by new
owners, is full of excellent plants very well grown
and many rare. It is also full of lessons for all
gardeners about the importance of siting plants and
choosing those that perform in every season. It is
especially strong on herbaceous plants and contains
the best collection of cultivars of hardy geraniums (a
National Collection) in the country. An excellent
nursery sells a very good range of the kind of plants

grown in the garden, chiefly herbaceous and many of them unusual, at excellent prices. A catalogue (50p) is produced and there is a mail order service; but it is much better to visit, admire, and buy, on the spot.

EDMONDSHAM HOUSE

Dorset

Edmondsham, nr
Wimborne BH21 5RE
17m SW of Salisbury
by A354 and B3081
Tel: 01725 517207

Owner: Mrs J. Smith

Open: Apr to Oct,
Wed and Sun, Bank
Hol 2–5. 6 acres

THE HOUSE at Edmondsham is marvellous, and splendidly two-faced – ornately Tudor and Jacobean on one side, suavely Georgian on the other, and framed by excellent old trees. The chief garden interest here is an old 1-acre walled kitchen garden, cultivated entirely organically. Fruit and vegetables are bursting with vigour, and broad double herbaceous borders flank a path. With its impeccable potting shed, its old well and pump and its beautifully restored pit house, this is a fascinating example of the kitchen gardens of the past.

FORDE ABBEY

Dorset

Chard TA20 4LU
7m W of Crewkerne by
B3165
Tel: 01460 220231

Owner: M. Roper

Open: Daily 10–4.30. 20
acres. House open

THE LATE medieval monastic buildings are spectacular, and near the house old yew hedges with wambly tops and a procession of sentinel clipped yews provide bold ornament. At some distance, across undulating turf with many fine specimen trees, a lake is overlooked by a curious summer house of pleached beech; beyond, is a fine bog garden. In the old kitchen garden The Abbey Nursery sells a wide range of excellent plants, emphasising the tender and unusual.

GARDEN HOUSE
Devon

Buckland Monachorum,
Yelverton PL20 7LQ
5m S of Tavistock by A386

Tel: 01822 854769

Owner: The Fortescue
Garden Trust

Open: Mar to Oct, daily
10.30–5. 7 acres

ON THE VERY edge of Dartmoor the Garden House is hidden in a wooded valley. Here, around some romantically decaying 16th-century ruins, Lionel Fortescue from 1945 onwards made a suitably romantic garden, surrounded by old walls and built on precipitous terraces from which there are lovely views over garden and country. Clematis and roses scale the stone walls and there are wonderful riches of plants, especially herbaceous, artfully disposed. Here are no cold and calculating vistas – everything depends on the quality of the planting and meticulous upkeep. Fortescue's successor, Keith Wiley, is now expanding the garden beyond the walls with ambition and skill. An impeccable nursery sells marvellous plants, none commonplace and all good value.

GLEBE COTTAGE PLANTS
Devon

Illustration: Geranium
pratense '*Mrs Kendall
Clark*'

Pixie Lane, Warkleigh,
Umberleigh EX37 9DH
6m W of South Molton by
B3226
Tel: 01769 540 554

Open: Apr to Oct, Wed to
Sat 10–5; also by
appointment

CAROL KLEIN specialises in herbaceous plants with a few woody herbs. She sells exactly the kind of plants that many people want to grow in their gardens and she has excellent collections of particular groups – campanulas, pinks, a long and distinguished list of hardy geraniums, many penstemons and a marvellous range of primulas. Most of these may be seen growing in her garden next to the nursery. An elegantly hand-lettered list (£1.00) is produced, plants may be supplied by mail.

GLENDURGAN GARDEN

Cornwall

Helford River, Mawnan
Smith, nr Falmouth
TR11 5JZ
4m SW of Falmouth on
road to Helford Passage
Tel: 01208 74281/01326
250906

Owner:
The National Trust

Open: Mar to Oct, Tue to
Sat and Bank Hol Mon
(closed Good Fri)
10.30–5.30. 25 acres

THE FOXES are a great Cornish family and their garden exploits contributed immensely to the horticultural life of the county. Glendurgan was bought by Alfred Fox in 1821 and his family have been here ever since. The glen is a deep ravine which tumbles down to the sparkling water of the Helford estuary. On either side of the steep banks paths follow the contours but the bottom of the valley is not so densely planted as to obscure the marvellous views across to trees and shrubs on the other side of the ravine. Deftly infiltrated into the informal planting is a wandering maze of cherry laurel, planted in 1833 by Alfred Fox, and making a lively evergreen garden ornament. Like other Cornish gardens Glendurgan is abundantly rich in camellias, magnolias and rhododendrons but it also has exceptional trees such as an unforgettable tulip tree with wide spreading branches, one of the largest in the country. It would be wrong to think of Glendurgan as merely a spring garden – the pleasures continue throughout the gardening season. In any season, the view from the terrace of the house, at the head of the glen, perfectly composed, is one the visitor will not quickly forget.

THE GNOME RESERVE

Devon

West Putford, nr
Bradworthy EX22 7XE
7 1/2m N of Holsworthy
by A388 and minor roads
(follow rose sign)
Tel: 01409 241435

Open: Daily, 21 Mar to
Oct, 10–6. 4 acres

IF THERE IS a larger collection of gnomes than this, I do not know it. Here in rural north Devon at least 1,000 of them live in comfort, doing their gnomely thing cushioned in moss or ivy under the shade of splendid beeches. Gravel paths snake through the woods and the visitor soon succumbs to the enchanted atmosphere; pointed felt hats are issued to make humans appear more congenial to the natives. A gnome museum traces their history, new gnomes are produced (if that is the word) on the premises and may be seen being dressed (i.e. painted). To one side the 2-acre Pixies' Wildflower Garden has a fine display of over 250 wildflowers, ferns, herbs and grasses arranged in appropriate habitats.

*Illustration opposite: The
Gnome Reserve*

GREENCOMBE

Somerset

Porlock TA24 8NU
1/2m W of Porlock by road
to Porlock Weir
Tel: 01643 862363

Owner: Greencombe
Garden Trust

Open: Apr to Jul, Sat to
Tue, 2–6. 3 1/2 acres

MUCH OF THE character of this remarkable garden is determined by its site – on slopes overlooking Porlock Weir and the Bristol Channel, with a very benign microclimate. The garden was started after World War II by Horace Stroud but it is under Miss Joan Loraine, who made the present garden and formed the Trust that now owns it, that it has come to full and unforgettable life. Near the house there are beds and flowing lawns with strong contrasts of shapely plants – mounds of Japanese maple and soaring spires of cypress. Above them, roses pour down slopes and walls; to the west, paths lead into ancient woodland in which immense hollies, oaks and old coppiced sweet chestnuts provide the background to wonderful magnolias, rhododendrons and maples underplanted with all kinds of shade- loving plants. There is nothing fiddly or fussy; the whole place has an air of marvellous inevitability.

HADSPEN GARDENS

Somerset

nr Castle Cary BA7 7NG
2m SE of Castle Cary by
A371
Tel: 01749 813707

Owner: N. and S. Pope

Open: Mar to Oct, Thur to
Sun and Bank Hol 9–6.
5 acres

THE VERY PRETTY late 18th-century house in its park-like setting is sheltered by wooded slopes rising to the north behind it. The garden beyond the house has 18th-century origins but most of its present distinction is more recent. Penelope Hobhouse restored and replanned it after 1968 and in 1987 a further impetus came from lively new gardeners from Canada, Nori and Sandra Pope. In the old walled kitchen garden a dazzling but subtle double border of yellow and white followed by hostas shaded with beech hedges descends the slope, and brilliant colour borders round the walls are alive with the Popes' new plantings of subtle harmonies. Nearby, above a huge rectangular pool, a high brick wall affords protection to many tender plants. A nursery sells excellent plants, some bearing the 'Hadspen' name, and new introductions are constantly being made. There is a catalogue (three 1st-class stamps) but no mail order.

THE HANNAYS OF BATH

Avon

Sydney Wharf Nursery,
Bathwick, Bath BA2 4ES
In Bath at bottom of
Bathwick Hill via Sydney
Mews
Tel: 01225 462230

Open: Mar to Oct, daily
except Tue 10–5

THE HANNAYS are mad about plants and a visit to their nursery is always rewarding because you will certainly find excellent and unfamiliar ones. Some may come from the Hannays' own collecting expeditions. They are especially good on herbaceous plants and on their wild forms; adenophoras, cimicifugas, dieramas, euphorbias and geraniums are well represented. Among woody plants cistus, phlomis and sages are outstanding. A very good catalogue (£1.40) is produced, with much valuable information, but there is no mail order.

HARE LANE POTTERY

Dorset

HANDMADE GARDEN POTS, made from local clay and fired in a wood-burning kiln were once common; today they are extremely rare. Jonathan Garratt makes a wide range of beautifully fashioned

nr Wimborne BH21 5QT
2m E of Cranborne on
Alderholt road
Tel: 01725 517700

Open: Sat and Sun 9–5 and
mostly during the week;
please 'phone to check

pots, alpine pans and various kinds of planter. They
vary in colour, some having an attractive darker
tinge, but all are finely made and are available only
at the pottery. All the pots are guaranteed against
frost damage; pots planted with bulbs having
withstood −12°C at the pottery.

HEADLAND
Cornwall

3 Battery Lane,
Polruan-by-Fowey
PL23 1PW.
In the centre of Polruan.
Park in main car park and
walk down St Saviour's
Hill, turning left at Coast
Guard Office.
Tel: 01726 870 243

Owner: Jean and John Hill

Open: 20 May to 30 Sept,
Thurs 2–8. 1 3/4 acres

JEAN AND JOHN HILL came to Headland in 1976
after several years of experience of gardening in
the south. Nowhere else, however, had quite the
same problems and possibilities as this. On a
splendid rocky promontory jutting out into the
mouth of the Fowey estuary, the Hills have made a
garden of vital interest to all gardeners who battle
against wind and salt-laden air. Paths wind along the
contours of precipitous slopes with marvellous
outcrops of natural rock. Hedges of escallonia,
euonymus and privet have proved their worth as
shelters. A few handsome mature trees, in particular
Monterey pine (*Pinus radiata*) and *Cupressus
macrocarpa*, although relishing the seaside climate,
suffered grievously from storm damage. Many other
woody plants – arbutus, cistus, cotoneaster, hebes –
provide wind- and salt-proof ornament. Frosts are
rarely severe and such herbaceous plants as aeonium,
lampranthus and osteospermum flourish. This is a
garden that will also be enjoyed by gardeners not
seeking practical guidance about coastal gardening;
the winding paths, well-kept plantings, and exquisite
views across the estuary give rare pleasure.

HELIGAN
Cornwall

nr Mevagissey, St Austell
PL26 6EN.
4m S of St Austell by
B3273; turn to right after
village of Pentewan.
Tel: 01726 844157/843566

Owner: The Heligan
Manor Gardens Project Ltd

Open: Daily 10.30–5.
57 acres

THE PRESIDING GENIUS of this extraordinary place, Tim Smit, is a man of such astounding energy that he could probably make a memorable event out of the restoration of a bus shelter. Here at Heligan, however, he has found a subject truly worthy of his skills. The lost garden of the Tremaynes, famous in its day, became neglected and forgotten. Tim Smit rediscovered it and with his partner John Nelson formed a trust to restore it. Work started in the spring of 1991 – paths were laid bare and resurfaced, immense brambles uprooted, glades cleared, and gradually a garden of fabulous enchantment was revealed. It is rich in rhododendrons (including several Hooker introductions of the 1840s), many rare and grown to exceptional size, and trees of exceptional beauty. It also possesses a unique range of garden buildings – a peach house, an ingenious pineapple pit, melon frames, bee boles and beautiful frames with fish-tail glazing. All these, and tool- and potting-sheds, are now restored. A magnificent walled flower garden and vast early glasshouses are now being tackled. Already the garden gives pleasure of the most varied kind. There is much to excite the most demanding of plant lovers, but the special quality of Heligan is that its wild and romantic atmosphere has been triumphantly preserved.

HESTERCOMBE
Somerset

Cheddon Fitzpaine, nr
Taunton TA2 8LQ
4m NE of Taunton off
A361
Tel: 01823 337222

Owner: Somerset County
Council

Open: Mon to Fri 9–5 (also
May to Sept, Sat and Sun
2–5). 8 acres

THE GARDEN at Hestercombe was designed by
Gertrude Jekyll and Edwin Lutyens just before
World War I and is one of their great masterpieces.
Since 1973 it has been rescued from the brink of
irretrievable collapse by Somerset County Council
who have restored it with authenticity. Here is a
marvellous distillation of the essence of the
Lutyens/Jekyll garden wizardry – an enclosed area of
shifting levels with lively stonework, a symmetrical
parterre-like 'Great Plat', iris-fringed rills fed by
water-spouting masks, and Miss Jekyll's boldly
unfussy planting of massed grey-leafed plants, glossy
bergenias, ramparts of rosemary and a pergola of
roses and clematis. In addition to all this, there is a
round pool in a round walled garden filled with
wintersweet and roses, a Dutch garden of lamb's
ears, lavender and roses, and the most beautiful
orangery of the 20th century. Everywhere there are
details of design and planting from which any
gardener can learn.

KELWAYS NURSERIES
Somerset

Langport TA10 9EZ
In Langport, 10m E of
Taunton by A358 and
A378
Tel: 01458 250521

Open: Mon to Fri 9–5, Sat
and Sun 10–5

THIS IS ONE of the best of all nurseries for daylilies,
irises and peonies, and the many cultivars bearing
the 'Langport' or 'Kelway' name are evidence of the
work of this famous place in the raising of
garden-worthy plants. A very wide range of bulbs
and herbaceous perennials is sold at the pretty new
plant centre. Excellent catalogues are issued twice a
year, from which orders are fulfilled by post.

KENWITH NURSERY
Devon

GORDON HADDOW, who moved here quite recently
from another site, sells only conifers, about
which he is immensely knowledgeable. There are
trees here, many of them dwarf, which you will not
often come across – for example his is the only

The Old Rectory,
Littleham, Bideford
EX39 5HW
In the village of Littleham
1m S of Bideford
Tel: 01237 473752

Open: Wed to Sat 10–12,
2–4.30

nursery in Britain to supply several different forms of
the dwarf American *Pinus banksiana*. He produces an
outstanding catalogue (three 1st-class stamps), rich in
background information about his plants, from which
he fulfils orders by mail. In front of the house, to one
side of the nursery, there are several display beds
containing many rarely seen specimens.

KILLERTON
Devon

Broadclyst, Exeter
EX5 3LE
5m NE of Exeter by B3181
and B3185; or by Jnct 28
on M5
Tel: 01392 881345

Owner:
The National Trust

Open: Daily dawn–dusk.
22 acres. House open

THE CHARMS of Killerton reveal themselves
gradually, and because of that tend to stick in the
mind. Behind the stucco house, land slopes up
towards the north and the garden lies chiefly to the
west. Near the house a gravel path leads between a
pair of fortissimo mixed borders – originally planted
with the advice of William Robinson – ornamented
with elegant Coade stone urns. Beyond, the lawn
unrolls, interrupted by countless trees and shrubs of
an acid-loving type – magnolias, rhododendrons,
stewartias, styrax and maples. A half-hidden rustic
summer house, with a touch of Grimm's fairy tales,
has a wonderful interior of rattan and wickerwork,
and a ceiling with patterns of pine cones. Behind it is
a masterly rock garden, recently restored, of a
naturalistic kind built in an old quarry; hellebores,
hostas, geraniums and many other herbaceous plants
flourish among mossy rocks under a canopy of old
camellias, maples and daphnes. In late spring the air
is scented with sheets of *Cyclamen repandum*. A good
plant shop also has a fine selection of pots.

KNIGHTSHAYES COURT
Devon

Bolham, Tiverton
EX16 7RQ
2m N of Tiverton by A396
Tel: 01884 254665

Owner:
The National Trust

Open: Apr to Oct, daily
11–5.30. 40 acres.
House open

THE GARDENS at Knightshayes have two faces,
both of them very handsome. Near the house are
generously planted borders and a formal garden with
yew hedges, standard wisterias, lead figures and a
cool pool overhung by a weeping pear. Looking away
from the house are marvellous rural views. East of
this is one of the best small woodland gardens in the
country, in which exceptional shrubs and ornamental
trees are disposed to brilliant effect. At first sight it

seems just a very attractive piece of woodland but the more you look the more you will see rare plants used with rare skill. A small selection of very good plants is for sale.

LANHYDROCK
Cornwall

Bodmin PL30 5AD
2 1/2m SE of Bodmin by
A38 or B3268
Tel: 01208 73320

Owner:
The National Trust

Open: Apr to Oct, daily
11–5.30 (5 in Oct). 25
acres. House open

THE HOUSE, a romantic mixture of the 17th and 19th centuries, is set in exquisite parkland, and an avenue of sycamores and beeches marches to the castellated entrance lodge. Beyond it a formal courtyard garden has rows of vast clipped Irish yews, beds of modern roses and ornate bronze urns. Behind the house and church is a yew-hedged circular garden with herbaceous beds containing the National Collection of crocosmias. Beyond this a woodland garden is rich in flowering shrubs and trees, especially rhododendrons and exceptional magnolias, of which there are 120 different kinds

LOWER SEVERALLS HERB NURSERY
Somerset

Lower Severalls, nr
Crewkerne TA18 7NX
1 1/2 NE of Crewkerne off
A30 on Haselbury–Merriott
road
Tel: 01460 732 34

Open: Daily except Thur
10–5 (Sun 2–5)

MARY PRING'S nursery is arranged in the garden of a very attractive Ham stone farmhouse. As well as medicinal and culinary herbs, she is particularly interested in those with especially good scents – of lemon, pineapple and so on. She also has a selection of tender and half-hardy plants for containers and bedding. There is a well chosen range of herbaceous perennials – including over 50 cranesbills and some very good sages (around 25 varieties). Orders are fulfilled by mail order and a catalogue (four 1st-class stamps) is produced

LYTE'S CARY MANOR
Somerset

Charlton Mackrell,
Somerton TA11 7HU
4m SE of Somerton by
B3151
Tel: 01985 847777

Owner:
The National Trust

Open: Apr to 28 Oct, Mon,
Wed and Sat 2–6 or dusk if
earlier. 3 acres. House open

THE ENTRANCE to the late medieval manor house is through a forecourt with a central path flanked by yew topiary clipped into cottage-loaf shapes. This mixture of formality and simplicity characterises the garden. A door leads through to a lavish mixed border of herbaceous plants under old roses, while, on the other side of the path, a yew hedge is clipped into buttresses with decorative finials. Beyond a formal orchard, open lawns and statues lead to a shady tunnel of hornbeam and a secret garden.

MALLET COURT NURSERY
Somerset

Curry Mallet, nr Taunton
TA3 6SY
In village of Curry Mallet
5m SE of Taunton by A358
and A378
Tel: 01823 480748

Open: Mon to Fri 9–1, 2–5

JAMES HARRIS is known among tree-lovers as 'Acer' Harris, and sells one of the finest selections of maples commercially available – almost certainly the largest in the country. His nursery is primarily devoted to trees and shrubs, with a particular emphasis on those grown from seed collected in the wild. He sells, for example, a vast range of oaks (120 kinds), many birches, rowans and magnolias, and shrubs, from China, Korea and Japan. There is a catalogue (£1 plus 29p s.a.e.) and mail order service but a visit is always worthwhile to discover treasures that have not yet found their way onto the list.

THE MANOR HOUSE
Avon

Walton-in-Gordano, nr
Clevedon BS21 7AN
2m NE of Clevedon by
B3124
Tel: 01275 872067

Owner: C.P.M. Wills

Open: Mid Apr to mid
Sept, Wed and Thur 10–4;
also by appointment. 4
acres

PROTECTED BY WOODED hills to the north, this
garden has a balmy microclimate which allows
the owners to grow a very wide range of plants. This
is a plant spotter's garden in which both herbaceous
and woody plants are well represented and where
something new is always happening. The garden
holds the National Collection of dodecatheon. A few
plants propagated in the nursery, some unusual, are
for sale at modest prices.

MAPPERTON GARDENS
Dorset

Beaminster DT8 3NR
2m SE of Beaminster by
B3163
Tel: 01308 862645

Owner: The Montagu
family

Open: Mar to Oct, daily
2–6. 12 acres. House open
by appointment to groups
only

TO THE EAST of the fine 17th-century house, the
garden, hidden in a long combe, comes as a
surprise – a splendid formal arrangement of
descending terraces and cross vistas. At the head of
the valley an orangery looks down flagged paths past
a rose-festooned pergola and along the central vista,
guarded by stone eagles, which ends with two long
rectangular pools. All this is copiously ornamented
with topiary of yew and box, handsome urns and
statues, and plenty of places to sit and admire the
garden and the gabled house rising above it. This
lively pastiche of a 17th-century garden, with all the
trimmings, was laid out as recently as the 1920s. It is
beautifully executed and makes an entirely
unexpected and wonderful contrast to idyllic views of
cattle grazing in the park-like countryside beyond.

PATRICIA MARROW

Somerset

Kingsdon, nr Somerton
TA11 7LE
In the middle of Kingsdon,
2m SE of Somerton off
B3151
Tel: 01935 840232

Open: Daily, dawn–dusk
but check by phone

A S SO MANY of the old-established nursery
gardens cut back on their stock, much smaller,
specialist nurseries have become one of the best
sources of more unusual plants. Mrs Marrow is a
gardening institution in the West Country – a demon
propagator who chooses her plants with great care.
There is nothing commonplace here and much that
you will not find easily elsewhere. She stocks a very
large number of hardy plants, woody and
herbaceous, some of which may not be quite so
hardy in the frozen north. She issues no catalogue
and provides no mail order service, but part of the
essential charm of the place lies in meeting her. She
does not bully customers but she talks about her
plants so seductively that you will certainly bear
away more than you bargained for.

MARWOOD HILL GARDENS

Devon

Barnstaple EX31 4EB
4m NW of Barnstaple by
A39 and B3230
Tel: 01271 42528

Owner: Dr J.A. Smart

Open: Garden: daily,
dawn–dusk; *Nursery:* daily
11–5. 20 acres

THERE ARE many reasons for visiting Marwood
Hill but the chief interest of the garden lies in the
very large number of plants grown in appropriate
habitats in the attractive valley setting. The garden
was started in 1949 by Dr Jimmy Smart who took
over the neglected garden of a Georgian house.
Flowering shrubs and ornamental trees clothe the

slopes of the upper garden and at the bottom of the valley small lakes are linked together by streams. A bog garden between two of the lakes burgeons with ligularias, candelabra primulas and irises. In high summer the banks are covered by the plumes of an immense number of astilbes – 135 different species and cultivars, a National Collection. There is also a large and excellent nursery whose chief speciality is camellias, of which it has one of the best selections commercially available. A catalogue (70p) is produced but there is no mail order, so a visit is essential.

MILTON LODGE
Somerset

nr Wells BA5 3AQ
1/2m N of Wells off A39
Tel: 01749 672168

Owner: D.C. Tudway
Quilter

Open: Good Fri to Oct,
daily except Sat 2–6. 12
acres

HERE IS a garden that takes full advantage of its exquisite position – with the city of Wells and its great cathedral below it to the south, and Glastonbury Tor in the distance beyond the vale of Avalon. On the south side of the 18th-century house a terrace overlooks the steeply sloping site with its mixed borders, yew hedges and vertiginous descents giving way to parkland with excellent ornamental trees. At some distance from the house, on the other side of the Old Bristol Road, is a real rarity – the Combe, a late 18th-century gentleman's arboretum now in splendid maturity. This walled and bosky valley, full of fine trees to which the present owner adds, has immense charm. Paths run along an upper level on either side, giving delicious views below.

MINTERNE
Dorset

Minterne Magna,
Dorchester DT2 7AU
9m N of Dorchester by
A352 in the village of
Minterne Magna
Tel: 01300 341370

Owner: Lord and Lady
Digby

Open: Apr to Oct, daily
10–7. 21 acres

AT MINTERNE THE rare quality of the garden lies in the gradual revealing of exotic flowering trees and shrubs in a beautiful setting. From the house there are wonderful views down a shallow valley to a sinuous lake set in parkland ornamented with superlative old trees. A path leads gently downwards into woodland which is rich in exceptional examples of *Davidia involucrata*, magnolias, maples and rhododendrons. A stream flows down the valley and its banks are richly planted – vast drifts of primulas

as well as exotic shrubs and trees, many of which
have grown to spectacular size. The visitor may
either follow the lower garden walk, nose-to-nose
with the plants, or take the upper walk which affords
unforgettable views across the densely planted valley.
Eventually the path arrives at a more open setting, a
stone bridge arches over the stream, and on the far
bank sheep graze among superb oaks and limes.
Spring, of course, is the obvious time to visit but for
those less besotted with the obvious, Minterne will
give unforgettable pleasure at any time.

MONTACUTE HOUSE

Somerset

Montacute TA15 6XP
In the village of
Montacute, 4m W of
Yeovil by A3088
Tel: 01935 823289

Owner:
The National Trust

Open: Daily except Tue
11.30–5.30 or dusk if
earlier. 12 acres. House
open

THE LATE Tudor house, a marvel of golden Ham
stone, is well situated in a garden to match. To
the east of the house a walled forecourt has good
herbaceous borders. The Tudor walls are ornamented
with stone finials and, in each corner, an airy
Elizabethan gazebo gives views to the deer park
beyond. North of the house a raised walk overlooks
a deep border planted with shrub roses, and a stately
lawn surrounded by clipped Irish yews with a
circular poool at its centre. All about are venerable
yew hedges, some handsomely blowsy with age, and
the view is constantly drawn to the great house.

MOUNT EDGCUMBE
Cornwall

Cremyll,
Torpoint PL10 1HZ
2 1/2m SE of Torpoint
Tel: 01752 822236

Owner: City of Plymouth
and Cornwall County
Council

*Open: Park and formal
garden:* daily dawn–dusk;
*Earl's Garden (entrance via
house):* Apr to Oct, Wed to
Sun and Bank Hol Mon
11–5.30. 865 acres. House
open

IT IS HARD to pin down the rare character of this place – but there is certainly nowhere like it. The site, on a sloping headland overlooking Plymouth Sound, is beautiful, and the castellated mansion turns its face to this, down an immense triple avenue of limes. The Edgcumbe family, also of Cotehele, came here in the mid 16th century and their estate became so famous that Admiral Medina Sidonia vowed that he would live there after his Armada had beaten the English. At the foot of the hill there are formal gardens – a French garden, an English garden, a conservatory and an Italianate garden with double staircase ornamented with flamboyant statuary, a pool, bedding schemes and orange trees in Versailles boxes. All this has recently been undergoing restoration. The parkland, laced with marvellous walks, runs to the very edge of the cliffs – interrupted with picturesque ruins and a columned temple from which there are lovely views of the sea.

OVERBECKS GARDEN
Devon

Sharpitor,
Salcombe TQ8 8LW
1 1/2m SW of Salcombe by
minor roads
Tel: 01548 842893/843238

Owner: The National Trust

Open: Daily 10–8 or sunset
if earlier. 6 acres

OVERBECKS IS a very unusual place, lost on the precipitous heights above Salcombe estuary. It was the creation of Otto Overbecks who left it to the National Trust in 1937. It enjoys a remarkably mild microclimate and, with views through trees of shimmering water, it is fairly easy to imagine yourself on the *corniche* on the Côte d'Azur. Even the steps leading down into the garden, with their sinuous handrail, have a Mediterranean feel to them. The garden is terraced and its very sharp drainage and abundant sunshine permits many tender plants to flourish as they do in few other places on mainland Britain – callistemons, Chusan palms, mimosa, olearias, olives and tender pittosporums. On the lower slopes, an old *Magnolia campbellii*, planted in 1901, is a famous sight in spring, covered with its hot pink flowers. The earlier part of the year is a wonderful time to visit, when the garden is extraordinarily floriferous and the air laden with sweet scents. In high summer it takes on the character of an exotic jungle.

PARNHAM HOUSE

Dorset

Beaminster DT8 3NA
1m S of Beaminster by
A3066
Tel: 01308 862204

Owner: John Makepeace

Open: Apr to Oct, Wed,
Sun and Bank Hol
weekends 10–5. 14 acres.
House open

SWARMING WITH decoration – gables, castellations and bristling chimneys – Parnham House is a Tudor mansion comprehensively done over by John Nash in the early 19th century. The estate was acquired by the famous furniture maker, John Makepeace, who has restored it with energy and imagination. To the south, a deep terrace with stone gazebos at each end overlooks an immense lawn with rows of giant yew cones and water runnels. Beyond, superb woodland is framed by great cedars of Lebanon. On the east side of the house the entrance forecourt has decorative walls crowned with finials, and borders planted with roses. Beyond the house, behind old yew hedges and brick walls, Jennie Makepeace has been breathing new life into herbaceous borders.

PENCARROW HOUSE
Cornwall

Washaway, Bodmin
PL30 3AG
3 1/2m NW of Bodmin by
A389
Tel: 0120884 369

Owner: The Molesworth-
St Aubyn Family

Open: Easter to mid Oct,
daily dawn–dusk. 50 acres

PENCARROW IS ONE of those rare places in which
the character of the whole amounts to much more
than the sum of the parts. It is set in a broad valley
with the very pretty 18th-century house facing south
along it. The Italian Gardens, an arrangement of
turfed terraces, urns and a fountain, lie immediately
south of the house (a plainer, country façade than the
more swagger east front). Beyond this, a vast
meadow opens out, edged on either side by ramparts
of magnificent trees and shrubs. From a Victorian
rock garden on one side of the Italian Gardens a path
leads through the woodland garden, a lake and an
American Garden. The visitor should return by the
path on the other side, with lovely views of the house
framed in great trees and old rhododendrons with, in
spring, an exquisite bluebell grove splashed with wild
garlic. The whole is a marvellous English scene – fine
house, formal gardens, enticing woodland and distant
views of cattle grazing on rich Cornish pasture.

PENJERRICK
Cornwall

Budock, nr Falmouth
TR11 5ED
3m SW of Falmouth by
minor roads
Tel: 01326 250 074/01872
870 105

Owner: Mrs R. Morin

Open: Mar to Sept, Wed,
Fri and Sun 1.30–4.30. 15
acres

FEW GARDENS HAVE the wonderful atmosphere of Penjerrick. It is another creation of the Fox family, the great Cornish master gardeners who also made Glendurgan and Trebah nearby. Like these, Penjerrick has a valley site sloping towards the sea. But here there is a character of wildness which provides exactly the right contrast to some of the more swaggering rhododendrons which are such a striking feature of the garden; many of these were bred here, bearing the name 'Penjerrick' or 'Barclayi'. Superlative old beeches, copper and ordinary, date from the early 1800s and provide a stately background to the more exotic planting that lies below. Here are exceptional tree ferns, many examples of the tender large-leafed rhododendrons, an exceptional *Davidia involucrata* and the most magnificent *Podocarpus salignus* in the country. There is a memorable group of the tender Chilean laurel (*Laurelia serrata*), with drooping branches and pungent leaves. In early spring many outstanding magnolias flaunt their flowers in the lovely jungle that surrounds them. The garden continues beyond a road, spanned by a bridge, and here in a jungle-like setting thickets of bamboos edge a lake and alluring fern-fringed paths wind up the side of the valley.

PROBUS GARDENS
Cornwall

Probus, nr Truro
TR2 4HQ
E of Probus village,
8m SW of St Austell by
A390
Tel: 01726 882597

Owner: Cornwall County
Council

Open: 2 Apr to 2 Oct, daily
10–5; 3 Oct to 31 March,
Mon to Fri 10–4

IT IS HARD to imagine any gardener failing to learn something interesting, diverting or useful at this ambitious and well organised place. It has many displays of particular groups of plants – roses, herbs, dahlias, conifers and so on – but also of plants for specific sites (e.g. windy places) and purposes (e.g. shrubs giving shade or acting as a mulch). There are many exhibitions showing horticultural techniques – for example comparing the results of different types of digging; different kinds of nourishment; the correct way to plant and prune trees; how to support and train climbers; and an immense number of other things. All this is vividly displayed and more quickly grasped than by reading dozens of gardening books.

ROSEMOOR GARDEN

Devon

Great Torrington
EX38 8PH
1m SE of Great Torrington
by B3220
Tel: 01805 624067

Owner: The Royal
Horticultural Society

Open: Mar and Oct, daily
10–5; Apr to Sept, daily
10–6; Nov to Feb, daily
10–4. 40 acres

THERE ARE two gardens at Rosemoor: one was made in the early 1960s by Lady Anne Palmer – an intimate woodland garden with less informal planting nearer the house; the other is a more razzamatazz affair complete with Visitors' Centre, ambitious formal rose gardens, giant borders and ornamental vegetable garden, all of which have been made by the Royal Horticultural Society since it became the owner in 1988. The two gardens, which have a fundamentally different character, are separated by the B3220 under which visitors may pass by a subterranean passage. A newly made lake and stream garden will make an attractive prelude to the tunnel. Lady Anne's garden has an excellent collection of trees and shrubs of the kind which relish the acid soil – dogwoods (a National Collection), eucryphias, maples, pieris, rhododendrons and vacciniums. By the house there are lawns, borders and a tennis court that has been transformed into a coniferous jungle. At the Visitors' Centre a shop sells a wide range of well grown plants and marvellous pots from the Whichford Pottery.

ROWDEN GARDENS

Devon

Brentor,
nr Tavistock PL19 0NG
NW of village of Brentor,
on road to Liddaton and
Chillaton
Tel: 01822 810275

Open: Apr to Sept, Sat, Sun
and Bank Hol Mon 10–5;
other times by appointment.

SOMETHING NEW always seems to be happening at Rowden Gardens nursery which has in the past specialised in aquatic plants but now has a wider range – in all, over 2,000 species and varieties with a strong emphasis on herbaceous perennials. There are particularly good collections of crocosmias, primulas and rheums. Some of the plants are very rare, including those bred at the nursery and bearing the 'Rowden' name. This is the home of probably the largest collection of polygonums in the country, of which Rowden holds the National Collection. Behind the nursery there are rows of slender canal-like pools, displaying the nursery's wares in very decorative fashion. An informative (£1.50) list is produced and there is a mail order service. Many plants that are not listed are to be seen at the nursery, and John Carter will probably seduce you into buying them.

SALTRAM

Devon

Plympton, Plymouth
PL7 3UH
3m E of Plymouth by A38
Tel: 01752 336546

Owner:
The National Trust

Open: Apr to Oct, daily
except Fri (but open Good
Fri) and Sat 10.30–5.30. 21
acres. House open

ALTHOUGH WITHIN sight of the urban sprawl of Plymouth, Saltram still preserves its character of a gentlemanly house set in parkland. The early 18th-century house was enriched by spectacular new rooms by Robert Adam for the Parker family. The parkland – in the 18th-century grazed by deer to the very walls of the house – is now embellished with ornamental trees, superb sweet chestnuts and the Spanish plane (*Platanus* × *hispanica*) among them. The lawn west of the house, smooth as finest Wilton carpet, is interrupted by thickets of shrubs, especially camellias, many fine magnolias and rhododendrons. From the stately pedimented orangery, built in 1775, paths lead to a dapper gothic pavilion. Beyond the house, a long avenue of limes, carpeted with pale narcissi in spring, forms a boundary. All this is understated and, of its kind, perfect.

SCOTT'S NURSERIES LTD

Somerset

Illustration: Rosa 'New Dawn'

Merriott TA16 5PL
2m N of Crewkerne by the
A356
Tel: 01460 72306

Open: Mon to Sat 9–5, Sun
10–5

THIS OLD-ESTABLISHED nursery is one of the best in the West Country. It sells a very wide range of plants, with especially good collections of old-fashioned and species roses and of fruit – there are many old cultivars of apples, pears, plums and soft fruit that are not often found. Good trees and flowering shrubs are stocked, as well as a wide range of herbaceous plants and alpines. An outstanding catalogue (£1.50) is issued, which is so full of useful information that many gardeners treat it as their bible. A mail order service is available.

TAPELEY PARK
Devon

Instow EX39 4NT
2m N of Bideford by A39
Tel: 01271 860528

Owner: N.D.C.I. Ltd

Open: Easter to Oct, daily
except Sat 10–5. 10 acres

TAPELEY PARK deserves to be much better known. The house, a mid 18th-century tycoon's mansion of pink brick, occupies an unforgettable position in parkland, with wonderful views down to the River Torrington. South of the house is a dazzling Italian garden designed by the neo-classical architect John Belcher in the early 20th century. Terraces gently descend the hill, with a sundial at the centre, and a row of sentinel Irish yews guards the lowest terrace to the west. Handsome statues decorate the walls, and others, on the far side of the lawn, gaze out towards the countryside. The lowest terrace wall is lined with lively borders in which tender plants such as *Sophora japonica* and *Feijoa sellowiana* flourish. To the east a pedimented brick and flint tool-house, with busts in niches, was designed by a former head gardener. To one side vertiginous steps flanked by statues climb up under the shade of old Monterey pines towards a sundial and a domed ice house. Beyond, is an old walled kitchen garden.

TINTINHULL HOUSE

Somerset

Tintinhull,
nr Yeovil BA22 8PZ
In village of Tintinhull, off
A303 5m SW of Yeovil
Tel: 01935 822545

Owner:
The National Trust

Open: Apr to Sept, daily
except Mon and Fri (open
Bank Hol Mon) 2–6. 3/4
acre.

THE DESIGN of this small garden is so clever that it provides an inexhaustible model for gardeners. Divided into separate 'rooms' by walls or hedges, each area has a distinctive atmosphere. The Eagle Court west of the Queen Anne façade of the house has a central flagged path edged with clipped mounds of box and, under the walls, richly planted borders. The path leads to a little white garden, hedged in yew, in which white anemones, roses and lilies glow under miniature silvery willows. An opening leads through to a decorative kitchen garden with an orchard beyond. The pool garden above it, with its slender canal planted with irises, and pillared summer house at one end, has a pair of masterly borders – one with hot colours of red and yellow, and the other with cool silvers and mauves. On either side of the summer house high walls give protection to tender plants, and pots decorate the terrace. The garden, chiefly the work of Phyllis Reiss between the wars, has recently been in the care of the well known garden designer and writer, Penelope Hobhouse.

TREBAH

Cornwall

Mawnan Smith,
nr Falmouth TR11 5JZ
4m SW of Falmouth,
tourism signs from A394
and A39 approaches to
Falmouth
Tel: 01326 250448

Owner: Trebah Garden
Trust

Open: Daily 10.30–5.
25 acres

TREBAH IS the creation of Charles Fox who came here in 1831, whose brother Alfred made the neighbouring Glendurgan which enjoys a very similar site. By 1981 when Major and Mrs Hibbert started to restore it, the place had suffered years of neglect. Set in a long, slender ravine, the garden sweeps down south to the Helford river. Paths run along each side of the valley, with vertiginous views over great rhododendrons, magnolias, groves of the great tree-fern *Dicksonia antarctica*, and palms. A stream runs along the bottom of the ravine, with a waterfall and pools in which koi carp lurk. Here, the moist ground provides a perfect site for an immense collection of hydrangeas and a grove of the giant Brazilian *Gunnera manicata*. Things grow well at Trebah and one of the attractions is the contrast of different exotic foliage, viewed from above or below. Plants and books are sold at the garden shop.

TRELISSICK GARDEN
Cornwall

Feock, nr Truro TR3 6QL
4m S of Truro by B3289
Tel: 01872 862090/865808

Owner:
The National Trust

Open: Mar to Oct, Mon to
Sat 10.30–5.30, Sun 1–5.30
(5 in Mar and Oct); Nov to
Mar, woodland walk open.
25 acres

THE GARDEN here is in the tradition of Cornish woodland gardens but it is a fairly recent creation and is a more manicured, gentler kind of place. The terrain is gently rolling, and smooth lawns, edged with sweeping mixed borders, give way to densely shaded woodland walks. There are many fine trees, outstanding rhododendrons, and a hydrangea walk leading from the main lawn, with many different species and cultivars. Near the house there is a collection of fig cultivars, and a sheltered garden of choice plants, many of them scented.

TRENGWAINTON GARDEN
Cornwall

Madron,
nr Penzance TR20 8RZ
2m NW of Penzance by
B3312
Tel: 01736 63021/68410

Owner: The National Trust

Open: Mar to Oct, Wed to
Sat, Bank Hol Mon and
Good Fri 10.30–5.30 (5 in
Mar and Oct). 15 acres

SIR EDWARD BOLITHO was the chief creator of this garden in the 1920s, when he added to it some of the spectacular new discoveries of the plant-hunters, especially those of Frank Kingdon-Ward. From the entrance lodge a very long drive provides the main axis of the garden. On one side an extraordinary walled kitchen garden now protects especially tender exotics. These flourish among rare magnolias and other ornamental trees and shrubs such as eucryphias, michelias, stewartias and *Styrax japonica* . Beyond the drive an excellent stream garden is beautifully planted with candelabra primulas, meconopsis, ligularias and skunk cabbage. In the woodland behind are immense rhododendrons – with spectacular examples of some of the large-leafed species such as *R. sino-grande*, *R. macabeanum* and *R. falconeri*. At the end of the drive the house looks out across a lawn to far views of St Michael's Mount, a splendid eye-catcher.

TRESCO ABBEY
Cornwall

Tresco,
Isles of Scilly TR24 0QQ
Access by helicopter or
ferry from Penzance
Tel: 01720 422849

Owner: R. Dorrien Smith

Open: Daily 10–4. 16 acres

THERE IS certainly no other garden like this in the world. Tresco, one of the Scilly Isles, has an extraordinarily benign microclimate with moderate rainfall but high humidity from the sea. The garden was started by Augustus Smith in 1834, who, after planting windbreaks, gradually built up terraces on which to cultivate a staggering range of plants, especially those of the Southern Hemisphere. This, greatly added to by his descendants, is the garden that visitors may see today. It is primarily a collection of plants, but it is craftily designed with gravel paths leading along terraces, and cross vistas giving thrilling views through the sub-tropical luxuriance. The garden contains countless plants which you will see in no other British garden. There are, however, emphatic repeated plantings – of different kinds of palms, of the splendidly architectural *Echium pininiana* with its soaring spires of flowers, and of the giant purple-flowered *Geranium maderense* – giving structure to the abundance. It is unlikely that you, or anyone else, will ever make a garden like this, and it gives unique and exhilarating pleasure.

TREWITHEN
Cornwall

Grampound Road,
nr Truro TR2 4DD
7m W of St Austell by
A390
Tel: 01726 882763/4

Owner: A.M.J. Galsworthy

Open: Mar to Sept, Mon to
Sat 10–4.30. 25 acres.
House open

TREWITHEN IS another Cornish garden with an outstanding collection of camellias, magnolias and rhododendrons, but it is strikingly unlike any of the others. Behind the elegant 1723 house there is an immense lawn, 200 yards long, with trees and shrubs crowding in on either side. From the far end of the lawn, this is seen to provide a marvellous setting for the house, like an immensely deep stage framed in wonderful plants. The garden was made by George Johnstone who came here in 1903 and cleared existing woodland, enriching the planting with many of the Asiatic plants newly introduced in the 1920s. Paths wind through this woodland and at every turn there is something wonderful to see. It is at its most spectacular in early to late spring but it has many pleasures to offer later in the year. Nor is it only a woodland garden. The formal walled garden should not be overlooked: with its wisteria-draped pergola, Irish yews and beautifully planted borders it is an admirable piece of work. An excellent plant shop sells many of the plants particularly associated with the garden (e.g. the beautiful *Ceanothus arboreus* 'Trewithen Blue').

WALL COTTAGE NURSERY
Cornwall

Illustration: Rhododendron genestierianum

Lockengate, Bugle,
St Austell PL26 8RU
6m N of St Austell by A391
Tel: 01208 831259

Open: Mon to Sat 8.30–5.
Best to telephone to check
if owners are there.

NURSERIES THAT SELL only a single genus of plant are very rare and, it must be said, sometimes of rather limited attraction. Mrs Clark sells only rhododendrons but her list is full of glittering treasures. You will not find, for example, the exquisite *R. genestierianum*, with dusty purple bell-flowers and intense scent of vanilla, in any other nursery in the country. The whole range is covered, from great tender species to brilliantly coloured Kurume azaleas. A catalogue (60p) is produced, mail order is available, and prices are very fair indeed.

WALES AND WEST-CENTRAL ENGLAND

Cheshire
Gloucestershire
Hereford and
Worcester
Shropshire

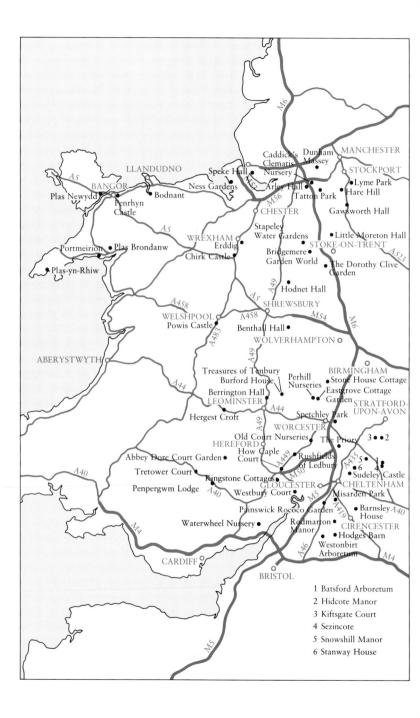

MANCHESTER
STOCKPORT
LLANDUDNO
Speke Hall
Caddick's Clematis Nursery
Dunham Massey
Ness Gardens
Arley Hall
Lyme Park
Hare Hill
BANGOR
Bodnant
Tatton Park
Plas Newydd
Penrhyn Castle
A5
Gawsworth Hall
CHESTER
A5
Stapeley Water Gardens
Little Moreton Hall
WREXHAM
STOKE-ON-TRENT
A523
Portmeirion
Plas Brondanw
Erddig
Bridgemere Garden World
Chirk Castle
The Dorothy Clive Garden
Plas-yn-Rhiw
A49
Hodnet Hall
A458
A5
SHREWSBURY
A458
M54
M6
WELSHPOOL
A458
Powis Castle
Benthall Hall
ABERYSTWYTH
A483
A49
WOLVERHAMPTON
BIRMINGHAM
Treasures of Tenbury
Perhill Nurseries
Stone House Cottage
A44
Burford House
Eastgrove Cottage Garden
Berrington Hall
STRATFORD-UPON-AVON
LEOMINSTER
A44
Spetchley Park
Hergest Croft
A49
WORCESTER
Old Court Nurseries
The Priory
3 • • 2
HEREFORD
How Caple Court
Rushfields of Ledbury
A435
1
A40
Abbey Dore Court Garden
A49
5
6 • 4
Tretower Court
A40
Kingstone Cottages
Sudeley Castle
CHELTENHAM
Penpergwm Lodge
A40
Westbury Court
GLOUCESTER
Misarden Park
M5
A419
Barnsley House
A40
Painswick Rococo Garden
Waterwheel Nursery
Rodmarton Manor
CIRENCESTER
M4
Hodges Barn
Westonbirt Arboretum
M4
A46
CARDIFF
M5
BRISTOL
1 Batsford Arboretum
2 Hidcote Manor
3 Kiftsgate Court
4 Sezincote
5 Snowshill Manor
6 Stanway House

ABBEY DORE COURT GARDEN

Hereford and Worcester

Abbey Dore,
nr Hereford HR2 0AD
11m SW of Hereford by
A465 and B4347
Tel: 01981 240419

Owner: Mrs C.L. Ward

Open: Mar to 3rd Sun in
Oct, daily except Wed 11–6
(also open before Mar for
hellebores; telephone for
dates). 5 acres

ABBEY DORE COURT on the banks of the River Dore has both an attractive garden and a nursery with a good range of the woody and herbaceous plants that may be seen growing in the garden. There is no catalogue and no mail order service, so a visit is essential. Abbey Dore keeps a National Collection of euphorbias, those fashionable and valuable greenery-yallery plants (78 species and cultivars). Throughout the garden the planting is of a very high standard; especially beautiful is a pair of mixed borders planted predominantly in yellow- and white-flowered plants, with gold and variegated foliage and the occasional sombre note of rich purple.

ARLEY HALL

Cheshire

Arley, nr Northwich
CW9 6NA
5m W of Knutsford by
minor roads; Jncts 19 and
20 of M6; Jnct 10 of M56
Tel: 01565 777353

Owner:
The Hon. M.L.W. Flower

Open: Apr to Oct, Tue to
Sun and Bank Hol Mon
12–5. 12 acres

A PAIR OF herbaceous borders was laid out at Arley in 1846, a great novelty, and they survive to this day, beautifully maintained: pairs of topiary yew 'dumb waiters' form entrances at each end, and a broad grass path separates the borders which have yew buttresses on each side, breaking up an otherwise uncomfortably long stretch of planting. From June to the end of the gardening season they are one of the great garden sights of England. A path leads from the borders to a procession of giant columns of clipped holm oak and views over fields. There are also borders of shrub roses, old walled gardens with good mixed borders, a simple terraced walk above a ha-ha, and much else to see. Still in private ownership, Arley Hall preserves the atmosphere of a garden kept for its own delight.

BARNSLEY HOUSE GARDEN
Gloucestershire

Barnsley, nr Cirencester
GL7 5EE
In Barnsley village 4m NE
of Cirencester by
A433/B4425
Tel: 01285 740281

Owner: Charles Verey

Open: Mon, Wed, Thur
and Sat 10–6 or dusk if
earlier. 4 acres

THIS IS a famous garden, made by David and Rosemary Verey since 1951. Influenced by her knowledge of garden history Mrs Verey contrived a heady mixture of ingredients – a pleached lime walk, knot gardens, an ornamental *potager*, temples and statuary. The real distinction, however, lies in the planting, especially in the use of herbaceous plants and subtle associations of form and colour. Barnsley House is well known through Mrs Verey's own excellent books – but there is no substitute for a visit to the garden itself, which is in a constant state of gentle but stimulating change as new discoveries are made. A nursery sells an excellent stock of choice and often rare plants of the sort grown in the garden.

BATSFORD ARBORETUM
Gloucestershire

Moreton-in-Marsh GL56 9QF
1m NW of Moreton-in-Marsh
by A44
Tel: 01386 700409 (weekends);
01608 650722 (weekdays)

Owner: The Batsford
Foundation

Open: Mar to early Nov, daily
10–5. 50 acres

THIS ARBORETUM, started in the 1880s, has recently been revitalised with an enormous amount of new planting. It is now well worth visiting at any time of the year and even demon dendrologists will find marvellous things – over 90 kinds of oak, for example, and many wonderful individual specimens. But for less rarified tastes the place is full of interest, with all trees well labelled and the landscape enlivened by statues (including a fine bronze Buddha) and ornamental buildings. There is also a large nursery which carries a good general stock.

BENTHALL HALL
Shropshire

Broseley TF12 5RX
6m SW of Telford by
minor roads
Tel: 01952 882159

Owner:
The National Trust

Open: 2 Apr to 27 Sept,
Wed, Sun and Bank Hol
Mon 1.30–5.30. 3 acres.
House open

BENTHALL HALL is a 16th-century gabled stone house which was inhabited in the 19th century by George Maw, a devoted amateur botanist with a particular passion for crocuses, on which he wrote a famous, very rare book. His naturalised plantings of spring and autumn crocuses survive to this day. He went on plant-collecting expeditions and made new introductions; the charming pale blue *Chionodoxa luciliae*, from western Turkey, first flowered in England at Benthall in 1877. A subsequent tenant was Robert Bateman, son of James Bateman of Biddulph not far away. Robert Bateman made the terraced Pixie Garden with a pool and topiary of yew and box. This is not a dramatic garden but it has many good plants and an agreeably intimate atmosphere.

BERRINGTON HALL

Hereford and Worcester

nr Leominster HR6 0DW
3m N of Leominster by
A49
Tel: 01568 615721

Owner:
The National Trust

Open: Apr to Sept, daily
except Mon and Tue (open
Bank Hol Mon, closed
Good Fri) 1.30–5.30; Oct,
Wed to Sun 1.30–4.30.
10 acres. House open

THE BROWN STONE mansion was designed by
Henry Holland and completed in 1781, and the
unspoilt landscape park was laid out by his partner
and father-in-law 'Capability' Brown. There was no
house or garden here before so this is an unusual
period piece. From the vast Arch of Triumph at the
entrance, an avenue of clipped mounds of golden yew
leads towards the front door of the house. On one
side a magnificent brick-walled 18th-century kitchen
garden has a recently planted collection of historic
varieties of apple and, leading up to the wrought-iron
entrance gate, a pair of good mixed borders. The
walls provide protection for some unusual tender
plants including the grandest of all buddlejas, *B.
colvillei*, with huge panicles of red flowers.

BODNANT

Gwynedd

BODNANT WAS started in the late 19th century at
the height of the rhododendron craze. The steep
slopes of the Conwy valley provided a wonderfully
romantic site for their cultivation, and with the
rushing waters of the River Hraethlyn at his feet, the
visitor today may convincingly imagine himself in a
dream-like valley of the Himalayas. Rhododendrons
and camellias flourish under a high canopy of
conifers. Nearer the house there is a completely

*Illustration opposite: Statue
at Bodnant*

Tenbury Wells WR15 8HQ
1m W of Tenbury Wells by
A456
Tel: 01584 810777

Owner: Treasures of
Tenbury Ltd

Open: Daily 10–5. 4 acres

paved terrace, a long straight vista through an
opening in a yew hedge, and double borders. Farther
from the house sweeping lawns are interrupted by an
ambling stream with excellent planting along its
banks, island beds of trees and shrubs fringed by
herbaceous plantings, and some fine specimen trees.
It is all beautifully kept, and everywhere there are
clematis: the National Collection is held here.

CADDICK'S CLEMATIS NURSERIES
Cheshire

Lymm Road, Thelwall,
Warrington WA13 0UF
At Thelwall village, just off
A56. 10 mins from Jnct 20
of M6 and Jnct 9 of M56
Tel: 01925 757196

Open: Daily except Mon
(but closed 15 Dec to 31
Jan) 10–5

CADDICK'S WAS STARTED only in 1984, by Harry
Caddick, a Lockmaster on the Manchester Ship
Canal. He now sells a a wonderful collection of
clematis, beautifully displayed in new premises.
Caddick's sells nothing but these essential garden
plants, and its catalogue (£1.00) of over 300 varieties
is one of the best. A mail order service is provided.

CHIRK CASTLE
Clwyd

Chirk LL14 5AF
1/2m W of Chirk village by
A5
Tel: 01691 777701

Owner:
The National Trust

Open: 2 Apr to Aug daily
except Mon and Sat (open
Bank Hol Mon) 11–6; Jul
and Aug also open Sat;
Oct, Sat and Sun 11–6. 5
acres. Castle open

CHIRK IS a 13th-century border castle, and its
massive defensive towers are echoed in the
billowing old topiary cones of yew that march down
its east side. An opening cut into a yew hedge
guarded by a pair of bronze nymphs leads through to
the upper lawn and a deep mixed border punctuated
by groups of flowering cherries. On this windy site

woodland provides protection for magnolias, rhododendrons and more unusual plants such as the Chilean firebush (*Embothrium coccineum*) with its scarlet flowers, and *Eucryphia glutinosa*.

THE DOROTHY CLIVE GARDEN

Shropshire

Willoughbridge, nr Market Drayton TF9 4EU
9m SE of Nantwich by A51
Tel: 01630 647237

Owner: Willoughbridge Garden Trust

Open: Apr to Oct, daily 10–5.30. 8 acres

Few gardens have such diversity of interest as this. The garden was started in 1940 by Col. Harry Clive who realised the attractions of the site: a former gravel pit with acid soil on a fine south-facing, well watered slope, which provides habitats for a very wide range of plants. At the very top of the hill, in the old quarry, Col. Clive's original woodland garden is now fully mature; it is rich with azaleas, maples, rhododendrons and other ornamental trees and shrubs. A rushing multi-tiered waterfall is a brilliant sight in high summer, fringed with the coloured plumes of astilbes and ligularias. On the slopes below the old quarry a garden of a completely different character, planned by the garden designer John Codrington, was developed after Col. Clive's death. In the upper reaches, broad grassy paths running along the contours of the hill divide mixed borders lavishly planted with woody and herbaceous plants. Paths then run downhill at a brisker pace, between informal and scree beds, with a lily pond at the bottom.

DUNHAM MASSEY
Cheshire

Altrincham WA14 4SJ
3m W of Altrincham by
A56
Tel: 0161 941 1025

Owner:
The National Trust

Open: Apr to 29 Oct, daily
11–5.30. 250 acres. House
open

ONE OF THE great successes of many National Trust gardens is their willingness to give full emphasis within a single garden to garden styles of different periods. At Dunham Massey, with its grand early 18th-century house, there are remains of a pattern of formal avenues of the same period, charging towards the horizon. Much replanting of beeches, limes and oaks has given this new life. From the house a double staircase leads to a sprightly Edwardian parterre, bedded in summer with zonal pelargoniums mixed with verbena and edged with rich blue lobelia. Clipped mounds of holm oak and hedges of golden yew give permanent ornament. To one side of the house informal lawns spread out, overlooked by an 18th-century orangery with, half-concealed in the woods behind, a well house disguised as a rustic retreat. Grassy walks lead along a moat whose banks are densely planted with astilbes, ferns, hostas, irises and rodgersias. The walk continues to a simple lawn, from which views are suddenly revealed of the house reflected in the tranquil waters of the moat.

EASTGROVE COTTAGE GARDEN
Hereford and Worcester

Sankyns Green, Little Witley WR6 6LQ
8m NW of Worcester, on the road between Shrawley (on B4196) and Great Witley (on A443)
Tel: 01299 896389

Owner: Malcolm and Carol Skinner

Open: Apr to Jul, Thur to Mon 2–5; Sept to 14 Oct, Thur to Sat 2–5 (closed throughout Aug). 1 acre

IF YOU DID NOT know what a cottage garden should look like this would be a good place to learn. The cottage itself, tiled and ancient, is set in lovely countryside and the garden, flawlessly kept, is full of lively planting and cunning design. There are formal ingredients – a splendid zigzagging hedge of the neatest possible *Lonicera nitida*, carefully placed benches in enclosures, and a great rose arbour; the garden itself is chiefly composed of curving borders and sweeps of lawn. A very wide range of plants, some extremely unusual, is grown. Malcolm and Carol Skinner, who made the garden, also run an outstanding nursery which concentrates on herbaceous perennials, hardy and half-hardy, and in which even the keenest gardeners will make discoveries. A very good list is produced (five 2nd-class stamps) but there is no mail order service.

ERDDIG
Clwyd

nr Wrexham LL13 0YT
2m S of Wrexham by A525
Tel: 01978 313333

Owner:
The National Trust

Open: 14 Apr to 1 Oct, daily except Thur and Fri 11–6; Oct, daily except Thur and Fri 11–5. 13 acres. House open

THE FORMAL GARDEN to the east of the long, low early 18th-century house is one of the very few in Britain to survive the craze for landscape gardens in the second part of the 18th century. It has now been sensitively restored by the National Trust and is full of delights. It is enclosed in brick walls on which are espaliered old varieties of fruit trees. These are underplanted with many varieties of daffodil, and the central area has formal orchards of apple trees. A gravel path leads from the Edwardian parterre under the east windows of the house, by tubs of Portugal laurel clipped into mushroom shapes, towards a slender canal flanked with old limes. At its end, exquisite wrought-iron gates give views of the country beyond. Parallel to this, to the south, a path runs along an avenue of Irish yews, with, on the north-facing wall, many varieties of ivy of which Erddig holds the National Collection. The path continues to the Dutch garden, a recreated flowery Victorian parterre with variegated maples, agapanthus, clematis and cheerful bedding. Beyond, the path continues to a pair of stone urns and a memorably gloomy moss walk in the woods of shady holly and laurel.

GAWSWORTH HALL
Cheshire

Gawsworth, nr
Macclesfield SK11 9RN
3m S of Macclesfield by
A536
Tel: 01260 223456

Owner: Mr and Mrs
Timothy Richards

Open: Apr to Oct, daily
2–5. 20 acres. House open

GAWSWORTH HALL is a lovely late Elizabethan half-timbered house of the characteristic Cheshire type. In front, lawns with specimen trees run down to a pool, and from the forecourt a paved path leads to a formal garden of rose beds, hedges of holly and yew and an ornamental bronze fountain. All this is quite modern but beyond the house lie the ghostly remains of a princely garden of the same date as the house. Magnificent Tudor brick walls survive, enclosing a great space, where a pattern of terraces, and the site of a wilderness garden and of a formal canal, are visible. All this has been the subject of an archaeological dig which is very well described in a booklet on sale at the house. No plants survive from this early garden but it still has great atmosphere.

HARE HILL
Cheshire

nr Macclesfield SK10 4QB
3m NW of Macclesfield by
B5087
Tel: 01625 828981

Owner:
The National Trust

Open: 29 Mar to 29 Oct,
Wed, Thur, Sat, Sun and
Bank Hol Mon 10–5.30; 12
May to 2 Jun, also daily
10–5.30. 10 acres

HARE HILL has a touch of the Marie Céleste about it – as though the inhabitants might return at any moment and the place would burst into life. It is a woodland garden, approached across meadows and parkland, with sandy paths running under a high canopy of beech, oak and sycamore, and glades of azaleas, maples and rhododendrons. Hidden in the middle of the wood is a large walled garden with rose beds, weeping silver pears and a trellis-work arbour draped in clematis. Deeper still into the woodland a rustic bridge spans the neck of a lake whose banks are densely planted with the wilder moisture-loving plants such as *Gunnera manicata*. From the path running along the southern edge of the wood, glades occasionally open out offering lovely views of the peaceful countryside.

HERGEST CROFT
Hereford and Worcester

THIS IS ONE of the best private collections of woody plants in Britain, and has an exceptionally attractive atmosphere. The house was built in 1896 by William Hartland Banks who also started the collection of plants, many of which were raised from seed gathered in the wild. The garden falls into two chief parts – that near the house and the separate

Kington HR5 3EG
1/2m W of Kington by A44
Tel: 01544 230160

Owner: W.L. Banks and
R.A. Banks

Open: Easter to Oct, daily
1.30–6.30. 50 acres

woodland garden which lies across some fields and
contains a fine collection of rhododendrons. It is
useless to attempt to list the great riches of this place.
There are marvellous plants everywhere, and of
particular interest are the National Collections of
maples (excluding *Acer japonicum* cultivars) and of
birches. There is also an exceptionally pretty kitchen
garden with good borders, peonies under old apple
trees, and proper vegetable beds. There are excellent
plants for sale at the garden, although no catalogue is
issued and there is no mail order.

HIDCOTE MANOR GARDEN
Gloucestershire

Hidcote Bartrim, nr
Chipping Campden
GL55 6LR
4m NE of Chipping
Campden by B4632
Tel: 01386 438333

Owner:
The National Trust

Open: Apr to Oct, daily
except Tue and Fri 11–7 or
sunset if earlier. 10 acres

Aᴌᴛʜᴏᴜɢʜ ᴀᴍᴏɴɢ the best-known gardens in
Britain, Hidcote still has the power to startle.
It was begun before World War I by an American,
Major Lawrence Johnston, who devised a type of
garden that many think of as quintessentially English.
First, it is a garden built up of separate 'rooms', each
connected to the next but often with dramatic
contrasts. For example, a pair of blazing red borders
leads through to a cool green alley of pleached
hornbeams. Second, the firm layout provides a
disciplined setting for an immense range of plants of

which Johnston was a pioneer rediscoverer – especially of old roses – and which he used in a swashbuckling manner in contrast with the crisp authority of his layout. Everywhere something enticing is glimpsed through an opening, across a pool, down steps or framed by a distant gate.

HODGES BARN
Gloucestershire

Shipton Moyne, Tetbury
GL8 8PR
E of the village of Shipton
Moyne, 2 1/2m S of
Tetbury by A433 and
minor road
Tel: 01666 880202

Owner: Mr and Mrs
Charles Hornby

Open: Apr to mid Aug,
Mon, Tue and Fri 2–5. 8
acres

HODGES BARN IS an exceptionally pretty house, a pair of lovely ancient domed dovecotes converted into an elegant house in the 20th century. The garden was started after 1946 by the present owner's grandmother who planted many trees and laid out an excellent, bold design which has been enriched by the present owners. Enclosed areas about the house, hedged or walled, are skilfully planted and make the most of lovely views of the house or of the rural countryside beyond. Everywhere there are excellent roses - climbers and shrubs near the house and the species and wilder types among trees. A naturalistic woodland garden is marvellous in spring and in a more formal woodland glade the former stew pond is edged with moisture-loving plants. Deft touches of formality – a procession of Irish yews, well placed ornaments or lively topiary – give crisp contrast to the lavish planting. All is impeccably kept and sparkles with the excitement of gardening.

HODNET HALL
Shropshire

Hodnet, nr Market
Drayton TF9 3NN
5 1/2m SW of Market
Drayton by A53; 12m NE
of Shrewsbury by A53
Tel: 01630 685202

Owner: Mr and the Hon.
Mrs Heber-Percy

Open: Apr to Sept, Mon to
Sat 2–5, Sun and Bank Hol
Mon 12–5.30. 70 acres

HEBERS HAVE been at Hodnet for an immense time but the garden can never have been in a better state than it is today. The main house is a neo-Elizabethan extravaganza built in 1870 by Anthony Salvin on an eminence with views south over a lake; a decorative Tudor dovecote forms an eye-catcher in the distance. Immediately below the south terrace of the house there are good mixed borders, and steps lead down towards the lake which is part of a chain of pools whose banks have been brilliantly planted with with moisture-loving plants –

astilbes, ferns, *Gunnera manicata*, hostas, rodgersias, and primulas. By the east end of the lake, partly concealed by woodland, is a circular bed with a figure of Father Time surrounded by concentric beds of hydrangeas, peonies and roses.

HOW CAPLE COURT GARDENS

Hereford and Worcester

nr Ross-on-Wye HR1 4SX
4m N of Ross-on-Wye by
A449 and B4224
Tel: 01989 86626

Owner: Mr and Mrs Peter
Lee

Open: Apr to Oct, Mon to
Sat 9–5.30, Sun 10–5. 11
acres

THIS MARVELLOUS PLACE is undergoing restoration but already so much has been done that it is well worth visiting. The house is an ancient one with medieval origins, rebuilt in the early 17th century and once again at the turn of the century. The present owner's grandfather was mad about gardens and laid out an ambitious and exciting scheme thoroughly appropriate to the spectacular site. On one side of the house he made a series of dramatic terraces linked by steps with views across the Wye valley towards the Brecon Beacons to the south. The bottom terrace has a pool, Italianate statues, sentinel Irish yews and cascades of old roses. In the wooded valley alongside the house there is a dell garden, a vast circular pool, a Florentine garden with a pattern of canals, the remains of a huge pergola and a loggia – all of which are undergoing restoration. A small nursery in the stable yard sells some good plants, particularly shrub roses.

KIFTSGATE COURT
Gloucestershire

Chipping Campden
GL55 6LW
3m NE of Chipping
Campden by B4632
Tel: 01386 438777

Owner: Mr and Mrs A.H.
Chambers

Open: Apr to Sept, Wed,
Thur and Sun 2–6; Jun to
Jul, also Sat and Bank Hol
Mon 2–6. 6 acres

THE NAME KIFTSGATE means to many gardeners that beautiful and embarrassingly vigorous rambling rose *R. filipes* 'Kiftsgate', but although the garden, started in the 1920s by Heather Muir, is certainly full of roses there is much else to admire. The house has a splendid setting, teetering on the edge of a precipitous valley across which, through the woods, are views of the Vale of Evesham. About the house is a series of enclosed gardens in which formality is blurred by generous planting. Four Squares has peonies, penstemons and rodgersias among berberis, indigofera and kolkwitzia. The rose borders have a central path hedged in *Rosa versicolor* behind which rise ramparts of shrub roses, and the 'Kiftsgate' rose zips 50 feet into the branches of a copper beech. Below all this, paths wind steeply down the valley side where, under the canopy of trees, cistus, hebes, phlomis and senecio relish the dry conditions. A choice selection of plants is for sale.

KINGSTONE COTTAGES
Hereford and Worcester

Weston-under-Penyard,
Ross-on-Wye HR9 7NX
2 m E of Ross-on-Wye by
A40 and minor roads
Tel: 01989 565267

Owner:
Mr and Mrs M. Hughes

Open: 4 May to 25 Jun,
Mon to Fri 9.30–4.30

SOPHIE HUGHES is an expert on pinks and at
Kingstone Cottages she holds the National
Collection of old garden varieties – over 140 species
and cultivars. Some are displayed in a little parterre,
like a bed in a physic garden, but many more are
used to great effect in the excellent mixed plantings
of her charming cottage garden. There are good
plants for sale, pinks, of course, but others too.

LITTLE MORETON HALL
Cheshire

Congleton CW12 4SD
4m SW of Congleton by
A34
Tel: 01260 272018

Owner:
The National Trust

Open: Apr to Sept, Wed to
Sun (closed Good Fri)
12–5.30; Bank Hol Mon
11–5.30; Oct, Sat and Sun
12–5.30 or dusk if earlier.
1 acre. House open

THE HALF-TIMBERED famously wambly 15th-century
house is surrounded by a moat. Little is known
about what sort of garden the house had in its
heyday but there are the remains of an artificial
mound of the sort that might have been used for
viewing a formal knot or parterre. With this in mind
Graham Stuart Thomas laid out a charming little
knot garden of box hedges, gravel and topiary yew
obelisks based on a 17th-century pattern. At each side
a pattern of square beds hedged in box contains a

standard gooseberry bush underplanted with blocks of a single herbaceous plant – germander, strawberries, London pride or woodruff. All this is perfectly appropriate to the setting and a model of what may be done in a small space.

LYME PARK
Cheshire

Disley,
Stockport SK12 2NX
6 1/2m SE of Stockport by A6
Tel: 01663 762023

Owner:
The National Trust

Open: Apr to Oct 11–5; Nov to 17 Dec, Sat and Sun 12–4. 15 acres. House open

AT LYME PARK the best parts of the garden have an exciting Victorian flavour that contrasts strikingly with the grand Frenchified house of the early 18th century. To one side of the house a well planted orangery of 1862 overlooks a parterre with Irish yews and urns, whose beds are planted in spring and summer with bright bedding schemes. On a terrace above, a rose garden with flagged paths and a central pool is enclosed in yew hedges and partly shaded by a pair of beautiful old limes. To one side a path sweeps uphill between deep herbaceous borders whose colour scheme modulates from oranges and yellows to blues and violets as it recedes from the house. North-west of the house, suddenly revealed below a high terrace, is an eye-stopping sight: the so-called Dutch garden, a dazzling arrangment of a fountain, statues of the four seasons, and a geometric pattern of beds edged in tightly clipped ivy and planted with single blocks of begonias, yellow or orange marigolds, santolina or purple verbena. For those who scoff at bedding this comes as a revelation.

MISARDEN PARK
Gloucestershire

Miserden, Stroud GL6 7JA
7m SE of Gloucester
Tel: 01285 821303

Owner:
Major M.T.N.H. Wills

Open: Apr to Sept, Tue to
Thur 9.30–4.30. 12 1/2 acres

THE HOUSE is of the early 17th century with additions in 1920 by Sir Edwin Lutyens who also influenced the style of the terrace garden and forecourt alongside the house. The site is marvellous, on the edge of a valley with long views over wooded country. South and east of the house are excellent ornamental trees, and pleasure gardens are disposed on the slopes above. At their heart is a long walk of yew hedges whose tops are decorated by a series of undulating topiary humps. On one side a pair of great mixed borders are separated by a broad grass walk, and on the other a formal rose garden is backed with elegant trellis fencing. The garden is extremely well kept and is full of interest. A nursery sells the kinds of plants seen in the garden.

NESS GARDENS
Cheshire

Ness, Neston, South Wirral
L64 4AY
11m NW of Chester by
A540
Tel: 0151 336 2135/7769

Owner: The University of
Liverpool

Open: Mar to Oct, daily
9.30–sunset; Nov to Feb,
daily (except 25 Dec)
9.30–4. 63 acres

NESS GARDENS WERE founded by A.K. Bulley, who sponsored the first expeditions of two of the greatest plant hunters of the 20th century – George Forrest to western China in 1904 and Frank Kingdon-Ward to Yunnan in 1911. Other expeditions followed and the plants that these men introduced are among the best specimens to be seen in the gardens to day. The site of the garden was good – with undulating land, acid soil and natural outcrops of stone. Bulley planted windbreaks of holly, evergreen oak, pines and poplars, and built up a very wide range of plants. Some parts of the collection – such as azaleas, rhododendrons and sorbus – are particularly good. From the gardener's point of view, however, there are other valuable features: a heather garden, herbaceous borders, a large rock garden, many roses, immense numbers of flowering trees and shrubs, and a woodland garden.

OLD COURT NURSERIES LTD
Hereford and Worcester

Illustration: Astrantia
'*George Chiswell*'

Colwall, nr Malvern
WR13 6QE
3m SW of Malvern by
A449 and B4218
Tel: 01684 40416

Open: Apr to Oct, Wed to
Sun 10–1, 2.15–5.30; Nov
to Mar, by appointment
only

THE GREAT GLORY of Old Court Nurseries is the collection of Michaelmas daisies, one of the National Collections and a wonderful sight in September and October. But the nursery also sells an excellent collection of herbaceous perennials and rock garden plants. These are handsomely displayed in the adjoining Picton Garden which is open at the same times as the nursery. Nursery and garden together make an extremely attractive place to visit. Paul Picton has an excellent eye for a good plant and any gardener will find something desirable. Michaelmas daisies only are sold by mail order and a list of them is issued for that purpose.

PAINSWICK ROCOCO GARDEN
Gloucestershire

THIS IS ONE of the most ambitious restorations of a private historic garden ever undertaken. The garden had all but disappeared but has now been almost entirely restored, using a painting of it by Thomas Robins of 1748. In a secret combe behind

Painswick,
nr Stroud GL6 6TH
1/2m N of Painswick by
B4073
Tel: 01452 813204

Owner: Painswick Rococo
Garden Trust

Open: 2nd Wed in Jan to
30 Nov, Wed to Sun and
Bank Hol Mon, 11–5. 10
acres

the house are wonderful garden buildings, woodland
walks, pools, and a snowdrop grove to take your
breath away. A mysteriously two-faced gothic gazebo
looks down a yew alley towards a distant pond.
Paths snake up and down the wooded slopes of the
combe, giving glimpses of alcoves, temples and pools.
Work continues – the Eagle House, filigree Gothic
Exedra and vegetable garden have recently been
reconstructed with great success.

PENPERGWM LODGE
Gwent

Abergavenny NP7 9AS
3m E of Abergavenny by
B4598; turn N opposite
King of Prussia
Tel: 01873 840208

Owner: Mr and Mrs Simon
Boyle

Open: mid Apr to mid
Aug, Thur to Sat 2–5. 3
acres

CATRIONA BOYLE INHERITED some good bones
when she took over the garden at Penpergwm
Lodge, to which she has added much finely judged
ornamental planting. Lawns by the house have
excellent trees and a recently made south-facing
paved terrace burgeons with *Carpenteria californica*,
cistus, diascias, indigofera, myrtle and penstemons.
This is a surprisingly mild part of the country and
the garden enjoys excellent frost drainage. On the far
side of the house a stately procession of 'rooms' is
hedged in yew: the former vegetable garden has

arches of roses and vines with ebullient herbaceous planting below (with the odd courgette or artichoke still lurking in a corner); a shady apple tunnel; a pair of rose borders backed with purple beech; and walks of magnolias and maples. There are some good plants for sale, chiefly herbaceous, and Mrs Boyle runs an organization called Catriona Boyle's Garden School which gives one-day courses on gardening, with lectures and demonstrations from very distinguished gardeners. The whole place seems to be buzzing with horticultural endeavour.

PENRHYN CASTLE

Gwynedd

Bangor LL57 4HN
1m E of Bangor by A5122
Tel: 01248 353084

Owner:
The National Trust

Open: 29 Mar to Oct, daily except Tue 11–6. 47 acres. House open

THE GIANT CASTLE – commissioned from Thomas Hopper in 1827 by a local millionaire quarry owner – is in neo-Norman style, built on a bluff with marvellous views north to Beaumaris Bay and south towards Snowdon. Parkland surrounds the castle but the chief horticultural interest lies in the old kitchen garden to the south. This is built on a steep slope with a formal terrace, parterres of roses and penstemons, and a rose arbour at the top; at a lower level are ornamental trees and shrubs – eucryphias, magnolias, sophoras and styrax; at the lowest level are trained fuchsias on a long pergola with clematis intertwining and views to the stream garden below, with, in summer, the huge leaves of *Gunnera manicata* splendidly placed against groves of elegant purple-leafed maples.

PERHILL NURSERIES
Hereford and Worcester

Illustration: Phygelius 'Winchester Fanfare'

Worcester Road, Great Witley WR6 6JT
On A443 1/4m SE of village
Tel: 01299 896329

Open: Mon to Sat 9–6, Sun 9–5. No mail order

ALPINES AND HERBACEOUS perennials are the speciality of this nursery, which carries a stock of over 2,200 different species and varieties. There are particularly good collections of campanulas, penstemons, phlox, pinks, salvias, silenes and sisyrinchiums. Perhill also has other interests including herbs – with, for example, a dozen different kinds of basil, sixteen lavenders and some marvellous sages. There are always too many plants to be listed so a visit and a rummage around will always reveal something new and desirable – all the more necessary because there is no mail order service. A plant list is produced (six 2nd-class stamps) and useful separate lists of plants for particular purposes or places.

PLAS BRONDANW GARDENS
Gwynedd

Llanfrothen, Penrhyndeudraeth LL48 6SW
3m N of Penrhyndeudraeth by A4085
Tel: 01766 770484

Owner: Trustees of the Second Portmeirion Foundation

Open: Daily 9–5. 4 acres

Illustration opposite: Plas Brondanw Gardens

TO MANY GARDEN VISITORS places that are completely unlike any other have an irresistible allure. Plas Brondanw belonged to the architect of Portmeirion, Sir Clough Williams-Ellis, who worked on the garden, on and off, from 1902 into the 1960s. On wooded slopes on the very fringe of Snowdonia, Plas Brondanw has one of the most magnificent natural settings of any garden in Britain. Williams-Ellis laid out an inventive formal garden enlivened by the cheerful panache that makes him such an attractive figure (who else could make such a

delightful pavilion out of *corrugated iron*, exquisitely
shaped and painted, as that which lurks in the
woodland here?). Bold axes of yew hedges connect
the house to the garden, and 'borrowed landscapes'
are given full emphasis, including a breathtaking view
of Snowdon which forms an eye-catcher to the main
vista, and a neatly framed picture of Cnicht through
a *claire voie*. The whole garden swarms with
architectural trimmings – a pretty orangery, terraces,
balustrades, urns, statues and irrepressible *jeux
d'esprit*. Under no circumstances miss the walk
through the woods behind the house to the
spectacular rocky ravine with its watchtower.

PLAS NEWYDD
Gwynedd

Llanfairpwll, Anglesey
LL61 6EQ
1m S of Llanfairpwll by A5
Tel: 01248 714795

Owner:
The National Trust

Open: 31 Mar to 29 Sept,
daily except Sat 11–5; Oct,
Fri and Sun 11–5. 31 acres.
House open

THE HOUSE of Plas Newydd is a famously
decorative piece of gothic fantasy built in 1793 by
James Wyatt overlooking the waters of the Menai
Strait. This is a mild but windy place and one of the
striking things about the garden is the decorative use
of unfamiliar hedging plants – fuchsia, grisellinia and
potentilla. There is a pretty little formal terraced
garden between the house and the strait but the real
garden excitement comes with the parkland to the
west, known as 'West Indies', in the design of which
Humphry Repton had a hand. Here countless good
ornamental trees and shrubs – camellias, magnolias,
maples and the Chilean firebush – flourish among

older cedars, an exceptional sycamore and Monterey cypresses. A rhododendron garden, three-quarters of a mile to the north of the house, has recently been restored and is open only during flowering time from the beginning of April to the end of May.

PLAS-YN-RHIW
Gwynedd

Rhiw, Pwllheli LL53 8AB
12m from Pwllheli on S
coast road to Aberdaron
Tel: 0175 888 219

Owner:
The National Trust

Open: 2 Apr to 29 Sept,
daily except Sat 12–5.
1 acre. House open

THE LLEYN PENINSULA is the most westerly part of Wales, and this enchanting little garden is one of the most remote on the mainland of Britain. The elegant stone house is built on precipitous wooded slopes giving beautiful views over Hell's Mouth Bay. Cobbled paths and box hedges divide the densely planted garden, and old plants of sweet bay, a fig, myrtles and artemisias give a Mediterranean air. The microclimate is very benign here so plants like *Euphorbia mellifera* grow to great size, and the tender climber *Lapageria rosea* flourishes.

PORTMEIRION
Gwynedd

Penrhyndeudraeth
LL48 6ET
2m SE of Porthmadog
Tel: 01766 770228

Open: Daily 9.30–5.30

IN A WOODED COMBE overlooking the estuary of Traeth Bach towards the Harlech hills the architect Clough Williams-Ellis let rip with a fantasy Italianate village. He incorporated old architectural fragments into his buildings – cupolas, colonnades, statues and enough balconies to meet the needs of the world's population of Romeos and Juliets. Among these buildings there is interesting planting with a

Mediterranean feeling – Chusan palms and Italian cypresses punctuate the scene, and cistus and artemisias flourish on the rocky slopes. Portmeirion has a mild microclimate so tender plants such as *Echium pininiana* do particularly well. There is a hotel in the village and houses are available for rent.

POWIS CASTLE

Powys

Welshpool SY21 8RF
1m S of Welshpool by
A483
Tel: 01938 554336

Owner:
The National Trust

Open: Apr to Jun, Sept to
Oct, daily except Mon and
Tue 11–6; Jul to Aug, daily
except Mon (open Bank
Hol Mon) 11–6. 24 acres.
Castle open

THERE ARE FEW historic gardens that have so much to offer the gardener as Powis Castle. The place is historic because it preserves the splendid remains of a great formal garden of the 17th century – with grand terraces and immense old yews. But on these terraces the National Trust has laid out a brilliant series of borders, with wall plants and climbers forming a background to fortissimo displays of border perennials; these are designed to provide interest throughout the summer into early autumn. Another particular interest in the gardens is the exceptional collection of pots, beautifully planted with carefully judged combinations. A small woodland garden below the castle has great atmosphere, where a mysterious sculpture by Vincent Woropay of a disembodied foot lies in the grass.

THE PRIORY
Gloucestershire

Kemerton GL20 7JN
6m S of Pershore by B4080
Tel: 01386 725258

Owner: The Hon. Mrs
Peter Healing

Open: Jun to Sept, Thur
2–7. 4 acres

THE HOUSE at Kemerton is an elegant Georgian box of Cotswold stone but the priory ruins are visible among the densely planted borders. On the south-facing slopes of Bredon Hill the garden has a protected site where Mrs Healing and her late husband devised brilliant borders in which colour harmony – some of it refreshingly bold – was the essential principle. Unusual plants chosen with an artist's eye fill these borders, and they flower over an extended period. Providing contrast are broad sweeps of lawn with beautiful ornamental trees (especially maples), yew hedges, a pergola of roses and vines. A nursery sells some excellent plants but there is no mail order.

RODMARTON MANOR
Gloucestershire

Rodmarton, nr Cirencester
GL7 6PF
In village of Rodmarton 6
miles SW of Cirencester by
A433
Tel: 01285 841253/841278

Owner: Mr and Mrs Simon
Biddulph

Open: 13 May to 26 Aug,
Sat 2–5; also by
appointment. 8 acres

THE ARCHITECT Ernest Barnsley started Rodmarton in 1909 and it became a shrine of the Cotswolds crafts movement. The grey, gabled house has an intricate garden, also designed by Barnsley, divided into 'rooms' and of a lively atmosphere. It is formal in spirit but the lavish planting has a cottage-garden informality. A flagged path separates double borders overflowing with old roses, peonies and campanulas, backed with stone walls and a yew hedge and enlivened with topiary of yew and box. Behind the house a pattern of enclosures separated by yew hedges and a pleached lime walk frames unspoilt views of the rural landscape.

RUSHFIELDS OF LEDBURY
Hereford and Worcester

Ross Road, Ledbury
HR8 2LP
1 1/2m SW of Ledbury by
A449
Tel: 01531 632004

Open: Wed to Sat 11–5

THIS IS A small nursery carrying a choice stock with an emphasis on herbaceous perennials. There are good collections of hardy geraniums, hostas, penstemons and interesting grasses. The very rare double-flowered sweet rocket is stocked, and there is a splendid selection of the exquisite hellebores cultivated by the legendary Helen Ballard. An informative catalogue is produced (s.a.e. 29p plus £1.00), from which plants may be ordered by post.

SEZINCOTE
Gloucestershire

nr Moreton-in-Marsh
GL56 9AW
1 1/2m W of
Moreton-in-Marsh by A44

Owner: Mr and Mrs D.
Peake

Open: Jan to Nov, Thur,
Fri and Bank Hol Mon 2–6
or sunset if earlier. 10
acres. House open

THE HOUSE at Sezincote was built in around 1810 by Sir Charles Cockerell and has a wonderful Indian character. At first the scene is quintessentially English – a sweeping drive and lovely parkland ornamented with exceptional cedars of Lebanon scarcely prepares the visitor for the exotic experience in store. Soon the drive runs over an Indian bridge surmounted by statues of bulls; below, a stream flows from a pool with an island bearing a curious column entwined with a three-headed snake. The banks of the stream are richly planted with hostas, rodgersias and skunk cabbage, relishing the moisture. On the far side of the bridge a figure of Souriya overlooks the temple pool. Old woodland spreads all around, studded with ornamental trees. Near the house a formal garden with a canal flanked by rows of soaring Irish yews is overlooked by a grand sweeping conservatory with minarets, ending in a domed pavilion. This heady mixture of subtle layout, excellent plants and orientalist decoration deep in the Cotswolds is a unique experience.

SNOWSHILL MANOR
Gloucestershire

Snowshill, nr Broadway
WR12 7JU
In village of Snowshill 3m
S of Broadway
Tel: 01386 852410

Owner:
The National Trust

Open: Apr and Oct, daily
except Tue 1–5; May to
Sept, daily exceot Tue 1–6.
2 acres. House open

CHARLES WADE, antiquarian and architect, was responsible for this extraordinary place where the garden was partly designed by the Arts and Crafts architect M.H. Baillie Scott. The house is a pretty stone-tiled Cotswold manor and the garden lies on steep west-facing slopes to one side. Wade terraced the slope and linked the separate spaces with stone steps and a bold descending avenue of Irish yews. Within the various garden enclosures Wade deployed a rich repertoire of garden ornaments – sundials, an armillary sphere, a gilt figure of George and the Dragon, pools, and benches painted in the distinctive 'Wade blue'. Flower beds and climbing roses look wonderful against the honey-coloured stone. The charm of this modestly sized garden lies in its different levels and endlessly shifting viewpoints.

SPEKE HALL
Merseyside

The Walk, Liverpool L24 1XD
8m SE of city centre by A561; follow signs to airport
Tel: 0151 427 7231

Owner: The National Trust

Open: Mar to 29 Oct, daily except Mon (but open Bank Hol Mon, closed Good Fri) 1–5.30; Nov to Mar, daily except Mon 12–4 (closed 24 Dec–1 Jan). 15 acres. House open

THE NORRISES WHO built Speke Hall in the late 16th century would be surprised to find their lovely half-timbered extravaganza cheek by jowl with Liverpool airport and threatened by encroaching suburbia. However, it is all impeccably cared for by the National Trust who have in recent years embarked on a programme of garden revitalization. A water garden, countless plantings of spring bulbs, a pretty formal rose garden, mixed borders by the house and rhododendrons in the woodland give pleasure in different seasons.

SPETCHLEY PARK
Hereford and Worcester

nr Worcester WR5 1RS
3m E of Worcester by A422
Tel: 01905 345224/345213

Owner: Mr and Mrs R.J. Berkeley

Open: Apr to Sept, Tue to Fri and Bank Hol Mon 11–5, Sun 2–5. 25 acres

THE HEART of the garden is a maze of walks, borders and hedged enclosures which are so full of excellent plants that one's attention is repeatedly drawn by some lovely specimen, making it easy to lose one's orientation. The Berkeleys have been here a long time but, from the gardening point of view, the most important event was the marriage in 1891 of Robert Berkeley to Rose Willmott of Warley Place, the older sister of the famous gardener Ellen Willmott, who designed the fountain garden at Spetchley. Here a fountain lies at the centre of four large squares, enclosed in yew hedges and densely planted. Running along one side is an immense border in which roses, philadelphus and other shrubs are generously underplanted with herbaceous perennials – campanulas, delphiniums, geraniums and peonies. The suave stone Georgian mansion overlooks a park with lake and clumped trees.

STANWAY HOUSE

Gloucestershire

Stanway, nr Cheltenham
GL54 5PQ
In the hamlet of Stanway,
11m NE of Cheltenham by
B4632 and B4077
Tel: 01386 584469

Owner: Lord Neidpath

Open: Jun to Aug, Tue and
Thur 2–5. 20 acres

IN STRAIGHTFORWARD GARDENING terms it would be hard to justify the inclusion of this exquisite place. But the setting for the wonderful Elizabethan and Jacobean house is unforgettably beautiful. Behind it, well-wooded land slopes up towards a pyramid-like folly which in the 18th century was at the head of a spectacular cascade whose remains have recently been excavated and which it is hoped to restore. It is essential to walk up to the pyramid; the view is breathtaking and, on the way, an exhilarating cross vista through the woods is revealed. Everywhere there are exceptional trees: old cedars of Lebanon and sweet chestnuts by the pyramid; an exceptional tulip tree by the house; and a pair of ancient spreading oriental planes past the medieval tithe barn as you enter. It's not a place for fiddly borders but any gardener will love it.

STAPELEY WATER GARDENS

Cheshire

THERE IS nothing at all quite like this anywhere in Britain. It is a tremendous celebration of water gardens and their plants, where the visitor may see and buy and, indeed, quite possibly spend the whole day. Although there is plenty of razzamatazz there is

London Road, Stapeley,
Nantwich CW5 7LH
1m SE of Nantwich by A51
Tel: 01270 623868

Open: Mon to Sat 9–6,
Sun and Bank Hol Mon
10–6.30; closes at 5 in
winter. 53 acres

also nurserymanship of a high order and the gardens
display the largest collection of hardy and tender
water-lily varieties in the world – over 160 varieties
are grown. Apart from these there are also very many
other water plants displayed in immense glasshouses
and out-of-doors. A mail order service is provided
and the very well illustrated catalogue (£1.00) tells
you probably all you need to know about making,
stocking and maintaining a water garden.

STONE HOUSE COTTAGE
Hereford and Worcester

Stone, nr Kidderminster
DY10 4BG
2m SE of Kidderminster by
A448
Tel: 01562 69902

Owner: Major and the
Hon. Mrs Arbuthnott

Open: Mar to Nov, Wed to
Sat 10–6 ; May to Jun, also
Sun 10–6. 3/4 acre

JAMES ARBUTHNOTT is a demon bricklayer and his
wife Louisa a brilliant propagator. The garden, an
old walled kitchen garden, now bristles with look-out
towers, gazebos, arcades and other charming
architectural geegaws which make ornaments as well
as supports for the countless climbing, twining and
ramping plants that are a speciality of the garden.
Hedges of yew and purple plum divide the space, and
at the centre there is a pair of burgeoning borders
culminating in a sundial. Ornamental trees and
shrubs are planted in grass, and near the house raised
beds contain alpines and smaller plants. There is an
excellent nursery which specialises in wall plants,
some very unusual, and many with reputations for
dubious hardiness that have proved remarkably tough
in this not very mild climate. A good catalogue
(s.a.e.) is produced but there is no mail order.

SUDELEY CASTLE
Gloucestershire

Winchcombe, nr
Cheltenham GL54 5JD
8m NE of Cheltenham by
B4075 and B4632
Tel: 01242 604357/602308

Owner: Lord and Lady
Ashcombe

Open: Apr to Oct, daily
10.30–5.30. 10 acres. Castle
open

THIS IS a spectacular place with a grand late
medieval castle with later additions, and a garden
that takes full advantage of the architectural setting.
Roses are the great thing at Sudeley and they look
wonderful against the old stone walls. At the
entrance a long lily pool runs in front of the ruins of
the 15th-century great barn whose roof-less walls are
draped with climbing roses and clematis. Beyond the
castle, a recently replanted formal Victorian garden
has a pool surrounded by L-shaped beds with old
shrub roses underplanted with herbs. On either side

nursery sells a general ~
distinguished collection of roses.

TATTON PARK
Cheshire

Knutsford WA16 6QN
3 1/2m N of Knutsford
signposted from the centre
of the town
Tel: 01565 654822

Owner:
The National Trust

Open: Apr to Sept, daily
except Mon (but open
Bank Hol Mon) 10.30–6;
Oct to Mar, daily except
Mon 11–4. 60 acres.
House open

THE HOUSE was designed in the early 19th century
for the Egerton family by Lewis Wyatt; he also
had a hand in the gardens which have an exuberant
19th-century flavour. South of the house, on a terrace
with grand views, a dapper parterre designed by
Joseph Paxton has recently been beautifully restored
and is brilliantly bedded out in summer. Her
Ladyship's Garden, by the house, is a sunken garden
with a pergola and rose-beds. Fine mixed borders
with buttresses of yew are backed by the formerly
heated walls of the kitchen garden. Nearby, a unique
fernery designed by Wyatt houses tender ferns, and

an orangery protects citrus plants and sub-tropical climbers. On sloping land south of the house a long walk pierces well wooded lawns, with glimpses to the west of a serpentine network of lakes. Humphry Repton landscaped the park soon after the house was built. By one of the lakes is an exceptional Japanese garden, built in 1910 by Japanese gardeners, in which maples, moss-covered stones, an arched bridge and a Shinto temple make a convincing picture under a canopy of old trees. In the walled former kitchen garden The Tatton Garden Society has its home. Its floriferous garden is open to the public on Thursdays from 2–4; it is delightful and beautifully kept.

TREASURES OF TENBURY
Shropshire

Tenbury Wells WR15 8HQ
1m W of Tenbury Wells by
A456
Tel: 01584 810777

Open: Daily 10–6 (or dusk if earlier)

T REASURES CARRIES a large general stock but it is for clematis that the nursery is best known: well over 200 species and varieties are stocked. The list is especially strong in the species and their choice forms, although it by no means disdains the glamorous large-flowered cultivars. A splendid list of clematis only is published (95p), with much detail on each variety and valuable information about cultivation, but there is no mail order. The late John Treasure's own garden at Burford House, next door to the nursery, with the National Collection of clematis, is also open (see p. 150).

TRETOWER COURT
Powys

Tretower, nr Crickhowell
In Tretower village, 3m
NW of Crickhowell by
A479
Tel: 01874 730279

Owner: Cadw: Welsh
Historic Monuments

Open: end Mar to end Oct,
daily 9.30–6.

O F THE VARIOUS ATTEMPTS to recreate a medieval garden, Tretower is quite one of the most attractive. The setting is a lovely one, beneath the windows and grey stone walls of the 15th-century manor house of the Vaughan family. Nothing is known about the garden that existed here in the late middle ages but what has been recreated is based on historical knowledge of gardens of that period. The garden is approached across an internal courtyard which affords beckoning glimpses of green through the entrance arch. Lattice-work fences enclose beds planted with correct plants of the period, and a

tunnel arbour is richly festooned with honeysuckle, roses and vines, with shade-loving herbaceous plants at their feet. A memorably atmospheric view of the garden is to be had through the old glass of the leaded windows of the first-floor rooms.

WATERWHEEL NURSERY

Gwent

Bully Hole Bottom, Usk Road, nr Shirenewton, Chepstow NP6 6SA
In the village of Bully Hole Bottom, 5m NW of Chepstow by B4235; nr Jnct 22 of M4
Tel: 01291 641 577

Open: Daily except Sun 9–6. Best to phone before making a special journey

DESMOND AND CHARLOTTE Evans's nursery always has for sale some mouthwatering plant which you certainly do not have in your garden. They carry a large stock but, as Desmond puts it, they 'specialize in not specializing'. Their range is wide, woody and herbaceous, within which are some exceptional groups – many euonymus (some you will find nowhere else), the very decorative *Poliothyrsis sinensis*, unusual kinds of *Skimmia japonica* and several viburnums. Among herbaceous plants are many euphorbias, the best geraniums, ornamental grasses and some very pretty, rarely seen cultivars of periwinkle. Although a list is produced, and a mail order is available in winter, this is pre-eminently a place to nose around in. Prices are indecently low.

WESTBURY COURT GARDEN

Gloucestershire

Westbury-on-Severn
GL14 1PD
9m SW of Gloucester by
A48
Tel: 01452 760461

Owner:
The National Trust

Open: Apr to Oct, Wed to
Sun and Bank Hol Mon
11–6 (closed Good Fri);
also by appointment.
4 acres

THIS LATE 17TH-CENTURY formal water garden, for a house that was destroyed, survived by the skin of its teeth and has now been beautifully restored. It was created by Maynard Colchester and many of the original bills survive, giving a valuable record of exactly what plants he used. On low-lying land on the banks of the Severn formality is given by two parallel canals edged with yew hedges whose crests are decorated with yew and holly topiary. An elegant Dutch-style pavilion overlooks the head of one canal, and a boundary wall is covered in pre-1700 varieties of espaliered fruit. In one corner is a secret walled garden, overlooked by a charming little summer house, in which box-edged beds burgeon with plants in cultivation before 1700, and the paths are shaded by an arbour of honeysuckle and clematis. Nearby a parterre of box topiary and annuals has been recreated from an 18th-century print. On the way out keep an eye open for an unforgettable sight behind the pavilion – an immense holm oak (*Quercus ilex*), probably the oldest in the country. It is a place of great delight – much more than merely a frigid exercise in historical restoration.

WESTONBIRT ARBORETUM

Gloucestershire

Westonbirt, nr Tetbury
GL8 8QS
3m SW of Tetbury by the
A433
Tel: 01666 880220

Owner: The Forestry
Commission

Open: Daily 10–8 or sunset
if earlier. 600 acres

THIS IS ONE of the greatest collections of trees in the country but it is far more than just a collection. It was started in 1829 by Robert Holford who had a brilliant eye for arranging the huge quantities of trees which he so energetically collected. Planting has been continued by subsequent members of his family and, since 1956, under the ownership of the Forestry Commission. Today it is not only a marvellous place to learn about and admire trees and shrubs but it is also a landscape of rare beauty. The arboretum has the National Collections of *Acer japonicum* and of *A. palmatum* cultivars, and of lowland species of willow (260 species and cultivars) but in most of the major groups it has wonderful trees, some of them fine old specimens. There is something lovely to see on every day of the year.

THE
HEART
OF
ENGLAND

Derbyshire
Leicestershire
Northamptonshire
Nottinghamshire
Staffordshire
Warwickshire
West Midlands

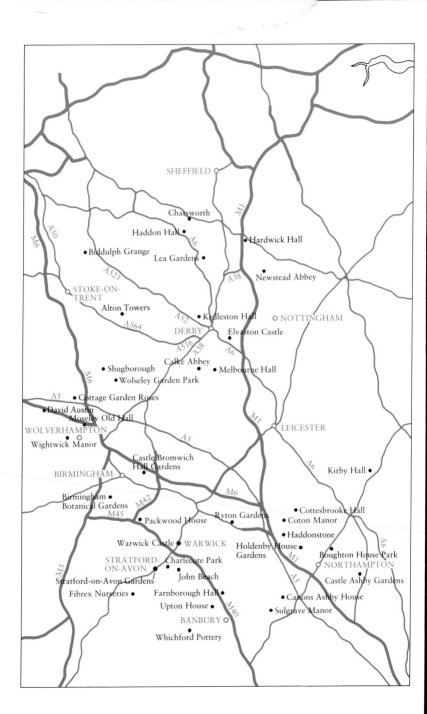

SHEFFIELD ○

M1

Chatsworth ●

Haddon Hall ●

A6

● Hardwick Hall

● Biddulph Grange

Lea Gardens ●

A523

A38

● Newstead Abbey

○ STOKE-ON-TRENT

Alton Towers

A53

● Kedleston Hall

○ NOTTINGHAM

A564

DERBY ○

Elvaston Castle ●

A516

A38

A6

Calke Abbey

● Shugborough

● Melbourne Hall

● Wolseley Garden Park

A5

● Cottage Garden Roses

M6

● David Austin

Moseley Old Hall

M1

● LEICESTER

WOLVERHAMPTON ○

Wightwick Manor ●

A5

Castle Bromwich
Hall Gardens

A6

BIRMINGHAM ○

Kirby Hall ●

Birmingham ●
Botanical Gardens

M42

M6

M45

● Packwood House

Ryton Gardens ●

● Cottesbrooke Hall

● Coton Manor

Warwick Castle ● WARWICK

● Haddonstone

Holdenby House
Gardens

A6

STRATFORD-
ON-AVON

Charlecote Park

M1

Boughton House Park

M5

John Beach

A5

○ NORTHAMPTON

Stratford-on-Avon Gardens

Castle Ashby Gardens

Fibrex Nurseries ●

Farnborough Hall ●

● Canons Ashby House

Upton House ●

M40

● Sulgrave Manor

BANBURY ○

Whichford Pottery ●

ALTON TOWERS
Staffordshire

Alton ST10 4DB
18m E of Stoke-on-Trent
Tel: 01538 702200

Owner: Madame Tussauds
Group of Companies

Open: Daily 9–6 (open
until 8 on some summer
evenings; check by 'phone).
100 acres

A RING-A-DING family leisure park, the busiest in Britain, is not a place where you would expect much by way of a garden. The gigantic house was designed for the 16th Earl of Shrewsbury in the first half of the 19th century by a bevy of architects of which the chief was A.W.N. Pugin whose wild gothic palace was said to sacrifice 'domestic comfort to showmanship'. The gardens were made on a similarly lavish scale. In a precipitous dell north of the house huge numbers of conifers clothe the slopes which are animated by exotic buildings, most of which were designed by Robert Abraham: a palatial mosque-like conservatory with many domes and beautiful stone work; a gothic prospect tower on the heights; a memorial to the 15th Earl; and, best of all, a fountain in a lake disguised as a Chinese pagoda. A shady terrace runs in front of the conservatory, with urns and a topiary tunnel of yew. J.C. Loudon thought the whole place was 'in excessively bad taste', and that is exactly what many people will love. The gardens are splendidly well cared for.

DAVID AUSTIN
West Midlands

Bowling Green Lane,
Albrighton,
Wolverhampton WV7 3HB
7m NW of Wolverhampton
by A41 and A464 nr Jnct 3
of M54
Tel: 01902 373931

Open: Mon to Fri 9–5, Sat,
Sun and Bank Hol Mon
10–6

Illustration: Rosa 'Mary
Rose'

A LTHOUGH DAVID AUSTIN grows other things (irises, peonies and daylilies, for example) he is overwhelmingly a rose specialist, and one of the very best in the country. He is known above all for old roses and his own 'English Roses' which combine the beauty of flower and form of the old varieties with the repeat flowering of the modern ones. In fact he does not disdain modern roses and has a carefully chosen selection of Hybrid Teas, some of which are now hard to find. Go, of course, in late June or July and be bowled over by the beauty and scent. He produces an excellent and informative catalogue and sells by mail order.

JOHN BEACH LTD
Warwickshire

Illustration:
Clematis *'Gravetye Beauty'*

9 Grange Gardens,
Wellesbourne CV35 9RL
(office); Case Lane, Five
Ways Island, Shrewley,
Warwick (nursery) 4m NW
of Warwick by A41 and
B4439
Tel: 01926 484506

Open: Daily except Sun
10–4 (or dusk in winter)

THE BEST PART of John Beach's nursery is the marvellous collection of clematis – well over 150 different kinds, with a particularly good selection of the species and smaller-flowered varieties. An excellent catalogue (£1.50) has invaluable information on the care and cultivation of these sometimes tricky customers. Although clematis loom largest on Beach's list he also sells shrubs, trees and herbaceous perennials. Among these there are some interesting things, with unusual selections of, for example, fuchsias and hibiscus cultivars, and an unexpectedly good range of grape vines – for both wine and dessert. A mail order service is provided.

BIDDULPH GRANGE GARDEN
Staffordshire

GARDENS THAT ARE snatched from the brink of extinction always have a special attraction, and Biddulph is an exceptionally fine example. It was made by James Bateman and Edward Cooke over a

Biddulph, nr
Stoke-on-Trent ST8 7SD
5m SE of Congleton by
A527
Tel: 01782 517999

Owner:
The National Trust

Open: Apr to 29 Oct, Wed
to Fri 12–6 (closed Good
Fri), Sat, Sun and Bank Hol
Mon 11–6 or dusk if
earlier; 4 Nov to 17 Dec,
Sat and Sun 12–4. 15 acres

long period from 1842, when tastes in garden design
turned to the exotic and a flood of newly introduced
conifers fuelled the gardening imagination.

A frightening rocky tunnel lit by a glimmer of
candle-light leads suddenly into a glittering gold,
scarlet and white interior of a Chinese pagoda
overlooking a pool fringed with maples. Stone
sphinxes and monumental clipped yews guard the
mysterious entrance to Egypt. A sprightly dahlia walk
marches up to a sombre avenue of deodars piercing
deeply into the woodland. This has been superbly
restored by the National Trust; more work is still
being done but the results already make Biddulph a
truly exciting place.

BIRMINGHAM BOTANICAL GARDENS AND GLASSHOUSES

Birmingham

T HERE IS a zip about the Birmingham Botanical
Gardens. First, they are beautifully gardened –
even the bedding schemes manage brilliantly to avoid
municipal plodding. Second, although they call
themselves botanical gardens, they are treated by
locals, and those from farther afield, as a public park
and there are plenty of horticultural diversions. They

Westbourne Road,
Edgbaston B15 3TR
2m SW from city centre
Tel: 0121 454 1860

Owner: Birmingham
Botanical and Horticultural
Society Ltd

Open: Daily except
Christmas Day 9 (10 on
Sun)–8 or dusk if earlier.
15 acres

were founded in 1829 on an attratively undulating site which was landscaped by J.C. Loudon. Glasshouses of several different climates protect a very wide range of tender plants which includes a collection of warm climate 'economic' plants. Collections of particular groups of plants – introductions by E. H. 'Chinese' Wilson (who had been a student here), rhododendrons, rock and water plants, and modern roses, are all well displayed.

BOUGHTON HOUSE PARK

Northamptonshire

nr Kettering NN14 1BJ
4m NE of Kettering by A43
by the village of Geddington
Tel: 01536 515731

Owner: The Duke and
Duchess of Buccleuch and
Queensberry

Open: May to Sept, daily
except Fri 1–5. 350 acres

THE GREAT HOUSE at Boughton has something decidedly French about it. It was started in the 1680s, an addition to a much older house, by the first Duke of Montagu who had been ambassador to Louis XIV. To his great palace the Duke added a formal garden of appropriate scale, designed by a Dutch gardener, Van der Meulen. In the 18th century the estate became a secondary residence of the Buccleuch family and the formal garden was not kept up. Today visitors may wander in this vast park of wonderful trees, lakes and canals, and exhilarating graze on the terraces of the old formal garden, now covered in turf, and there are marvellous glimpses of the distant house. The character of the place today is essentially that of a landscaped park, but always visible, like the underpainting of an old master, are the smudged but distinguished traces of the earlier garden.

CALKE ABBEY
Derbyshire

Ticknall DE7 1LE
9m S of Derby by A514
Tel: 01332 863822/864444

Owner:
The National Trust

Open: Apr to Oct, Sat to Wed 11–5.30 (closed Good Fri). Park only open throughout the year dawn–dusk. House open

THE EARLY 18th-century grey stone mansion seems almost like an after-thought when the visitor has traversed the many acres of wonderfully unspoilt ancient parkland that surrounds it. The garden, at some distance from the house, as was often the case in the 18th century, consists of a walled formal garden with a pattern of borders containing bedding schemes of Victorian appearance. In one corner a rare 'auricula theatre' – shelves on which to display auriculas in pots – is used for pelargoniums in summer. In the restored walled kitchen garden many old varieties of vegetables and fruit are grown.

CANONS ASHBY HOUSE
Northamptonshire

Canons Ashby, Daventry NN11 6SD
11m NE of Banbury by A361, A422 and B4525
Tel: 01327 860044

Owner:
The National Trust

Open: Apr to Oct, Sat to Wed 1–5.30 or dusk if earlier. 70 acres. House open

THE BEGUILING brick and stone house, the home of the Dryden family, was started in the 1550s and substantially rebuilt in the early 18th century. The essential layout of the garden as it is today is a rare

survival from the same period. The Green Court by the west façade, with its decorative stone walls and gates, is ornamented with giant cones of clipped yew and a lead statue of a fluting shepherd boy which was probably made by John Van Nost. A door leads under a vast cedar of Lebanon to the garden proper in which terraces descend towards decorative gates. Here there has been much replanting with formal rows of Portugal laurels and ancient varieties of fruit trees. The Drydens were an old-fashioned family and rejected the late 18th-century craze for landscaping, so preserving the gentlemanly formality of an earlier period that may be seen today.

CASTLE ASHBY GARDENS
Northamptonshire

Castle Ashby NN7 1LQ
5m E of Northampton by
A428
Tel: 01604 696696

Owner: The Marquess of
Northampton

Open: Daily 10–one hour
before sunset. 25 acres.
Terrace garden by
appointment only

CASTLE ASHBY was built for the Compton family between 1574 and 1640 and it is still in their hands. The Marquess of Northampton has recently undertaken a strikingly successful restoration of house and garden. A Victorian terraced garden below the house has been brilliantly restored with scalloped fountains, ribbon carpet bedding and elaborate arabesques of gravel cut into the turf. Marvellous parkland to the south-west was laid out by 'Capability' Brown in 1761, and much replanting of trees has been carried out. The Italian garden has a glamorous conservatory designed by Matthew Digby Wyatt, overlooking formal gardens with a pond, yew topiary and terracotta urns. A path leads downhill to an arboretum with some fine trees, especially the specimens of weeping beech.

CASTLE BROMWICH HALL GARDENS
Birmingham

CASTLE BROMWICH HALL is a fine brick mansion built in the 17th century for the Bridgeman family. The gardens are an exciting survival from the heyday of English formal garden design of the late 17th and early 18th century and are in the process of restoration by a privately formed trust. Already much

Old Chester Road, Castle
Bromwich B36 9BT
6m NE of city centre by
A47, near Jnct 5 of M6
(exit northbound only;
entry soutbound only)
Tel: 0121 749 4100

Owner: Castle Bromwich
Hall Gardens Trust

Open: Apr to Sept, Mon to
Thur 1.30–4.30, Sat, Sun
and Bank Hol Mon 2–6.
10 acres

has been done and this is a very rare opportunity to
see an authentic restoration of a garden of this period
in a mavellous setting of old brick walls and fine
garden buildings. The site is a west-facing slope
divided down the centre by a holly walk – a broad
path lined with regularly spaced variegated hollies – a
replanting of the 'Gilded ever Green' mentioned in
surviving records. One end of the walk is punctuated
by an elegant pedimented brick orangery and the
other by the remains of a corresponding music room.
Above the walk is an area of 'wilderness', formal
shubberies with winding walks, and below, kitchen
gardens and a holly maze. Work on other features is
going ahead and it will be fascinating to follow this
restoration as it progresses.

CHARLECOTE PARK
Warwickshire

Wellesbourne, Warwick
CV35 9ER
5m E of Stratford-on-Avon
by B4086
Tel: 01789 470277

Owner:
The National Trust

Open: Apr to Oct, Fri to
Tue (closed Good Fri)
11–6. 30 acres. House open

THE APPROACH to Charlecote – across an ancient
park with grazing fallow deer – has wonderful
atmosphere. The house, originally an Elizabethan
mansion, was comprehensively done over in the 19th
century. The garden has been revitalised in recent
years by the National Trust, with lively mixed
borders in the walled forecourt with its ornate
turreted gate-tower. Charlecote has associations with
Shakespeare – he is supposed to have poached here
as a lad – and a border of flowers mentioned in his
plays commemorates him. Behind the house the River
Avon curves across flat parkland with avenues

radiating into the distance. An admirable park walk of about one mile runs along the banks of the river, girdling the estate, and gives wonderful shifting views of the house and its lovely setting.

CHATSWORTH
Derbyshire

Bakewell DE4 1PP
4m E of Bakewell by A6 or
A619 and minor roads
Tel: 01246 582204

Owner: Chatsworth House
Trust

Open: Easter to Oct, daily
11–5. 100 acres. House open

THE CAVENDISHES first made a garden at Chatsworth in the 16th century, and it was subsequently added to by many of the greatest garden designers and architects of the day. In the late 17th century London and Wise were called in; in the 18th century 'Capability' Brown landscaped the garden, undoing one of the greatest of all formal gardens; in the 19th century Joseph Paxton was head gardener, adding great conservatories and rockeries. Today, the garden is full of reminders of the past – a handsome formal scheme of lime walks and pools to the south; Paxton's 'conservative' wall; an exquisite orangery of 1698; the dazzling cascade house of 1703 over whose domed roof water pours as though off an umbrella. But this is not a museum and there are lively new borders in front of the orangery shop and the charming caprice of a miniature ornamental *potager*. The 1 1/2-acre working kitchen garden is now visitable, and the great yew maze planted in 1961 is once again open. Above all, views across the valley beyond the great house to exquisite pastoral scenery, provide an incomparable setting. Good plants are sold at the plant centre, and Chatsworth makes its own garden furniture which is of very high quality.

COTON MANOR
Northamptonshire

nr Guilsborough NN6 8RQ
10m NW of Northampton
by A50
Tel: 01604 740219

Owner: Mr and Mrs Ian
Pasley-Tyler

Open: Easter to Sept, Wed
to Sun 12–8 (also Bank Hol
Mon). 10 acres

AT COTON MANOR the gardens are adorned by many different kinds of rare birds, some enclosed in aviaries and others, black-necked swans, for example, at home in one of the many pools in the garden. The land slopes away from the old gabled stone house and is divided into enclosures of varying character. Terraces, overhung with the 'Seven Sisters' rose, with cerise flowers changing to the palest of pinks, lead to a long herbaceous border hedged in holly. Behind this is a formal rose garden. At a lower level a peaceful pond is edged with lawns with an old 'Kanzan' cherry, and paths lead through a water garden well planted with moisture-loving plants. A small nursery has excellent hebes, hepaticas, roses and viburnums. There is no mail order.

COTTAGE GARDEN ROSES
Staffordshire

Illustration: Rosa *'Souvenir du Docteur Jamain'*

THIS NURSERY was formerly known under the delightful name of Roses du Temps Passé and specialised in the very best old and wild roses. To this original collection have been added modern roses of high quality, all possessing the virtues of beautiful flowers and lovely scent found in the older kinds.

Woodland House, Stretton,
nr Stafford ST19 9LG
9m SW of Stafford by
A449; 2m from Jnct 12 of
M6
Tel: 01785 840217

Open: Daily 9–6

John Scarman, who runs the nursery, knows an
immense amount about these plants and has
produced one of the best catalogues ever assembled,
beautifully illustrated in colour and with a great deal
of background information about roses and their
cultivation. He describes it as a selective guide to the
most interesting and reliable roses. Roses may be
bought in containers at the nursery or supplied
bare-rooted by post. The Rose Garden School at the
nursery runs attractive residential courses on practical
rose gardening, with visits to other gardens.

COTTESBROOKE HALL
Northamptonshire

nr Northampton NN6 8PF
9m NW of Northampton
by A50 (A14–A1M1 link
road)
Tel: 01604 505 808

Owner: Captain John
Macdonald-Buchanan

Open: Easter to Sept, Thur
and Bank Hol Mon 2–5.30.
25 acres. House open

SOME GARDENS DESERVE to be better known and
Cottesbrooke is a prime example. The beautiful
early 18th-century brick and stone house has a
garden which matches it for beauty and interest. It
looks out over wonderful 18th-century parkland and
a central vista is aligned on the distant spire of
Brixworth church. The garden today is the result of
many different influences – the present owner's
mother, Lady Macdonald-Buchanan, the Arts and
Crafts designer Edward Schultz, Dame Sylvia Crowe
and Sir Geoffrey Jellicoe. Around the house there is a
cornucopia of formal gardens: a pair of fortissimo
herbaceous borders; a stately walk with yew hedges
and wrought-iron gates with fine piers; enclosed
gardens with pools and a pergola; and a south-facing
terrace with statues and plantings of roses and

agapanthus. All about is splendid parkland and countless good trees. At a distance from the house, but not to be missed, is a wild woodland garden with a beautifully planted stream; arched bridges and many Japanese maples give an eastern atmosphere. There are few gardens anywhere with so much to admire as Cottesbrooke.

ELVASTON CASTLE
Derbyshire

Elvaston, Derby DE72 3EP
6m SE of Derby by A6 and
B5010
Tel: 01332 571342

Owner: Derbyshire County
Council

Open: Daily 9–sunset.
200 acres

THE GOTHIC CASTLE is the work of James Wyatt in the early 19th century and sets the scene for the thoroughly romantic if slightly dishevelled gardens which were laid out for a reformed Regency buck, 'Beau' Petersham, in the 1830s. They were designed by a Scot, William Barron, who concocted a heady mixture of the latest conifers, Italianate parterres and 'bowers', and much topiary of box and golden yew. A new addition is the 'old English garden' of herbaceous and rose borders, in the walled former kitchen garden.

FARNBOROUGH HALL
Warwickshire

nr Banbury, Oxfordshire
OX17 1DU
6m N of Banbury off A423
Tel: 01295 89 202

Owner:
The National Trust

Open: Apr to Sept, Wed
and Sat 2–6; also 7 and 8
May 2–6. 16 acres

FARNBOROUGH is a very unusual intimate landscape garden laid out in the 18th century – delicate chamber music rather than resounding symphony. William Holbech inherited the estate with its handsome late 17th-century house in 1717 and, with the help of the elusive Sanderson Miller, laid out the grounds in the new landscape taste. Behind the house a half-mile long terrace of grass curves up a slope. Woodland presses in on one side and, on the other, there are occasional views of the countryside and parkland. The terrace is embellished with two pavilions, one of which is an unusual oval in section, with an open loggia, and the other in the form of a columned temple. Hidden in the woods a game-larder is built in the form of an exquisite temple and has idyllic views over fields towards the village. The very end of the terrace is marked by a slender obelisk. It is one of the most original and memorable landscape gardens in the country.

FIBREX NURSERIES LTD
Warwickshire

Honeybourne Road,
Pebworth, nr
Stratford-upon-Avon
CV37 8XT
5m NW of Chipping
Camden by B4081 and
minor roads
Tel: 01789 720788

Open: Jan to Mar, Sept to
Nov, Mon to Fri 12–5; Apr
to Aug, Tue to Sun 12–5;
closed Dec

THE NURSERY has four specialities, in each of which it offers marvellous collections. First, its pelargonium list is enormous, essential browsing for anyone with an interest in those plants. Second, there is a rich selection of ivies with, for example, over 200 different varieties of *Hedera helix*. Third, it has a particularly attractive collection of hardy ferns for which a good catalogue is issued with much valuable information. Lastly, there is a unique selection of very rare cultivars of *Helleborus orientalis*, known as the Raithby hybrids, with lovely and unusual colouring. Mail order is provided and lists (two 2nd-class stamps) of each speciality are published.

HADDON HALL
Derbyshire

Bakewell DE4 1LA
2m SE of Bakewell by A6
Tel: 01629 812855

Owner: The Duke of
Rutland

Open: Apr to Jun, Sept,
Tue to Sun 11–6 (open
Bank Hol Mon); Jul and
Aug, Tue to Sat (open
Bank Hol Mon) 11–6. 6
acres. House open

HADDON HALL is an intensely romantic place: a vast castle, built between the 12th and 17th centuries, with turrets, crenellations and tracery windows. It is set in hilly wooded countryside and the garden still has some of the character of the formal gardens of the 17th century. The south garden, a series of terraces with balustrades, dates from the very early 17th century. Buttresses at the lowest level make an attractive and protected setting

for roses and other flowering shrubs and climbers. There is a fountain and an immense collection of roses but the eye is constantly drawn to the old stone of the castle and to the river looping through the rural landscape below.

HADDONSTONE LTD
Northamptonshire

The Forge House, Church Lane, East Haddon, Northampton NN6 8DB 8m NW of Northampton off A428
Tel: 01604 770711

Open: Mon to Fri 9–5.30 (closed Bank Hol Mon)

G ARDEN ORNAMENTS and buildings made of reconstituted stone have a long and honourable history. Haddonstone is one of the leading manufacturers and produces a very wide range of statues, urns, columns, garden buildings and architectural detailing. It also undertakes to make individual pieces to customers' specifications. Many of the designs are faithful copies of surviving examples in historic gardens. A beautifully kept show garden displays many of the products in a setting planned to display their ornamental use. An elegant catalogue is produced and ornaments may be supplied by Haddonstone's own delivery service.

HARDWICK HALL
Derbyshire

Doe Lea, Chesterfield S44 5QJ
6 1/2m W of Mansfield by A6175 and minor roads, nr Jnct 29 of M1
Tel: 01246 850430

Owner:
The National Trust

Open: Apr to Oct, Wed, Thur, Sat, Sun and Bank Hol Mon 12.30–5 or sunset if earlier. 7 acres. House open

B ESS OF HARDWICK married successfully (four times) and this is her final architectural flourish, built in the late 16th century when she was in her seventies and Countess of Shrewsbury. She ornamented the

parapet of her great house with her initials, E.S., carved in fretted stone against the sky. The gardens are disposed in the Elizabethan stone courts to the west and south of the house. The entrance court, with a fine old cedar of Lebanon on the lawn, has splendid new mixed borders in which colour and foliage have been cunningly chosen. Repeated plantings of the sprawling, elegant *Aralia elata* 'Aureovariegata', and in late summer of the arching plumes of miscanthus, give structure to a dashing colour scheme – hot reds, oranges and yellow near the house, and blues, whites and yellow farther away. The south court is divided into four by yew and hornbeam hedges. One of the divisions is a virtuoso herb garden in which pillars of golden and ordinary hop rise magnificently from a sea of angelica, lavender, sage, sweet cicely and thyme.

HOLDENBY HOUSE GARDENS
Northamptonshire

Holdenby, nr Northampton
NN6 8DJ
6 1/2m NW of
Northampton by A428 and
minor roads; signposted off
A428 and A50
Tel: 01604 770074

Owner: Mr and Mrs James
Lowther

Open: Easter to Sept, Mon
to Fri 1–5, Sun and Bank
Hol Mon 2–6. *Note:*
Entrance through falconry
centre. 10 acres

HOLDENBY WAS BUILT in the 16th century by the Hattons who also owned Kirby Hall. In its day it was one of the great houses of England and had a spectacular garden of which tantalising traces remain today. The present house is Victorian although two magnificent Elizabethan stone arches survive in a field at a distance from the house. By far the best feature of the garden today is a dazzling little evocation of a 16th-century garden. Enclosed in yew hedges, with a sundial at the centre, surrounding beds are decorated with lollipops of variegated box or holly, mounds of santolina and hedges of lavender or artemisia. In summer there are drifts of white, mauve and purple *Salvia viridis*, and the surrounding beds are filled with culinary herbs. The whole is overlooked by a shady gazebo of clipped yew.

KEDLESTON HALL
Derbyshire

Derby DE6 4JN
5m NW of Derby by A52
and minor roads
Tel: 01332 842191

Owner:
The National Trust

Open: Garden: Apr to Oct,
Sat to Wed 11–6; *Park:* Apr
to Oct, daily 11–6; Nov to
18 Dec, Sat, Sun 12–4.
7 acres of garden. House
open

KEDLESTON is the grandest and possibly the prettiest of Robert Adam's houses, built for Nathaniel Curzon in the 1760s. Adam also had a hand in the park which forms a lovely approach for the house. To the north, a long serpentine lake is spanned by a three-arched bridge with a rocky cascade below it, and nearby, on the banks, a charming Fishing Room with a Venetian window is flanked by a pair of pedimented boathouses. Behind the house, in the well wooded old pleasure grounds, a circular garden of beds of roses radiating from a central pool is hedged in laurel and overlooked by a domed hexagonal temple. Shrubberies of dogwoods, rhododendrons and roses are embellished by a fine stone urn and, round a corner, the Medicean Lion rises up with a roguish grin.

KIRBY HALL
Northamptonshire

THIS IS A GHOSTLY place on the edge of the industrial sprawl of Corby – the uninhabited remains of an exquisite late 16th-century palace built for one of Queen Elizabeth's favourite courtiers, Sir

4m NE of Corby by minor roads
Tel: 01536 203230

Owner: English Heritage

Open: Daily 10–6. 5 acres

Christopher Hatton. In the late 17th century Charles Hatton made a great garden here, which was restored after excavations in the 1930s. But this was highly inauthentic – full of HT roses and with a jolly Victorian flavour. Hatton's garden is particularly well documented, including detailed lists of the plants. English Heritage is now in the process, rather slowly, of redoing it and it will be fascinating to see what it achieves. In the last two years the turf plats and gravel paths in front of the house have been re-made and a few old varieties of fruit trees planted. If what is eventually achieved is anything like as beautiful as the house it will be wonderful to see.

LEA GARDENS
Derbyshire

Lea, Matlock DE4 5GH
5m SE of Matlock by A6 and minor roads
Tel: 01629 534380

Owner: Mr and Mrs J. Tye

Open: 20 Mar to Jun, daily 10–7. 4 acres

THIS GARDEN, inspired by Bodnant and Exbury, although quite small by comparison, was started in 1935 by John Marsden-Smedley. It is a marvellous site, high up on south-facing wooded slopes that run down to the valley of the River Derwent. It makes a splendid setting for the excellent collection of rhododendrons which Marsden-Smedley built up. Subsequent owners have developed the garden even further and added many new trees and herbaceous plants. A wide range of bulbous plants of an alpine kind are displayed in a large scree bed. They have also started a nursery which sells alpines, conifers, azaleas, rhododendrons and kalmias by post, of which a list is issued (s.a.e. and 30p).

MELBOURNE HALL
Derbyshire

Melbourne D73 1EN
9m S of Derby by A453
Tel: 01332 862502

Owner: Lord Ralph Kerr

Open: Apr to Sept, Wed,
Sat, Sun and Bank Hol
Mon 2–6. 16 acres. House
open Aug only

MELBOURNE IS a fascinating place. The house, of grey stone, presents its most glamorous façade, of 1744, to the garden which was laid out in the early 18th century. Giant steps of turf descend to the Great Basin, a curved pool that crisply reflects the house. On one side is the 'Birdcage', Robert Bakewell's airy arbour of wrought-iron of exquisite delicacy. To the south lies a pattern of lime alleys, unchanged in almost 300 years, with grassy walks punctuated by urns and statues of marvellous quality, some of them by John Van Nost, the greatest maker of garden ornaments of the early 18th century. Of the same period, leading to the west, is an immense tunnel of yew between whose gnarled trunks the visitor may walk. On its south side are some very good new mixed borders, showing that the spirit of gardening at Melbourne is still alive and kicking.

MOSELEY OLD HALL
Staffordshire

AROUND AN UNASSUMING Elizabethan and 17th-century house the National Trust has made a little formal garden rich in the features of the 17th century. The old windows overlook a parterre with a geometric pattern of box hedges, coloured pebbles and lollipops of clipped box – all this was taken from a design of 1640. On one side a nut walk leads to a

Moseley Old Hall Lane,
Fordhouses,
Wolverhampton
WV10 7HY
3 1/2m N of
Wolverhampton, between
A460 and A449, S of M54
Tel: 01902 782808

Owner:
The National Trust

Open: Apr to 29 Oct, Wed,
Sat, Sun and Bank Hol
Mon 2–5.30 (Bank Hol
Mon 11–5); Jul to Aug,
also Tue 2–5.30. 1 acre.
House open

paved path flanked by pairs of medlars, mulberries
and quinces. Running down one side of the parterre
is a 'carpenter's work' tunnel, festooned with
purple-leafed vines and Virgin's Bower clematis (*C.
flammula*) and underplanted with aquilegias,
geraniums and lavender. A wrought-iron gate leads
into the enclosed front garden which has box topiary
clipped into cones and spirals and lively borders. All
the planting here and elsewhere in the garden is of
varieties known to have been in gardens before 1700.

NEWSTEAD ABBEY
Nottinghamshire

Linstead NG15 8GE
9m N of Nottingham by
A60
Tel: 01623 793557

Owner: Nottingham City
Council

Open: Daily 10–sunset. 25
acres. Abbey open

L ORD BYRON'S family, the Gordons, acquired the
Augustinian abbey at the Dissolution, and the
decaying monastic ruins were immensely attractive to
Byron's romantic imagination; but the oak he planted
in 1798, whose stump remains to this day, never grew
well. Much of the romanticism survives, but although
there are medieval touches such as the monks' stew
pond, most of the garden is a 20th-century creation.
In the heart of the abbey building, laid out in the
former cloister yard, is a reconstructed, enclosed
medieval 'Mary' garden. The abbey lawns are
ornamented with fine trees, some of them unusual,
such as a variegated sweet chestnut. Beyond them an
elaborate rock garden has a good collection of
heathers, from which a Japanese garden is seen
across a lake, with a curved pergola of roses and
wisteria, rushing streams, hump-backed bridges, snow
lanterns and Japanese maples.

PACKWOOD HOUSE
Warwickshire

Lapworth, Solihull
B94 6AT
11m SE of Birmingham by
A34
Tel: 01564 782 024

Owner:
The National Trust

Open: Apr to Sept, Wed to
Sun and Bank Hol Mon
(closed Good Fri) 2–6; Oct,
Wed to Sun 12.30–4.30.
5 acres. House open

A SOLEMN GROUP of immensely tall clipped yews,
known as the Multitude and the Apostles,
surrounds a mount covered in box. A mysterious
spiral path leads to the top which is crowned by a
clipped parasol shape of yew. Some of these giant
topiary pieces date back to the 17th century and have
an unforgettable atmosphere. Nearer the house, a
stately gabled brick mansion of the late 16th century,
there is a completely different mood with a
pronounced Arts and Crafts feel. A fine wrought-iron
gate leads down into in a handsomely walled garden
overlooked by a long terrace edged with flowery
borders and with a gazebo at each end. A decorative
sunken garden with a pool is hedged in yew and has
lively summer bedding schemes.

RYTON ORGANIC GARDENS
Warwickshire

THIS IS the home of the National Centre for
Organic Gardening. As well as being the leading
research centre of its subject, it is a fascinating
display garden, showing the techniques of
ecologically friendly gardening. Regarded by some
until recently as the province of cranks, this is now
seen to be the best way to garden, working with
nature rather than zapping it with chemicals. At

Ryton-on-Dunsmore,
Coventry CV8 3LG
5m SE of Coventry by A45
Tel: 01203 303517

Owner: The Henry
Doubleday Research
Association

Open: Daily 10–5.30
(except Christmas holiday).
10 acres

Ryton, demonstration areas show techniques of vegetable growing, how to make compost, how to control weeds and pests and many other things. A wildflower meadow is rich in native plants; a rose garden is planted with varieties that are resistant to disease. This is not only muck and magic – there are also some attractively laid out pleasure gardens. Any gardener will learn from the insights of this unique place.

SHUGBOROUGH
Staffordshire

Milford, nr Stafford
ST17 0XB
6m E of Stafford by A513
Tel: 01889 88 1388

Owner:
The National Trust

Open: 25 Mar to 27 Oct,
daily 11–5. 18 acres. House
open

SHUGBOROUGH is a dream-like picturesque landscape garden in which marvellous ornaments and garden buildings float into view at every turn. From the house, largely built by Samuel Wyatt for Viscount Anson in the 1790s, a series of shallow terraces descend to the River Sow, decorated with golden yew topiary and rose beds. A wild picturesque ruin designed in 1750 by Thomas Wright crouches on the water's edge. To one side a rose garden with an Edwardian flavour has roses trained on arches and pillars. A path now winds away into the informal heart of the garden where an arched scarlet Chinoiserie bridge leads to the pagoda-like Chinese house (1747). In the woods there is a mysterious Cat's Monument; the riddling Shepherd's Monument; a dapper Doric temple; and, in front of the house, handsome parkland with James 'Athenian' Stuart's Temple of the Winds. Do not miss, on the way out, Brackenside Nurseries which has taken up residence in part of Wyatt's superb old walled kitchen gardens.

STRATFORD-UPON-AVON GARDENS
Warwickshire

STRATFORD IS, of course, thoroughly given over to the celebration of Shakespeare's life and work. Some of the various old houses associated with him in and around the town have gardens of considerable charm. **Shakespeare's Birthplace** (Henley Street. *Open:* Mar to Oct, daily 9–5.30 (Sun 10–5.30); Nov to Feb, daily 9.30–4 (Sun 10.30–4)). A lawn at the back is ornamented with trees such as a fig, hawthorn, medlar and quince, all of which are mentioned in the plays. A pair of pretty, mixed borders is planted to give interest throughout the year. **Hall's Croft** (Old Town. *Open:* Mar to Oct, daily 9.30–5 (Sun 10.30–5); Nov to Feb, daily 10–4 (Sun 1.30–4)). The garden is walled and has a splendid old mulberry and borders running from a sundial to the back of the half-timbered house. **New Place** (Chapel Lane. *Open:* Mar to Oct, daily 9.30–5

(Sun 10.30–5); Nov to Feb, daily 10–4 (Sun 1.30–4)). A knot garden follows Elizabethan patterns in its layout of low hedges of box, hyssop and santolina and its surrounding apple tunnels, but is planted in thoroughly 20th-century summer bedding. The Great Garden behind has topiary of box and yew and burgeoning herbaceous borders. **Anne Hathaway's Cottage** (in the village of Shottery, 1 1/4m NW of Stratford by A422. *Open:* Mar to Oct, daily 9–5.30 (Sun 10–5.30); Nov to Feb, daily 9.30–4 (Sun 10.30–4)). At the front a profusion of planting gives a vision of the English cottage garden. There is an orchard to one side and, behind it, the Shakespeare Tree Garden is a nice idea but still in its infancy.

SULGRAVE MANOR
Northamptonshire

Sulgrave, nr Banbury
OX17 2SD
7m NE of Banbury by
B4525
Tel: 01295 760205

Owner: The Peoples of
England and America

Open: Apr to Sept, daily
except Wed 10.30–1, 2–5.30
(closed 19 Jun); Oct, daily
except Wed 10.30–1, 2–4;
Nov, Dec and Mar, Sat
and Sun 10.30–1, 2–4
(closed 25 and 26 Dec).
2 acres. House open

GEORGE WASHINGTON'S ancestors lived here and the American connection is proudly emphasised, with the stars and stripes flying above the roof. The house is a 16th-century stone-tiled manor and the garden was designed by Sir Reginald Blomfield in 1927, who laid out a crisply formal entrance of yew hedges. The entrance to the house lies across an orchard with gravel walks and the forecourt has lawns decorated with topiary yew birds and herbaceous borders flanking the porch. A little herb parterre on a terrace above is shaded by an old walnut tree. To one side a rose garden is edged in box and a sundial stands in the middle, fringed with lavender. There is no attempt at historical planting here but the garden makes an attractive setting for the old house.

UPTON HOUSE
Warwickshire

Banbury, Oxfordshire
OX15 6HT
7m NW of Banbury by
A422
Tel: 01295 87 266

Owner:
The National Trust

Open: Apr to Oct, Sat to
Wed 2–6. 19 acres. House
open

THE HOUSE, finished in 1695 and built of golden Hornton stone, lies on the edge of a steep combe; on its slopes the garden is spread like a patchwork quilt. Formal steps and a balustrade entwined with wisteria lead downwards towards areas enclosed in wavy old yew hedges. An impeccable kitchen garden, like a celestial vision of the perfect allotment, benefits from the southerly exposure. Sweeping down the hill are a pair of herbaceous borders with accents of hot red and a cool turf path running down between them to the pool at the bottom. A mile from the house is a delightful piece of landscape gardening dating from the 1760s – a lake and Doric temple (possibly by Robert Adam) deftly slipped into the countryside, the very essence of 18th-century elegance.

WARWICK CASTLE
Warwickshire

THIS SPECTACULAR CASTLE was until 1978 the home of the Earls of Warwick. In front of the orangery there is a hexagonal parterre designed in 1869 by Robert Marnock, with vivid contrasts of golden and common yew and blood-red roses. Peacocks preen and fit well with the mood of the place. The land falls steeply away and, framed by 18th-century cedars of Lebanon, there is one of the best garden views in

Warwick CV34 4QU
In the centre of Warwick
Tel: 01926 495421

Owner: Pearsons plc

Open: Daily 10–6 (5 in
winter); closed Christmas
Day. 60 acres. Castle open

England – 'Capability' Brown's breathtaking park
sweeping down to a curve in the River Avon 200 feet
below. Robert Marnock also designed a great rose
garden which has very recently been beautifully
restored; old roses with irresistible names like
'Adélaïde d'Orléans' and 'Variegata di Bologna' are
draped in festoons, arched over tunnels and rise in
columns to produce unforgettably swoony scents in
late June and July.

WHICHFORD POTTERY

Warwickshire

Whichford, nr
Shipston-on-Stour
CV36 5PG
22m NW of Oxford E of
A3400
Tel: 01608 684 416

Open: Mon to Fri 9–5, Sat
and Bank Hol Mon 10–4

JIM KEELING, trained in the traditional craft of
hand-throwing terracotta pots, now leads a team
of potters making a very wide range of different
styles. From plain flower pots to giant Florentine
vases dripping with swags and foliage, all are
beautifully made in local clay and are guaranteed
frostproof. There is nowhere in Britain quite like this
and it is very well worth visiting. Outside the pottery
are displayed immense numbers of pots and planters,
some beautifully planted up to show their
effectiveness in the garden. An excellent catalogue is
produced and pots may be delivered by carrier.

WIGHTWICK MANOR

West Midlands

WIGHTWICK MANOR is a piece of ripe High
Victoriana – a decorative Pre-Raphaelite
mansion made for a paint millionaire – with a garden
in keeping. It was laid out in 1887, partly by the

Wightwick Bank,
Wolverhampton WV6 8EE
3m W of Wolverhampton
by A454
Tel: 01902 761108

Owner:
The National Trust

Open: Mar to Dec, Thur
and Sat, Bank Hol Mon
and preceding Sun
2.30–5.30. 10 acres. House
open

watercolourist Alfred Parsons and partly by the architect and garden designer T.H. Mawson, who was responsible for the south terrace and the dramatic procession of great clipped drums of yew that marches purposefully away from it. On one side a 'writers' bed' is filled with plants from the gardens of Dickens, William Morris, Shelley and Tennyson. A formal garden of zig-zag yew hedges, yew topiary and rose beds leads to a walk of variegated holly.

WOLSELEY GARDEN PARK
Staffordshire

Wolseley Bridge, Stafford
ST17 0YT
8m SE of Stafford by A513
Tel: 01889 574888

Owner: Sir Charles and
Lady Wolseley

Open: Apr to Oct 10–6.30;
Nov to Mar, 10–dusk.
45 acres

WOLSELEY GARDEN is a new phenomenon – a garden designed specifically to open to the public. The site had advantages to start with – a winding stream, fine old beeches and an old walled kitchen garden. An immense amount of new planting had been done and there is much to admire: a very large rose garden in the kitchen garden; a shady woodland area with camellias, rhododendrons and lilies; a formal garden with an avenue of cypresses; a romantic dell. New additions are constantly being made and there is an air of horticultural bustle about the place. At the entrance there is a large branch of Wyevale-Cramphorn Garden Centre.

THE
EAST
OF
ENGLAND

Bedfordshire
Cambridgeshire
Essex
Hertfordshire
Lincolnshire
Norfolk
Suffolk

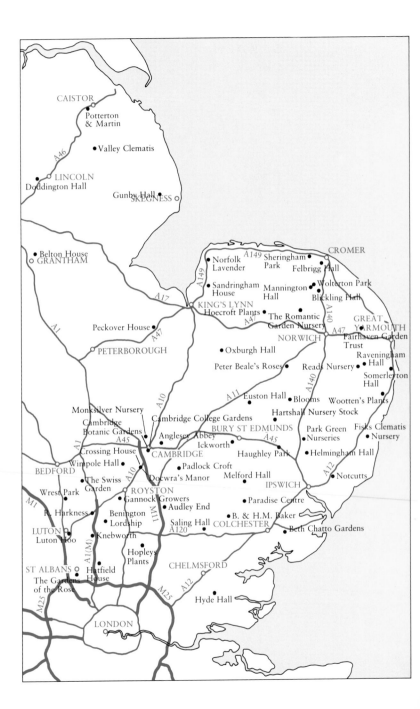

CAISTOR

● Potterton
& Martin

● Valley Clematis

A46

● LINCOLN
Doddington Hall

● Gunby Hall
SKEGNESS ○

● Belton House
○ GRANTHAM

A149 ● Sheringham CROMER
● Norfolk   Park
Lavender   ● Felbrigg Hall
A149
● Sandringham   ● Wolterton Park
House   ● Mannington
            Hall   ● Blickling Hall
A17   A140
KING'S LYNN
Hoecroft Plants ● ● The Romantic
A47   Garden Nursery
● Peckover House   GREAT
A1   NORWICH A47 YARMOUTH
A47   ● Fairhaven Garden
○ PETERBOROUGH   ● Oxburgh Hall   Trust
                             ● Raveningham
● Peter Beale's Roses ● Reads Nursery ● Hall
A10   ● Somerleyton
                                Hall
A140
● Euston Hall
A11 ● Blooms ● Wootten's Plants
Monksilver Nursery   ● Hartshall Nursery Stock
Cambridge   Cambridge College Gardens
Botanic Gardens   BURY ST EDMUNDS   Fisks Clematis
A45 ● Anglesey Abbey A45   ● Park Green   ● Nursery
Crossing House   Ickworth   Nurseries
BEDFORD ● Wimpole Hall CAMBRIDGE ● Haughley Park ● Helmingham Hall
A1   A10   ● Padlock Croft
● The Swiss   ● Docwra's Manor ● Melford Hall   ● Notcutts
Garden   A12
● Wrest Park ○ ROYSTON   IPSWICH
● R. Harkness ● Gannock Growers
M1   ● Audley End ● Paradise Centre
LUTON ○   Benington ● B. & H.M. Baker
Luton Hoo   ● Lordship Saling Hall COLCHESTER
● Knebworth A120   ● Beth Chatto Gardens
ST ALBANS ○ ● Hopleys
A1(M)   Plants CHELMSFORD
The Gardens ● Hatfield
of the Rose House
M25
M25 A12
● Hyde Hall

LONDON
○

ANGLESEY ABBEY AND GARDEN
Cambridgeshire

Lode, Cambridge CB5 9EJ
In the village of Lode 6m
NE of Cambridge by B1102
Tel: 01223 811200

Owner:
The National Trust

Open: 29 Mar to 9 Jul,
Wed to Sun and Bank Hol
Mon 11–5.30; 10 Jul to 5
Sept, daily 10–5.30; 6 Sept
to 29 Oct, Wed to Sun
11–5.30. 100 acres. House
open

ANGLESEY ABBEY was an Augustinian priory and its buildings, with many additions, form an alluring ornament at the heart of gardens that Lord Fairhaven started to lay out in 1930. He deployed a marvellous collection of statues and garden ornaments, giving them their full decorative presence in subtly contrived settings of alleys, vistas, hedged enclosures and distant prospects. Handsome parkland and some exceptional old trees – particularly limes – give his scheme a rich background. The statues and bold formal designs are what makes Anglesey famous, and walking among them is indeed an exciting experience. But contrasting with these grand formal schemes are more intimate areas – gardens devoted to dahlias and hyacinths, some exceptionally good borders in the herbaceous garden enclosed in a great horseshoe hedge of beech, and a river walk with grassy banks and a mill-house of rural atmosphere.

AUDLEY END
Essex

AUDLEY END is a much fiddled with Jacobean mansion set in splendid parkland designed by 'Capability Brown' from 1762 onwards. Shortly after this Robert Adam added various splendid buildings to the estate – a three-arched bridge over the Cam, a

near Saffron Walden
1m W of Saffron Walden
by B1383
Tel: 01799 522842

Owner: English Heritage

Open: Apr to Sept, Wed to
Sun and Bank Hol Mon
12–6.
50 acres House open

Temple of Victory and Lady Portsmouth's Column. Newly restored is a great flower parterre east of the house, which was designed in 1832 by William Gilpin. A vast geometric pattern of beds spreads out below the windows of the house. The planting is a mixture of old shrub roses, herbaceous perennials and annuals; all the plants are known to have been available when the parterre was originally laid out.

B. & H.M. BAKER

Essex

Greenstead Green,
Halstead CO9 1RJ
6m NE of Braintree by
A131 and minor roads
Tel: 01787 472900/476369

Open: Mon to Fri 8–4.30,
Sat to Sun 9–12, 2–4.30

THE BAKERS' SPECIALITY is fuchsias and their fuchsia-red list is a connoisseur's delight. There has been an explosion of new fuchsia cultivars in recent years and some of the best old varieties have been trampled to death in the rush to buy new ones. Baker's fascinating catalogue (20p plus stamp) lists varieties going back to the early 19th century and gives the dates of introduction and the names of their breeders. Many of these represent the best varieties of the past – very few are the latest. Most of the list consists, of course, of tender varieties but there is also a section devoted to hardy kinds as well as a

PETER BEALES ROSES

Norfolk

Illustration: Rosa '*Gruss an Aachen*'

PETER BEALES is the author of one of the best rose books of recent times, *Classic Roses*, and here at Attleborough may be seen one of the best rose nurseries in Britain. It sells all kinds of roses but the heart of the business is old-fashioned, species and

London Road,
Attleborough NR17 1AY
15m SW of Norwich by
A11
Tel: 01953 454707

Open: Mon to Fri 9–5, Sat
9–4.30, Sun 10–4

modern shrubs, of which it sells a staggering range. If
you are searching for an old rose this is probably the
best place to start with; a visit in late June will
provide an unforgettable sight. A wonderful
catalogue is produced, a model of such things, full of
information about the history and cultivation of
roses. Plants may be supplied by post.

BELTON HOUSE
Lincolnshire

Grantham NG32 2LS
3m NE of Grantham by
A607
Tel: 01476 66116

Owner:
The National Trust

Open: Apr to Oct, Wed to
Sun and Bank Hol Mon
(closed Good Fri) 11–5.30.
Free access on foot to park
only, all the year from Lion
Lodge gates. 100 acres.
House open

BELTON HOUSE is an exquisite mansion dating from
the 1690s. The park was landscaped in the late
18th century by William Emes in the style of
'Capability' Brown, but traces of an earlier formal
garden survive – including a slender canal at the head
of which is a pretty pedimented temple. Between the
house and the church a grand conservatory designed
by Sir Jeffry Wyatville in 1811 overlooks a formal
garden with a circular pool and fountain surrounded
by a low hedge of purple plum and pale pink roses.
Columns of Irish yew, mounds of clipped box and
stone urns give vertical emphasis. To the north of the
house a walk of golden and common yew columns
and mounds is backed by borders with a ghostly
planting of white roses, cream petunias and lavender
edging. This might have been a pompous and
overwhelming setting for a very grand house but
cheerfulness keeps breaking through.

BENINGTON LORDSHIP
Hertfordshire

Benington, nr Stevenage
SG2 7BS
4m E of Stevenage by
minor roads; signposted
from Watton-at-Stone
Tel: 0148 869 668

Owner: Mr and Mrs
C.H.A. Bott

Open: Apr to Aug, Wed
12–5 and Sun 2–5; Sept,
Wed 12–5. Easter, spring
and summer Bank Hol
Mon 12–5. 7 acres

A T BENINGTON the remains of a Norman castle, a neo-Norman gatehouse and a 1700 brick mansion give character that is in every way matched by the garden. The house looks across a gentle valley to lakes below, fed by a stream edged with acanthus, astilbes, ferns, geraniums and primulas. To one side, descending the slope, a pair of dazzling herbaceous borders has a colour scheme of cream, white, yellow and blue, with touches of orange and red. Beyond it, the walled kitchen garden has more borders, vegetables and a small nursery. On the other side of the house a formal garden has pink and white roses underplanted with irises, aquilegias and catmint.

BLICKLING HALL
Norfolk

B LICKLING HALL – turreted, gabled and irresistible – was built in around 1620 by Robert Lyminge. The chief part of the garden lies to the east of the house, where a parterre of four square herbaceous beds is

Blickling, Norwich
NR11 6NF
15m N of Norwich
Tel: 01263 733084

Owner:
The National Trust

Open: 25 Mar to 5 Nov,
daily except Mon and Thur
(open Bank Hol Mon and
preceding Sun, closed Good
Fri) 11–5; Jul and Aug,
daily 11–5. 46 acres. House
open

brilliantly contrived: the planting rises towards the
centre, giving, in late July, the shape of a pyramid.
Colours are subtly graded – the beds near the house
in yellow and cream, those farther away in blue, pink
and red. Rounded cones and curious 'grand-piano'
shapes of clipped yew, fine urns and a central
fountain decorate the parterre. A pair of sphinxes
starts a long gravel walk, backed by azaleas and
woodland, leading to a classical temple, from which
on either side oak avenues plunge into the woods.

BLOOMS OF BRESSINGHAM
Norfolk

nr Diss IP22 2AB
3m W of Diss by A1066
Tel: 01379 88 464

Open: Daily 10–5.30

FEW FAMILIES choose their occupation to suit their
name so happily as the Blooms of Bressingham.
Although best known for a very wide range of
herbaceous plants (more, probably, than any other
nursery in the country) they also sell choice alpines,
bamboos, hardy ferns, bamboos, conifers, grasses,
rhododendrons, shrubs and heathers. Many varieties,
especially of herbaceous plants, bear the name
'Bressingham' and give some idea of the liveliness
and enterprise of this influential nursery. Although
the nursery itself is primarily wholesale there is still
plenty for individual gardeners to see, admire and
buy. A very well planned catalogue is produced twice
a year, packed with detailed information about the
cultivation of the plants. New cultivars are
constantly being added, particularly in the perennial
department. Orders may be supplied by mail order.

BRESSINGHAM GARDENS
Norfolk

Bressingham, Diss
IP22 2AB
3m W of Diss by A1066
Tel: 01379 88 464/8138

Owner: Alan Bloom

Open: Apr to Oct, daily
10–5.30. 5 acres

ALAN BLOOM has, through his nursery and his books, had a great influence on garden taste. In his own garden, alongside the nursery, visitors may see these ideas put into practice. There is, of course, a huge range of herbaceous perennials grown in his famous sweeping island beds. Over 5,000 species and cultivars of herbaceous plants, including 200 or so new plants introduced by the nursery, are displayed in an informal setting. There are very few places where such a range of plants is to be seen and there is the added interest that most of them may be ordered from the nursery next door.

CAMBRIDGE BOTANIC GARDEN
Cambridgeshire

Cambridge CB2 1JF
3/4m S of city centre by
Trumpington Road (A10)
Tel: 01223 336265

Owner: The University of
Cambridge

Open: Mon to Sat 10–dusk
(6 in summer, 4 in winter),
Sun 10–dusk. 35 acres

ALTHOUGH the primary purpose of botanic gardens is to provide material for study, many of them are both beautiful and instructive places for gardeners to visit. This is no exception, and at any time of the year there is much to be seen. Of special interest to gardeners are a particularly good rock garden in which plants are grouped according to country of origin; comprehensive collections of tulips and cranesbills; a huge collection of European species of saxifrage (of which the garden holds the National Collection); and glasshouses protecting different types of plant, from alpines to tropical food plants. There are beds of herbaceous plants and of shrubs, and everywhere there are fine trees, many rare, well displayed in the attractively laid out grounds.

CAMBRIDGE COLLEGE GARDENS
Cambridgeshire

CAMBRIDGE IS STRIKINGLY rich in planted space and the Backs running along the west bank of the Cam provide an exquisite setting for the great college buildings. Within the colleges there is some excellent

Illustration: Clare College Fellows' Garden

gardening, and in many cases these more intimate enclosures connect harmoniously with the larger landscape of the Backs. The garden at **St John's College** (St John's St; *Open:* Daily 10.30–5.30 but closed May and Jun) is approached through marvellous 16th-century courts, across the Wren Bridge which has the best view of the most glamorous Cambridge bridge, the Bridge of Sighs. Bold borders run along the gothic screen of New Court, and, in the distance, fine trees mark the Scholars' Garden hedged in yew with an old weeping ash, ornamental trees and mixed borders. **Clare College** (Trinity Lane; *Open:* 2–4) has large and varied gardens of which the best part is the Fellows' Garden, redesigned in 1947 by Professor Willmer. It lies off the Avenue, which has wonderful 18th-century wrought-iron gates, and its most spectacular feature is a dazzling pair of beautifully kept herbaceous borders in blue and yellow, with daylilies, delphiniums, thalictrum and verbascums. **Newnham College** (Sidgwick Avenue; *Open:* 9–4) has fine late-Victorian buildings by Basil Champneys and preserves gardens that are touched with the same atmosphere – yew hedges, lively borders and some excellent trees, among them several *Ailanthus altissima* and a fine *Sorbus latifolia*.

BETH CHATTO GARDENS

Essex

Elmstead Market,
Colchester CO7 7DB
1/4 mile E of Elmstead
Market by A133
Tel: 01206 822007

Owner: Mrs Beth Chatto

Open: Mar to Oct, Mon to
Sat 9–5; Nov to Feb, Mon
to Fri 9–4

BETH CHATTO'S garden and nursery make a most attractive place to visit. Her nursery is particularly strong on herbaceous plants and plants with ornamental foliage. She also fully recognises the importance of a plant's natural habitat, as she has shown in her excellent books on the dry and the damp garden. The former car park has recently been transformed into a brilliant gravel garden. Beyond the nursery a series of pools runs along a hollow edged with moisture-loving plants. Farther up the slopes are sweeping beds containing immense numbers of bulbs and herbaceous perennials backed with shrubs and trees. No gardener could come here and fail to discover something seductive and unfamiliar. An informative catalogue (£2.50) is produced and plants are sold by mail.

CROSSING HOUSE

Cambridgeshire

THE URGE to make a garden can often be so overwhelming that the small matter of a railway line running through one's plot may easily be brushed aside. Mr Fuller was in charge of the railway crossing and Mrs Fuller made a garden, at first immediately

78 Meldreth Road,
Shepreth, Royston SG8 6PS
In Shepreth village 8m S of
Cambridge off A10
Tel: 01763 261071

Owner: Mr and Mrs
Douglas Fuller

Open: Daily, dawn–dusk.
1/4 acre

about the house, but increasingly along the railway line itself – which she is no longer allowed to tend. Although in general appearance a cottage garden, signs of serious plant collecting are soon detected. Here is an immense range of plants, many exceedingly rare and beautifully grown. Alpines are grown on raised beds and there are some excellent groups of particular plants – several varieties of witch hazel, for example. Winding paths and decorative ornaments and a yew arbour give the impression of space. The level of interest is unflagging and there are very many far bigger gardens in which there is much less to admire.

DOCWRA'S MANOR
Cambridgeshire

Shepreth, nr Royston
SG8 6PS
In Shepreth village 8m S of
Cambridge off A10
Tel: 01763 261473/260235

Owner: Mrs John Raven

Open: Mon, Wed and Fri
10–5; Apr to Oct, 1st Sun
2–5; Bank Hol Mon 10–5.
2 1/2 acres

COLLECTIONS OF PLANTS can be extremely boring to gardeners if they are not given a harmonious setting. Mrs Raven and her late husband took a particular interest in natural species, especially those from Mediterranean countries, and gave them a home in this cold but very dry part of England. Many of them flourished and the Ravens designed a layout which would provide both a satisfactory habitat for the plants and make an attractive garden for non-botanists. In this they were triumphantly successful. There is just enough formality, such as a decorative tunnel of pears and clematis, to prevent a mere jungle but there is no artificial regimentation of plants. Old outhouses and courtyards give protection from the wind on this flat and well drained site. An excellent nursery sells plants propagated in the garden.

DODDINGTON HALL
Lincolnshire

Doddington,
nr Lincoln LN6 4RU
5m W of Lincoln by B1190;
signposted off A46 Lincoln
bypass
Tel: 01522 694308

Owner: Mr and Mrs A.G.
Jarvis

Open: 19 Mar to 30 Apr,
Sun 2–6 (open Easter Mon;
closed Easter Day); May to
Sept, Wed, Sun and Bank
Hol Mon 2–6. 12 acres

ROBERT SMITHSON, the greatest Elizabethan architect, designed this lovely brick mansion which casts its spell over the gardens that surround it. Rare Elizabethan garden walls enclose the courts at back and front, making a wonderfully ornamental background to the varied planting that they enclose. To the front, with its simple pattern of lawns edged with box, ornament is added by cherry trees shaped into lollipops, and mounds of clipped yew. In the courtyard on the west side ebullient box parterres make a brilliant display, in which crown imperials and many irises are followed by roses, and where deep herbaceous borders line the walls. Beyond this a wild garden has excellent old trees, including some superb ancient sweet chestnuts, and many decorative incidents – a turf maze, an elegant Temple of the Winds and a water garden.

EUSTON HALL
Suffolk

EUSTON HALL was built by the Earl of Arlington in the 1670s, and in the early 18th century a pioneer landscape garden was laid out by William Kent; later in the century 'Capability' Brown was consulted by the 3rd Duke of Grafton. South of the house a formal terraced garden is ornamented with summer planting in urns, and a balustrade. To one side, the

Euston, Thetford IP24 2QP
3m S of Thetford by A1088
Tel: 01842 766366

Owner: The Duke and
Duchess of Grafton

Open: 1 Jun to 28 Sept,
Thur 2.30–5; also Sun 25
Jun and Sun 3 Sept 2.30–5.
70 acres. House open

King Charles Gate, a survival from the 17th century,
leads out into the park, and in the far distance Kent's
exquisite domed temple rises on an eminence. From
the formal garden a beautiful wrought-iron gate leads
through a high wall with a very successful mixed
border. Beyond, to the west, the remains of a great
lime avenue stretches out towards Kent's arched
lodge. The present Duke has added new borders to
the east of the house and contrived a charming
setting for a wooden William Kent summer house.

THE FAIRHAVEN GARDEN TRUST

Norfolk

c/o G. Debbage, 2 The
Woodlands, Pilson Green,
South Walsham, Norwich
NR13 6EA
9m NE of Norwich by
B1140, E of the village of
South Walsham
Tel: 01603 270449

Owner: The Fairhaven
Garden Trust

Open: May to Sept, Tue to
Sun 11-6 (Sat 2–6). 170
acres

WITH AN EXCEPTIONAL setting on the broads, this
unique woodland garden was started in 1947 by
Lord Fairhaven of the same family that made the
garden at Anglesey Abbey. In marvellous old
woodland of beech and oak, some of great age and
beauty, exotic plantings are unostentatiously slipped
into the scenery – azaleas, cherries, dogwoods,
enkianthus and mahonias. In the spring immense
spreads of bluebells are followed by candelabra
primulas glittering along shady walks. Occasional
glades and clearings give calm views of South
Walsham Inner Broad. This is not a place for great
rarities or fortissimo displays of flower power. But
there is no other garden quite like it – where a lovely
piece of natural landscape has been gently shaped by
the restrained hand of the gardener.

FELBRIGG HALL
Norfolk

Roughton, nr Norwich
NR11 8PR
2m SW of Cromer by A148
and B1436
Tel: 01263 837444

Owner:
The National Trust

Open: 25 Mar to 5 Nov,
daily except Tue and Fri
11–5. Parkland open daily
except 25 Dec dawn–dusk.
1/2 acres. House open

A WINDY PLAIN surrounds the mansion at Felbrigg with its curious contrasting Jacobean and mid Georgian façades. Handsome parkland – dating from the 17th century and with some survivals from that time – is planted with beech, oak and sweet chestnut, but the object of chief interest is the magnificent old walled kitchen garden at a distance from the house. Gravel paths and low box hedges divide the area in which productive plants – vines, figs, pears and plums – are trained against the walls. Borders line the walls – peonies and lilies under shrub roses. An orchard is underplanted with spring bulbs and there is a collection of thorns planted in formal rows in grass. An octagonal dovecote with white doves stands in the centre of the north wall, forming an eye-catcher at the end of the central path. Of particular interest is the collection of colchicums of which Felbrigg has the National Collection.

FISKS CLEMATIS NURSERY
Suffolk

IT IS HARD to imagine any garden not possessing at least one or two clematis. Here at Jim Fisk's admirable nursery, which has its own display garden, the visitor can see an immense range of varieties. The large-flowered hybrids as well as the species and other small-flowered sorts are stocked in variety, and

Westleton, Saxmundham
IP17 3AJ
5m NE of Saxmundham by
A12 and minor roads
Tel: 0172 873 263

Open: Mon to Fri 9–5; also
Sat and Sun summer only,
10–1, 2–5

many of them are rare – such as 'Louise Rowe' with frilly double and single mauve flowers. There is always something of interest flowering from spring to late autumn. A model catalogue (four 1st-class stamps), well illustrated in colour, gives much valuable information on cultivation. Fisks supply by mail order, with meticulous planting instructions.

GANNOCK GROWERS
Hertfordshire

Illustration: Campanula
takesimana

Gannock Green, Sandon,
Buntingford SG9 0RH
Turn SE off A505 towards
Sandon mid way between
Baldock and Royston.
Nursery is 2 1/3m from
A505 and 1/2m NW of
Sandon church
Tel: 01763 287 386

Open: Mar to Oct, Tue to
Sat and Bank Hol Mon
10–4; also by appointment

GANNOCK GROWERS specialises in unusual hardy herbaceous plants. The range is wide, with many plants suitable for the border and some smaller items verging on alpines. Penny Pyle has several aquilegias, good campanulas, an unusual range of centaureas, species dianthus, eryngiums, one of the very best ranges of geraniums, lychnis, several species penstemons, a rare collection of silenes and some decorative sedges and grasses. There are countless individual plants, rarely seen in nurseries, that will seduce any gardener. Most plants are priced by pot size and prices are modest. A list is published (three 1st-class stamps) and plants are sold by mail order.

THE GARDENS OF THE ROSE
Hertfordshire

THOUSANDS OF ROSES, including well over 1,500 varieties, are displayed here, and although there is a strong emphasis on modern varieties there are also interesting reference collections of the main

Chiswell Green AL2 3NR
2m SW of St Albans by
B4630
Tel: 01727 850461

Owner: Royal National
Rose Society

Open: Mid Jun to mid Oct,
Mon to Sat 9–5, Sun and
Bank Hol 10–6. 25 acres

historic groups. The site is flat and windswept, and
some vertical emphasis is given by Irish yews and
pergolas on which the climbing roses are trained.
Modern roses are generally arranged in large beds,
often with a single block of one variety making a
vast splash of colour. The Royal National Rose
Society, one of the leading specialist plant societies,
publishes a journal and provides advice to members.

GUNBY HALL

Lincolnshire

nr Spilsby PE23 5SS
7m W of Skegness by A158
Tel: 01909 486411

Owner:
The National Trust

Open: Apr to Sept, Wed
and Thur (also Tue, Thur
and Fri by written
appointment) 2–6. 7 acres.
House open

GUNBY PRESENTS an elegant pastoral scene – the
Georgian brick mansion looking out over serene
parkland. In the old walled kitchen garden there is
more excitement, with a rumpus of roses, burgeoning
herbaceous borders, apples trained over arches and
underplanted with irises, and a dinky domed gazebo
painted a celestial blue. A second walled garden has
beds of fruit and vegetables and old pear trees
growing out of herbaceous borders. There is a rose
walk, a bed of hydrangeas and, hidden behind a yew
hedge, a stately walk of Irish junipers along a canal.
On the far side of the house lawns are ornamented
with specimen trees and there is a wild flower walk.

R. HARKNESS & CO LTD

Hertfordshire

HARKNESS SELL chiefly roses with the emphasis on
modern cultivars, of which they are constantly
making new introductions, but they also stock a
worthwhile selection of old varieties. Immense

The Rose Gardens,
Hitchin SG4 0JT
On A505 between Hitchin
and Letchworth
Tel: 01462 420402

Open: Mon to Sat 9–5, Sun
and Bank Hol Mon 10–5

numbers of all these are available in containers at the
nursery, but more energetic visitors are also allowed
to visit the growing fields nearby. An especially
informative and well produced catalogue is issued
free; it includes, for example, information about the
origin of every rose. A mail order service is provided,
orders are sent between November and March.

HARTSHALL NURSERY STOCK
Suffolk

Hartshall Farm,
Walsham-le-Willows, Bury
St Edmunds IP31 3BY
1 1/2m SE of
Walsham-le-Willows off
Westhorpe road
Tel: 01359 259238

Open: Tue to Sat 10–4.30.
Closed Jul and all Bank
Hols

LIKE SOME MUCH-LOVED, but elderly, actress
Hartshall keeps threatening to retire, but popular
acclaim repeatedly brings it back from the brink.
Trees and shrubs are the best part of the stock but it
does carry carefully chosen examples of just about
every kind of plant you would want for your garden.
In the tree department it has notable ranges of
birches, cherries, maples, oaks and willows. There is
no mail order but in any case the chief merit of the
nursery is the excitement of exploration and chance
discoveries. Lists are issued (three 1st-class stamps).

HATFIELD HOUSE
Hertfordshire

Hatfield AL9 5NQ
In the centre of Hatfield
village, 20m N of London
by A1 and A1(M) Jnct 4
Tel: 01707 262 823

Owner: The Marquess of
Salisbury

Open: 25 Mar to Jul, daily
except Sun (closed Good
Fri) 11–6; Aug to 8 Oct,
daily 11–6; East Garden
Mon 2–5 (closed Bank Hol
Mon). 30 acres. House open

HATFIELD HOUSE, a Jacobean extravaganza of pink
brick, was started in 1607 by Robert Cecil, and
the family has owned it ever since. There has always
been a notable garden here, but over the last twenty
years the present Marchioness of Salisbury has
brought dazzling new life to it. Near the house there
are formal gardens, most of which have ancient
origins. By the Old Palace Lady Salisbury has made a
new knot garden with old varieties of plants,
including many of those introduced by John
Tradescant the Elder who worked for the Cecils
when the garden was started. The privy garden and
the scented garden to the west of the house have been
replanted, and in summer are very beautiful. The East
Garden is decorated with formal rows of clipped
holm oaks (*Quercus ilex*), Italian statues and
brimming beds of shrubs, especially roses,
underplanted with herbaceous plants. Beyond are
avenues of apple trees, a Victorian yew maze (alas,

not open) and the New Pond which is full of
atmosphere. There are few great historic gardens that
demonstrate so visibly the excitement of gardening. A
shop, at the entrance, sells a few good plants.

HAUGHLEY PARK
Suffolk

nr Stowmarket IP14 3JY
4m NW of Stowmarket by
A45
Tel: 01359 240205

Owner: The Williams
family

Open: May to Sept, Tue
3–6. 8 acres plus woodland

THE GABLED HOUSE was built in 1620, with a pretty
gothic wing added in 1820 and the whole
restored by A.J. Williams after a fire in 1961.
Handsome old woodland, with some exceptional
individual specimens, makes a fine setting for the
gardens which are almost entirely of the 20th
century. North of the house a broad apron of grass
opens out, edged with mixed borders, and, to one
side, an immense hollow oak which is at least 1,000
years old. The vista is continued by an old lime
avenue stretching across fields into the distance.
A dell has shady walks fringed with hostas, and the
woodland garden, ablaze with bluebells in spring, has
many azaleas and rhododendrons planted among
majestic beeches and Scots pines.

HELMINGHAM HALL
Suffolk

nr Stowmarket IP14 6EF
9m N of Ipswich by B1077
Tel: 01473 890363

Owner: Lord Tollemache

Open: 30 Apr to 10 Sept,
Sun 2–6. 2 acres

AT HELMINGHAM, house, parkland and garden
together create an exceptional work of art. The
brick house, with its romantic moat and drawbridge,
is of several periods, starting in 1500, and has always
been owned by the Tollemaches. It overlooks a deer
park with a double avenue of oaks and, to one side,
also moated, a walled kitchen garden has been turned
to ornamental purposes. At the entrance a box-edged
parterre with summer bedding is surrounded on three
sides by borders of old roses and hedges of lavender.
Winged horses cap the piers of the gates into the
walled garden, which is divided into four parts by
two superb double herbaceous borders running down
and across. Leading off them are paths through
tunnels of sweet peas, runner beans or marrows, and
behind the ornamental borders fruit and vegetables
grow in impeccable beds. On the banks of the moat a

grassy walk with narrow borders encircles the walls. On the far, eastern, side of the house a herb and knot garden made since 1982 is hedged in yew. Within are low hedges of clipped box or lavender and several beds of old roses which are underplanted with bulbs and herbaceous perennials. Few great historic houses have gardens so exquisite as those at Helmingham.

HOECROFT PLANTS
Norfolk

Severals Grange, Holt Road, Wood Norton, Dereham NR20 5BL
6m E of Fakenham by A1067 and B1110
Tel: 01362 860179/844206

Open: May to Sept, Mon, Wed and Sat 10–4

THIS ADMIRABLE NURSERY used to be near Bath but has now reappeared, with rekindled vigour, in Norfolk. Margaret Lister sells wonderful ornamental grasses, and plants with especially distinguished foliage – both herbaceous and woody. It is the grasses, though, that are the special excitement of her list. These are really valuable border plants, mixing easily with any other plantings. Hoecroft carries a very wide range, some of which you will scarcely find

in any other nursery in the country. Over 160 varieties include reeds, sedges and bamboos. The catalogue (£1.00) is outstanding, with much valuable information on the garden use of the plants.

HOPLEYS PLANTS
Hertfordshire

High Street, Much Hadham SG10 6BU
5m SW of Bishop's Stortford by B1004
Tel: 01279 84 2509

Open: Mon to Sat (closed Tue) 9–5, Sun 2–5; closed Jan

Y OU WOULD HAVE to be a gardener of steely resolve to avoid buying something at Hopleys. They have introduced into commerce some of the most successful new garden plants of recent years – including, for example, *Potentilla* 'Red Ace' and *Lavatera* 'Barnsley'. Their list ranges widely and every year new and exciting plants – hardy and non-hardy – are offered. Some groups are especially well represented (for example, salvias) but the striking quality of Hopleys is the very careful choice of particular cultivars of a single species (e.g. 14 different varieties of *Argyranthemum frutescens*). The beautifully kept 4-acre garden, alongside the nursery, is open to visitors. There is an impeccable catalogue (£1.20) and a mail order service in the autumn only.

HYDE HALL
Essex

W HEN THE ROBINSONS came here to farm in 1955 there was no garden, merely a handful of trees on top of a famously windswept hill in one of the driest parts of the country. The garden they made is now enormous, full of wonderful plants in diverse

Rettendon, nr Chelmsford
CM3 8ET
7m SE of Chelmsford by
A130
Tel: 01245 400256

Owner: The Royal
Horticultural Society

Open: 26 Mar to 29 Oct,
Sat, Sun, Wed, Thurs and
Bank Hol Mon 11–6.
24 acres

habitats – a brilliant tribute to their gardening skill. An immensely wide range of plants is grown – daylilies, irises, peonies, roses, snowdrops and countless ornamental trees and shrubs. Hyde Hall has two National Collections: of crab apples (*Malus*) and of viburnums. This is not merely a plant collection, for many parts of the garden have carefully worked out colour harmonies – e.g. a gold garden and a series of herbaceous borders with hot or cool schemes. No gardener could come here without being informed and delighted. A nursery sells excellent plants but there is no mail order. Hyde Hall is now owned by the RHS and it is hoped that the charm of the Robinsons' style will survive intact.

ICKWORTH
Suffolk

Horringer, Bury St
Edmunds IP29 5QE
3m SW of Bury St
Edmunds by A143
Tel: 01284 735270

Owner:
The National Trust

Open: 25 Mar to 5 Nov,
daily 10–5 (closed Good
Fri); 6 Nov to Feb, daily
10–4. Park open daily
throughout year 7–7. 33
acres. House open

THERE IS no house like Ickworth – a dumpy, domed cylinder with curving wings designed in the late 18th century by Francis Sandys with help from his patron, the Earl of Bristol, Bishop of Derry. The garden is influenced by the shape of the house. At the front, a sweeping herbaceous border, echoing the wings, is well planted in blues and purples – acanthus, campanulas, geraniums and sage – with clumps of purple-leafed cotinus. Behind the house there is a more formal arrangement, again related to the shape of the house, with a curved terrace and box-hedged alleys. A marvellous walk about the estate of Ickworth affords splendid views back to the house and to the Earl's obelisk in the distance. The park is a wonderful combination of ancient woodland and the tactful hand of 'Capability' Brown.

KNEBWORTH
Hertfordshire

Knebworth SG3 6PY
28m N of London by
AI(M) Jnct 7
Tel: 01438 812661

Owner: Lord Cobbold

Open: Easter to end May,
Sat, Sun and Bank Hol
12–5; Jun to Aug, daily
except Mon (but open
Bank Hol Mon) 12–5; Sept,
Sat and Sun 12–5. 25 acres.
House open

THE LYTTONS have lived here since the late Middle
Ages and the house, a wild and woolly gothic
fantasy, was partly designed by Bulwer Lytton, the
best-selling Victorian novelist. Edwin Lutyens married
a Lytton daughter and between 1907 and 1911 he
simplified the immensely complicated Victorian
garden. From the façade of the house a pair of cool
pleached lime walks leads to a formal rose garden
flanked by herbaceous borders. Beyond a screen of
clipped yew, with statues half-embedded in niches, a
circular pool has gold borders on either side and a
path leads to a garden of old roses underplanted with
artemisias, catmint and lamb's ears. To one side of
the house an attractive little herb garden has been
recreated from a Gertrude Jekyll design of
interlocking circles.

LUTON HOO
Bedfordshire

THE MANSION at Luton Hoo was designed by
Robert Adam in 1764 and revised by Sir Robert
Smirke in 1827. It is a palatial affair and the terraced
gardens which lie below it to the south are
appropriately glamorous. At the upper level, lawns
on either side of the path have fine stone urns which
in summer are filled with pale pink petunias and
helichrysum; behind them are mixed borders of pale
colours. In the middle of the lower terrace, hedged in

Luton LU1 3TQ
1 1/2m SE of Luton by
A6129; Jnct 10 of M1
Tel: 01582 22955

Owner: The Wernher
Family

Open: 29 Mar to 16 Oct,
daily except Mon (open
Bank Hol Mon 10.30–6)
12–6. 10 acres. House open

yew, a circular water-lily pool has a central fountain
with a bronze boy and dolphin on a rock. Box-edged
rose beds surround it, ornamented with box topiary
cones and spirals. On either side domed temples
mark the corners, and splendid old cedars of
Lebanon rise up behind. At some distance from the
house a romantic rock garden has a series of pools
overhung with fine old Japanese maples, planted
round about with conifers and rhododendrons. The
cascades are now working again after 30 waterless
years. The superb park at Luton Hoo is the work of
'Capability' Brown who dammed the River Lea to
make two lakes and planted huge numbers of trees.

MANNINGTON HALL
Norfolk

nr Saxthorpe NR11 7BB
18m NW of Norwich by
B1149 and minor roads
Tel: 0126 387 4175

Owner:
Lord and Lady Walpole

Open: Apr to Oct, Sun
12–5; Jun to Aug, also
Wed to Fri 11–5. 20 acres

MANNINGTON HALL, with its moat, towers and
crenellations, has a wildly romantic air. It dates
from the late 15th century but was much changed in
the 19th century. The moat is splashed with
water-lilies and walled with yew on the inner bank.
Behind the hedges are beds of modern roses and
stone busts on plinths surveying the scene. Lawns and
specimen trees – some fine cedars of Lebanon – lie
on the far side of the moat, and a classical pavilion
with a statue of Diana gives architectural contrast to
beds of shrub roses. In a large walled garden a little
distance from the house, the Heritage Rose Garden
has a very large collection of roses of all the
representative types, trained on pergolas or walls and

in beds. Part of the garden is laid out to show the use of roses in different period styles. A visit at rose time is a heady experience but the beauty of house and setting is worth seeing at any time. A nursery sells a good selection of roses.

MELFORD HALL
Suffolk

Long Melford, Sudbury
CO10 9AH
In village of Long Melford
4m N of Sudbury by A131
Tel: 01787 880286

Owner:
The National Trust

Open: Apr, Sat, Sun and
Bank Hol Mon 2–5.30;
May to Sept, Wed to Sun
(except Fri) and Bank Hol
Mon 2–5.30; Oct, Sat and
Sun 2–5.30. 9 acres. House
open

IF IT WERE NOT for the gazebo at Melford Hall the garden would only just be worth visiting – but what a gazebo! It is octagonal, built of brick, and it bristles with pediments and finials. Gertrude Jekyll visited it and, recognizing its architectural distinction, criticised it for being smothered in ivy. Today it is revealed in its full eccentric glory. Steep steps lead up to it, and from tall sash windows there are views on one side over the dry moat and on the other of the garden with its curving herbaceous borders, old weeping ash and mulberry, and a pretty little herb parterre planted with low hedges of yew and patches of purple sage, germander, lavender and rue.

MONKSILVER NURSERY
Cambridgeshire

Illustration: Centaurea
macrocephala

HERE IS ONE of the most fascinating collections of herbaceous plants that you will find anywhere. The Monksilver list (six 1st-class stamps) is the sort you take to bed on a winter's evening for a long, happy and richly inspiring browse. There are rare plants here, some exceedingly rare, but there are also

Oakington Road,
Cottenham CB4 4TW
In the village of Cottenham
4 1/2m N of Cambridge by
B1049

Open: Apr to Jun, Fri and
Sat 10–4. Also open for the
National Gardens Scheme
from Apr to Oct, on the
second Sat of each month
10–4

countless more common (or garden) things that
should not be overlooked. The catalogue describes
the plants well, and in terms of naming and botanical
precision has the highest standards. National
Collections of *Galeobdolon*, *Lamium* and *Vinca* are
held at the nursery. Chiefly a mail order business, the
nursery has fairly restricted opening times. Prices are
very fair, although in a few cases, for extreme
rarities, they do not quote a price, but invite bids (of
money or *even rarer plants*). Do not miss the chance
of a visit to this unique place.

NORFOLK LAVENDER
Norfolk

Caley Mill, Heacham
PE31 7JE
13 1/2m N of King's Lynn
on A149
Tel: 01485 570384

Open: Daily 10–5 (closed
23 Dec to 14 Jan)

L AVENDER USED to be very widely grown on a
commercial scale in southern England but
Norfolk Lavender is the only remaining lavender
farm in England and it holds a National Collection
(55 different species and varieties). Display beds
show vividly the variations in foliage and flower, and
in late summer fill the air with their scent. Many
lavenders, and a few other plants, are sold in a small
nursery, and a mail order service is provided.

NOTCUTTS NURSERIES LTD
Suffolk

N OTCUTTS is an institution and carries an immense
general stock. In every department gardeners will
find excellent things. New introductions are
constantly being made and medals relentlessly won at
the best shows. A mail order service is provided and

Ipswich Road, Woodbridge
IP12 4AF
Tel: 01394 383344

Open: Mon to Sat
8.45–5.30, Sun 10–5

the oustanding catalogue is a valuable gardening reference book, 300 pages long and very detailed. The main section, called 'Plants for a Purpose', gives lists of plants grouped under every imaginable heading. Apart from the Woodbridge branch there are also centres in the east of England at Orton Waterville, nr Peterborough (01733 234600); Smallford, St Albans (01727 53224), Ardleigh, Colchester (01206 230271); and Daniel's Road, Norwich (01603 53155). All these have similar opening times to the main branch.

OXBURGH HALL
Norfolk

Oxborough, nr King's
Lynn PE33 9PS
In Oxborough 9m E of
Downham Market by
A1122 and A134
Tel: 01366 328258

Owner:
The National Trust

Open: 25 Mar to 5 Nov,
daily except Thur and Fri
12–5.30. 18 acres. House
open

R ISING FROM its moat, the 15th-century manor house is wonderfully romantic. It was built by the Bedingfields who gave it to the National Trust in 1952. To the east of the hall a splendid Frenchified parterre was made in the 19th century after the Bedingfields saw a similar one on a visit to France in 1845. Against a background of gravel, swirling beds hedged in box are filled with a permanent planting of rue and santolina, which is enlivened by summer bedding of ageratums, marigolds and pelargoniums. Parterres of this sort were intended to be viewed from above, as this one can be from the windows of the hall or from the terrace to one side. A yew hedge separates a very handsome long mixed border from the parterre. A 19th-century brick-walled kitchen garden has been planted with a formal orchard of medlars, mulberries and different varieties of plum, with clematis and roses trained on the walls.

PADLOCK CROFT

Cambridgeshire

Illustration: Campanula punctata *'Pallida'*

19 Padlock Road, West Wratting, nr Cambridge CB1 5LS
14m SE of Cambridge by A1307, A604 and minor roads
Tel: 01223 290383

Open: Apr to Oct, Wed to Sat, and Bank Hol Mon 10–6. 1 acre

SUSAN AND PETER Lewis are famous for campanulas, of which their garden houses the National Collection; their splendid list (four 2nd-class stamps) leads with no less than fifteen pages of them, and nearly 300 different kinds may be seen growing in the garden. In addition they hold National Collections of the related genera of Adenophora, Platycodon and Symphyandra. Garden and nursery blend indistinguishably at Padlock Croft, forming a maze of alpine troughs, glasshouses and packed beds. Alpines and smaller border plants are the speciality of the nursery, and there are very good collections. In every part of the list there are desirable things – a choice range, for example, of species digitalis. A mail order service is provided but a visit is especially rewarding to see the many unlisted plants growing in the garden.

PARADISE CENTRE

Suffolk

Twinstead Road, Lamarsh, Bures CO8 5EX
In village of Lamarsh 4m S of Sudbury by minor roads
Tel: 01787 269449

Open: Sat, Sun and Bank Hol Mon 10–5; also by appointment

THE HEART of this unusual nursery garden is its collection of bulbs and herbaceous perennials. Among the bulbs are exceptionally long lists of alliums, crocuses, erythroniums, many fritillaries and species narcissi and tulips. Among the herbaceous plants are excellent groups of epimediums, a good range of ferns, hardy geraniums, hostas, a wonderful list of primulas and several saxifrages. All the plants are well chosen and are available by post from an attractive and informative catalogue (four 1st-class stamps). As with many small and interesting nurseries, there are always excellent plants available at the nursery which have not been listed. The nursery is, in effect, the owners' own garden – made by them from virtually nothing – and it is delightful.

PARK GREEN NURSERIES
Suffolk

Wetheringsett, Stowmarket
IP14 5QH
6m NE of Stowmarket
E of A140
Tel: 01728 860139

Open: Mar to Oct Thur to Mon 10–5.30

RICHARD AND MARY Ford grow over 150 different species and varieties of hosta, and there are few garden sites for which an appropriate and beautiful specimen cannot be found. Many of the plants are hard to come by, and some are available only here. As well as their chief speciality, the Fords also have a choice collection of astilbes, of which they have many named varieties of both tall and dwarf kinds. Plants are sold by mail order and are despatched from October to March when dormant. A good catalogue (three 1st-class stamps) is produced, with excellent descriptions of the plants. Seeds are also sold and, as hostas cross-pollinate with abandon, you may well germinate something new and interesting yourself.

PECKOVER HOUSE
Cambridgeshire

WHEN YOU HAVE got over the surprise of finding a garden as big as this behind an elegant town house in the middle of Wisbech, you can get down to admiring its distinctive charms. Lawns slope away

North Brink, Wisbech
PE13 1JR
In the centre of Wisbech
Tel: 01945 583463

Owner:
The National Trust

Open: Apr to Oct, daily
except Thur and Fri
2–5.30. Parties at other
times by arrangement with
tenant. 2 acres. House open

from the back of the house, with many substantial
specimen trees of a Victorian character, and a rustic
summer house adds to the period flavour. To one
side of the main lawn, hidden behind brick walls, a
pair of mixed borders leads up to a pool and an
elegant little gazebo. The borders are ornamented
with slender metal pillars with roses and clematis,
and a pair of topiary yew peacocks. In a separate
part of the garden a conservatory houses oranges,
daturas and other tender plants, and there is an
unusual 19th-century fern house.

POTTERTON & MARTIN
Lincolnshire

Moortown Road,
Nettleton, Caistor
LN7 6HX
18m NE of Lincoln by A46
and B1205
Tel: 01472 851792

Open: Daily 9–5

POTTERTON & MARTIN call themselves 'The Cottage
Nursery', which is misleading. In fact they sell a
wide range of alpine plants, dwarf bulbs, ferns and
orchids, with interesting excursions into such oddities
as carnivorous plants, some of which are hardy and
make good plants for the edges of ponds. There is
generally a strong emphasis on species and forms,
with an exceptionally good list of anemones; dozens
of crocuses; virtually every species of cyclamen that is
hardy out-of-doors (and some that are not), including

some of the forms with especially pretty foliage; a good collection of the smaller irises; an excellent range of primulas; a long and interesting selection of saxifrages; and all sorts of other tempting things of the smaller kind. Catalogues are issued (50p stamp), and a mail order service is provided.

RAVENINGHAM HALL GARDENS
Norfolk

Raveningham, nr Norwich
NR14 6NS
14m SE of Norwich by
A146 and B1136
Tel: 0150 846 222

Owner:
Sir Nicholas Bacon Bt

Open: Garden: mid Mar to
mid Sept, Wed 1–4, Sun
and Bank Hol Mon 2–5.30;
Nursery, conservatory,
arboretum and vegetable
garden: Mon to Fri 9–5;
Mar to Oct, also Sat 9–4

THE NURSERY attached to the garden is a full-scale commercial enterprise with an excellent general stock, very largely propagated from the plants in the garden. Many of these are unusual without being modish, and are of exactly the kind that give so many old-established country house gardens their distinctive character. There is a good range of agapanthus, several ceanothus, cistus, euphorbias, snowdrop cultivars (some hard to come by), many penstemons and pulmonarias. A good catalogue is produced (three 1st-class stamps) and there is a mail order service. The garden itself, lying mostly to the south of the gentlemanly 18th-century brick mansion, has many grey and tender things such as *Buddleja crispa* doing surprisingly well in this part of the world. A rose garden is enclosed in brick walls and hedges of yew, a long deep herbaceous border runs along the outside of the walled kitchen garden, and to the south views open out over parkland.

READS NURSERY
Norfolk

Hales Hall, nr Loddon
NR14 6QW
10m SE of Norwich by
A146
Tel: 01508 548395

Open: Tue to Sat 10–1, 2–5
or dusk if earlier; May to
Oct, also Sun and Bank
Hol Mon 2–5

THIS OLD-ESTABLISHED (1890) nursery specialises in fruit, especially citrus fruits, of which the Reads have the largest selection commercially available in Britain – not just oranges and lemons but all sorts of exotics like mandarins and kumquats. They also sell a very large selection of desert and wine grapes, several different varieties of figs, mulberries and tender climbing plants. The nursery holds one of the most exotic of all National Collections – that of cultivars of the fig (*Ficus carica*). All this makes Reads especially worth visiting, the more so because it occupies a particularly attractive group of buildings – the potting shed is housed in the largest medieval brick barn in England. A very informative catalogue (four 1st-class stamps) is produced and plants are supplied by post.

THE ROMANTIC GARDEN NURSERY
Norfolk

The Street, Swannington,
Norwich NR9 5NW
In the village of
Swannington, 9m NW of
Norwich by A1067 and
minor roads
Tel: 01603 261488

Open: Wed, Fri and Sat
10–5

THE ROMANTIC GARDEN NURSERY swarms with ready-made topiary – a menagerie of animals clipped of box. More unusual are many standard-trained and mop-headed plants – *Arbutus unedo*, bay, holly, privet and others. Plants for the conservatory are also sold, including curious oleanders with three-part trunks plaited exotically together. A range of hand-thrown frost-proof Italian terracotta pots is sold. A list is produced (four 1st-class stamps) and there is a mail order service.

SALING HALL

Essex

Great Saling, nr Braintree
CM7 5DT
6m NW of Braintree by
A120
Tel: 01371 850141

Owner: Mr and Mrs
Hugh Johnson

Open: May to Jul, Wed
2–5. 12 acres

SOME GOOD GARDENS fall too easily into genteel ossification but at Saling Hall there is a constant buzz of horticultural activity. The present owners came in 1971 and found an old garden already full of interest surrounding the long, curvaceously gabled brick house of the early 17th century. They redefined the best parts (including a very pretty walled garden west of the house and a decaying water garden) and expanded boldly into the woodland with new ventures. Here is an excellent collection of trees, many rare, skilfully deployed with vistas and ornaments (including a recently made Tuscan Temple of Pisces), and a deft sketch of a Japanese garden with a stream, billowing mounds of clipped box and a snow-lantern. If you don't like what you see here you have probably lost interest in gardening.

SANDRINGHAM HOUSE

Norfolk

Sandringham, King's Lynn
PE35 6EN
9m NE of King's Lynn by
B1440
Tel: 01553 772675

Owner: H.M. The Queen

Open: Easter to late Jul,
early Aug to Oct, Mon to
Sat 10.30–5, Sun 11.30–5.
House open

THERE ARE NOT many gardens belonging to the Royal Family that are regularly open to the public so this is one of the very few places where its taste in gardening may be seen. First, it is on a huge scale and the chief impression is one of immense and impeccable lawns punctuated with specimen trees, many of which are 19th-century plantings of conifers. On this sandy, acid soil rhododendrons do well and they flourish in the protection of the trees. Nearer the house there is an attractive formality with pleached lime walks, hedges of yew and a series of herbaceous

beds enclosed in tall box hedges. On the other side of
the house a stream feeds two lakes whose fringes are
richly planted with conifers, maples and other
ornamental trees and shrubs.

SHERINGHAM PARK
Norfolk

Upper Sheringham
NR26 8TB
2m SW of Sheringham by
A148
Tel: 01263 823778

Owner:
The National Trust

Open: Daily dawn–dusk.
90 acres

HUMPHRY REPTON was the genius behind this place
of woods and rambling walks around a shallow
combe by the sea. It was commissioned by Abbot
Upcher's family, for whom Repton also built a new
house between 1812 and 1819 in a more picturesque
position embowered by trees – many of them
marvellous 18th-century oaks – on one side of the
valley. In the woods across fields to the south of the
house is a collection of rare rhododendrons started
by Abbot Upcher's son Henry who helped finance
plant-hunting expeditions to the Himalayas. Many of
these rhododendrons have grown to great size in the
sheltered combe. In 1975 Thomas Upcher built an
arcaded temple to Repton's design, on an eminence
with lovely views to the house and the sea beyond.

SOMERLEYTON HALL
Suffolk

SOMERLEYTON HAS a big, bold Victorian house and
a garden to suit. The garden entrance leads
through the former kitchen garden which now has a
spanking pair of herbaceous borders marching down
the middle. The well maintained glasshouses were

nr Lowestoft NR32 5QQ
5m NW of Lowestoft by
B1074
Tel: 01502 730224

Owner: Lord and Lady
Somerleyton

Open: Easter Sun to Sept,
Thur, Sun and Bank Hol
Mon 12.30–5.30; Jul to
Aug, also Tue and Wed
12.30–5.30. 12 acres. House
open

designed by Joseph Paxton, and on the outside south walls of the kitchen garden there are rare peach cases awaiting restoration. Wellingtonias and monkey puzzles on the lawn beyond the kitchen garden were part of the 19th-century layout but among them are much older trees, including some superb sweet chestnuts. From the Victorian parterres by the house, planted with roses and columns of clipped yew, there are views of the remains of an ancient avenue of limes disappearing towards the horizon. There is also a hedge maze of yew built in 1846 and a magnificent winter garden of the same date in which the tea-room is now housed.

THE SWISS GARDEN
Bedfordshire

Old Warden,
nr Biggleswade
2 1/2m W of Biggleswade
by minor roads; signposted
from A1 and A600
Tel: 01767 627666
Owner: Managed by
Bedfordshire County
Council

Open: Mar to Jul, Sept,
Sat, Sun and Bank Hol
Mon 10–6, Mon, Wed,
Thur, Fri 1.30–6; Aug,
daily except Tue 10–6; Jan,
Feb and Oct, Sun 11–4.
9 acres

IN THE EARLY 19th century there was a fashion for everything Swiss, and here at Old Warden the Lord Ongley made an enchanting 'Swiss' garden full of rustic thatched houses, precipitous rocky descents and picturesque views. The site, well wooded and gently undulating, has interconnected ponds with ornamental islands, and paths wind about, revealing views of garden houses, delicate iron-work arched bridges, a kiosk with stained glass, statues and urns, a grotto and a fernery. All around are excellent trees and the garden has been beautifully restored by the county council.

VALLEY CLEMATIS
Lincolnshire

Illustration: Clematis *'Perle d'Azur'*

Willingham Road, Hainton
LN3 6LN
17m NE of Lincoln, S of
Hainton on the road to
South Willingham
Tel: 01507 313398

Open: Daily 10–6 (closed
24 Dec to 1 Jan)

OTHER NURSERIES sell clematis, but none with quite the panache of Keith and Carol Fair. They win medals at all the best shows and have an outstanding range of plants for sale – including several unique to them. Over 350 varieties are grown, although not all of these will be available at any one time. The illustrated list (£1.00) is a delight, not only for the exceptional plants but also for the valuable suggestions for cultivation and the use of clematis in the garden. A mail order service is available.

WIMPOLE HALL
Hertfordshire

Arrington, Royston
SG8 0BW
8m SW of Cambridge by
A603
Tel: 01223 207257

Owner:
The National Trust

Open: 25 Mar to 5 Nov,
daily except Mon and Fri
1–5 (open Bank Hol Mon
and preceding Sun 11–5); 4
Aug to 28 Aug, also open
Fri 1–5. 20 acres. House
open

ON THIS WINDY, open site on the borders of Hertfordshire and Cambridgeshire the 18th-century house rises on a slight eminence, commanding wide and distant views. In the very early 18th century there had been a great formal garden here, and an immense avenue of elms, planted by Charles Bridgeman in the 1720s, survived until it was killed by the elm disease; it has now been replanted in limes. In the 1750s the formal garden began to be dismantled, and later both 'Capability' Brown and Humphry Repton worked here, naturalising the landscape even further. In recent years the National Trust has restored some of the formality (including parterres on the north side) but has respected the different layers of garden style that give Wimpole its interest.

WOLTERTON PARK
Norfolk

nr Erpingham NR11 7LY
2m N of Aylsham by A140
Tel: 0126 387 4175

Owner: Lord and Lady
Walpole

Open: 9–5 or dusk if earlier

WOLTERTON PARK is a handsome house of orange brick and stone built in the 1730s for Horatio Walpole. It has remained in the family but was abandoned in the 19th century, lived in once again in the 20th century and badly damaged by fire in 1952. Now the present Lord Walpole has taken it in hand and a programme of restoration is under way. The visitor starts with a wonderful rural amble, skirting fields and woods, passing a romantically ruined church tower and eventually emerging in a vast open space dotted with exceptional oaks. The south front of the house is then revealed, embowered in trees, overlooking in the far distance a great lake. Hedges and trees are being replanted in the park. The formal gardens south of the house, glimpsed from the park, are open only on occasional Sundays (advertised in the local press).

WOOTTEN'S PLANTS
Suffolk

MICHAEL LOFTUS STARTED his nursery in 1991 and already it has a distinctive, and distinguished, character. He sells chiefly herbaceous plants, not all hardy, and what makes the nursery different is the meticulous choice and the care with which they are

Blackheath, Wenhaston,
Halesworth IP19 9HD
3m SE of Halesworth by
A144 and minor roads
Tel: 0150 270 258

Open: Daily 9.30–5. Closed
25 Dec–2 Jan

grown. The plants are regularly potted on and all visitors will be struck by their size and vigour. Here are many campanulas, diascias, euphorbias, geraniums, lychnis, penstemons, salvias and countless other things such as large daturas in pots, and the very finest pelargoniums. Virtually everything is something you would like to possess, but you will have to go to the nursery as there is no mail order and no list. Michael Loftus's own very attractive garden alongside the nursery is occasionally open.

WREST PARK
Bedfordshire

Silsoe MK45 4HS
3/4m E of Silsoe by A6
Tel: 01525 860152

Owner: English Heritage

Open: Apr to Sept, Sat,
Sun and Bank Hol Mon,
10–6. 80 acres

THE GARDEN at Wrest Park has only fragments – but they are wonderfully attractive. The de Grey family had lived at Wrest since the 13th century but the present palatial house was built in the 1830s in the French style. A Frenchified parterre south of the house dates from the same time and has bedding schemes and fine classical statues. Of the elaborate formal garden of the early 18th century all that remains is a slender canal and a swagger domed classical pavilion designed by Thomas Archer in 1710. Between the pavilion and the canal is a lead figure of William III. A garden of woodland vistas and a serpentined pool has a pretty Chinese gazebo and traces of 'Capability' Brown who worked here from 1758 to 1760. One of the charms of the place is the mixture of his informal landscaping overlaid on the fine survivals of the earlier formal garden.

THE
NORTH
OF
ENGLAND

Cumbria
County Durham
Humberside
Lancashire
Northumberland
Yorkshire

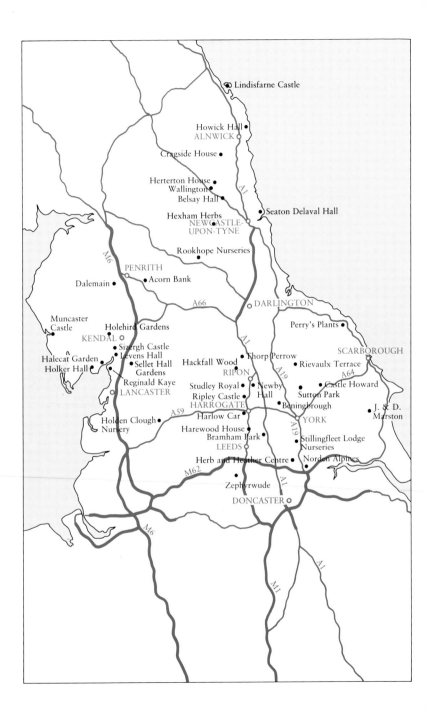

Lindisfarne Castle

Howick Hall
ALNWICK

Cragside House

Herterton House
Wallington
Belsay Hall

Hexham Herbs
NEWCASTLE-
UPON-TYNE

Seaton Delaval Hall

Rookhope Nurseries

M6

PENRITH

Dalemain   Acorn Bank

A66

DARLINGTON

A1

Muncaster
Castle

Holehird Gardens

KENDAL

Perry's Plants

SCARBOROUGH

A64

Sizergh Castle
Levens Hall

Halecat Garden
Holker Hall

Sellet Hall
Gardens

Hackfall Wood   Thorp Perrow

Rievaulx Terrace

RIPON

A19

Castle Howard

Reginald Kaye

LANCASTER

Studley Royal   Newby
Ripley Castle   Hall

Sutton Park

J. & D.
Marston

HARROGATE

Boninbrough

A59   Harlow Car

YORK

Holden Clough
Nursery

Harewood House
Bramham Park

A19

Stillingfleet Lodge
Nurseries

LEEDS

Herb and Heather Centre

Norden Alpines

M62

Zephyrwude

A1

DONCASTER

M6

M1

ACORN BANK GARDEN

Cumbria

Temple Sowerby,
nr Penrith CA10 1SP
6m E of Penrith by A66
Tel: 017683 61893

Owner:
The National Trust

Open: Apr to Oct, daily
10–5.30. 2 1/2 acres

To ONE SIDE of the brown stone 18th-century mansion a herb garden is beautifully laid out in the former kitchen garden, finely enclosed in 17th-century brick and sandstone walls. Three long borders run the length of the herb garden, and although this is primarily a reference collection – the largest in the north of England, with well over 200 species – it has been laid out in a very decorative fashion. A booklet describes the medicinal and culinary uses of the plants. Above the herb garden, in a further walled enclosure, a formal orchard is divided by a yew alley flanked by rows of cherry trees – the sour cherry (*Prunus cerasus* 'Rhexii') with lovely double white flowers. Narrow beds under the walls have mixed plantings of shrubs and perennials, with clematis, roses and espaliered fruit trees.

BELSAY HALL

Northumberland

Belsay, nr
Newcastle-upon-Tyne
NE20 0DX
14m NW of Newcastle by
A696
Tel: 01661 881636

Owner: The Belsay Trust.
In guardianship of English
Heritage

Open: Apr to Oct, daily
10–6; Nov to Mar, daily
except Mon 10–4 (closed
Christmas Day, Boxing
Day and New Year's Day).
House open

THE NEO-CLASSICAL brown stone mansion at Belsay was built to the design of its owner, Sir Charles Monck, in the early 19th century. The stone was quarried on the site and the resulting rocky hollows and ravines were made by Sir Charles into an unforgettable wild and romantic garden. The planting is boldly appropriate to the setting, with the striking foliage of Chusan palms, the larger-leafed rhododendrons, *Gunnera mannicata* and the handsome angelica tree (*Aralia elata*) looking wonderful against the cliffs and outcrops. A path winds gently upwards between the walls of stone fringed with ferns, and emerges in meadows above the quarry. Here is a surprise – the substantial remains of 14th-century Belsay Castle rising up in the long grass. Near the house formal terraced gardens with yew hedges overlook woodland of conifers with a large collection of rhododendrons, and an unusual 'winter garden' is planted with different kinds of heathers for winter colour.

BENINGBROUGH HALL
North Yorkshire

Shipton-by-Beningbrough,
York YO6 1DD
8m NW of York by A19
and minor roads
Tel: 01904 470666

Owner:
The National Trust

Open: Apr to Oct, daily
except Thur and Fri (open
Good Fri) 11–5; Jul to
Aug, daily except Thur
11–5. 7 acres. House open

BENINGBROUGH HALL in flat country west of York is a very glamorous house built of fine brick and stone in the early 18th century for John Bourchier. The gardens are surrounded by water meadows and a hint of landscaping, although no known landscaper ever worked here. The chief garden interest now lies in the formal arrangements near the house. A long tunnel of pleached pears underplanted with herbs runs down the middle of the walled kitchen garden, now a picnic area. At the end of the walled garden a mixed double border is planned for all-season flowering. On either side of the house are elegant little formal gardens: to the west brick paths separate knots of box filled with apricot or red roses and pansies; to the east a rectangular lily pool is surrounded by clipped domes of box and lilies in pots, with clematis and roses scaling the walls behind.

BRAMHAM PARK
West Yorkshire

Wetherby LS23 6ND
5m S of Wetherby by A1
Tel: 01937 844265

Owner: Mr and Mrs
George Lane Fox

Open: Easter weekend,
spring Bank Hol weekend,
May Day weekend
1.15–5.30; 19 Jun to 4 Sept,
Sun, Tue, Wed and Thur
and Bank Hol 1.15–5.30.
100 acres. House open

A GARDEN LIKE BRAMHAM is an exciting place, giving unique and special pleasure. There are borders and rose beds but the really wonderful thing here is the great formal garden with its immense alleys of clipped beech, distant views of lonely statues, exquisite garden buildings commanding wide views, and refreshing vistas out into the surrounding countryside. It was designed in the very early 18th century for Robert Benson, the 1st Lord Bingley, who probably masterminded the building of the beautiful house as well as the making of the garden. On the Grand Tour he had seen the latest French gardens and

wanted to make something of the sort for himself. The garden he made has a definite French accent – but with an attractively playful English irregularity. Still owned by descendants of its maker, Bramham is maintained to wonderfully high standards; of its kind, there is nothing in England to touch it.

CASTLE HOWARD
North Yorkshire

nr York YO6 7DA
14m NE of York by A64
Tel: 01653 648444

Owner: The Hon. Simon Howard

Open: Mid Mar to late Oct, daily 10–5. Castle open

Bᴵɢ ɪꜱ ᴛʜᴇ ᴡᴏʀᴅ for Castle Howard but the garden gives pleasures that are both grand and intimate. Vanbrugh's gigantic early 18th-century palace is set in dramatic country that is matched for drama by the house. To the south a vast formal arrangement of clipped yew hedges surrounds a fountain with a figure of Atlas supported by Tritons, designed by W.A. Nesfield in 1850. To one side, in a secluded walled garden, yew hedges and screens of hornbeam divide rose beds edged in dwarf box, lavender and purple berberis. The very large collection of roses – old and new – is beautifully arranged, underplanted with grey and silver artemisias, phlomis, pinks and

santolina. On the slopes far beyond the house a completely different atmosphere reigns. Ray Wood is an immense woodland garden with winding walks and a marvellous collection of trees and shrubs – including very recent new introductions – in a naturalistic setting with colonies of cowslips, narcissus, and willow gentian.

CRAGSIDE HOUSE
Northumberland

Rothbury, Morpeth
NE65 7PX
13m SW of Alnwick by
B6341
Tel: 01669 20333/20266

Owner:
The National Trust

Open: Apr to Oct, daily
except Mon (open Bank
Hol Mon) 10.30–5.30; Nov
to Dec, Tue, Sat and Sun
10.30–4. 1,000 acres. House
open

CRAGSIDE WAS DESIGNED by Norman Shaw for the industrialist Lord Armstrong and built in 1870. The very name makes one think of a Grimm fairy tale, and the appearance of the house rising high above a rocky bluff overlooking the Debdon Valley has more than a touch of Wagner. This is no place for genteel borders, and below the house a precipitous rockery cascades down the slopes. This has very recently been restored with plantings of heathers, rowans and the wilder kinds of rose. Giant steps lead down to a sombre and beautiful pinetum spreading along the banks of the river below.

DALEMAIN
Cumbria

nr Penrith CA11 0HB
3m SW of Penrith by A66
and A592
Tel: 01768 486450

Owner: R. Hasell McCosh

Open: Easter Sun to Sept,
daily except Fri and Sat
11.15–5. House open

O N ONE SIDE of the handsome 18th-century house
at Dalemain a broad gravelled terrace, fringed
with tumbling shrub roses, looks out over fields.
Behind the house a knot of box-edged compartments
is filled with artemisias, astilbes, campanulas,
penstemons and violas, and in summer pots of lilies
are arranged about a pool. A gravel walk with a
border of shrub roses leads under old fruit trees to a
door. Beyond this is Lobb's Wood where a wild
woodland walk follows the banks of the Dacre beck.
On the other side of the beck the wild garden is
occasionally revealed, with azaleas, rhododendrons
and ornamental trees. This is the kind of garden,
unpretentious and filled with good plants, that many
think of as quintessentially English.

HACKFALL WOOD
North Yorkshire

Grewelthorpe, nr Ripon
1/2m NW of the village of
Grewelthorpe, 6 1/2m NW
of Ripon

Owner: Woodland Trust

Open: Daily, dawn to
dusk. 112 acres

T HIS WONDERFUL WILD landscape garden was
conjured out of a piece of dramatic country by
William, son of John Aislabie of Studley Royal,
between 1730 and 1750. A natural wooded gorge, 100
metres deep, overlooks a lovely loop of the River
Ure. Aislabie added buildings, paths, waterfalls and
rills to animate the woods of beech and oak. Today
you may wander at will, pushing through thickets of
bracken, and marvel at the romantic prospects within

the woods or high above them from the crest of the gorge. A famous beauty spot until the 1930s, it fell into decay; rediscovered by local enthusiasts, it is now cared for by the Woodland Trust and accessible to all. It has a secret atmosphere and its present state of controlled dishevelment seems perfectly in tune with its exceptional character.

HALECAT GARDEN NURSERIES

Cumbria

Witherslack,
Grange-over-Sands
LA11 6RU
5m NE of
Grange-over-Sands by
B5277 and A590
Tel: 015395 52 229

Open: Mon to Fri 9–4.30,
Sun 2–4

HALECAT HOUSE is an early 19th-century mansion looking south over terraced gardens and fields to exquisite, far-reaching views of Arnside Knott. This private garden is open to visitors, which gives an additional reason for coming to the very good nursery. Stone-paved terraces run along the south side of the house and a path skirts an unadorned lawn edged on two sides with generously planted mixed borders. A handsome gothic gazebo designed by Francis F. Johnson clings to the slope and provides an eye-catcher for a pair of borders with many shrub roses and a background of dark purple cotinus. In the nursery, on the far side of the house from the garden, an especially choice collection of over 60 varieties of hydrangea is the star of the list but there are many good things, herbaceous and woody, in other departments. A well produced catalogue is issued but there is no mail order.

HAREWOOD HOUSE
West Yorkshire

Harewood, Leeds
LS17 9LQ
7m N of Leeds and 7m S
of Harrogate by A61
Tel: 01532 886331

Owner: The Earl and
Countess of Harewood

Open: 25 Mar to 31 Oct,
daily 10–5. 36 acres. House
open

HAREWOOD HOUSE is a palatial mansion designed by John Carr of York and Robert Adam, and built in the 1760s. In the 19th century there were many changes by Sir Charles Barry who also laid out the Italianate south terrace which survives today. A parterre with arabesques filled with sempervivums, stone urns and cones of clipped yew is embellished with a recent statue by Astrid Zydower – a nobly proportioned bronze figure of Orpheus with a leopard draped over his shoulders and standing on a black marble plinth veiled with falling water. But the view from the terrace over 'Capability' Brown's landscape park is the most beautiful thing at Harewood. A lake is masked by trees and the land rises and falls with belts and clumps of trees alternating with meadows in which cattle graze. No building or ornament is visible and the simplicity of it is a splendid foil to the imposing house.

HARLOW CARR BOTANICAL GARDENS
North Yorkshire

THIS IS THE NORTHERN equivalent of Wisley Gardens and is crammed with the same sort of garden attractions. The site is a very handsome one, a shallow valley with a stream and well wooded on

Crag Lane, Harrogate
HG3 1QB
1 1/2m W of Harrogate by
B6162
Tel: 01423 565418

Owner: The Northern
Horticultural Society

Open: Daily 9.30–6 or dusk
if earlier. 60 acres

its south-western slopes. There are sections devoted
to particular groups of plants – a rose garden, a bulb
garden and an arboretum. Display areas have three
different kinds of rockeries – peat, limestone and
sandstone – and a winter garden. Much space is
devoted to vegetables and a fruit cage. Something
different is arranged for each season in the trial
gardens, with displays of new cultivars. A seasonal
leaflet is produced, giving background information
about what is going on in the season in question, and
about the plants displayed.

HERB AND HEATHER CENTRE
North Yorkshire

West Haddlesey, nr Selby
YO8 8QA
4m SW of Selby by A19
Tel: 01757 228279

Open: Daily except
Christmas week 9.30–5.30
(dusk in winter)

HERB GARDENS spring up all the time and vary
considerably in their interest. Carole Atkinson's
is a particularly good one, and apart from herbs she
sells a wide range of heathers (over 200 varieties) and
a good collection of conifers. All her plants are raised
organically, and most may be seen in the adjacent
display gardens which contain over 500 varieties of
herbs and a National Collection of cotton lavender
(*Santolina*). A list (three 1st-class stamps) is issued
and orders are supplied by mail order.

HERTERTON HOUSE
GARDENS AND NURSERY
Northumberland

FEW GARDENS so small give so much pleasure and
interest as Herterton. Stone outhouses and
beautifully made walls frame a series of enclosed
gardens, each with distinctive character. A flower

Hartington, nr Cambo
NE61 6BN
2m N of Cambo by B6342
Tel: 01670 774 278

Owner: Frank and
Marjorie Lawley

Open: Apr to Sept, daily
except Tue and Thur
1.30–5.30. 1 acre

garden has hedges of box and yew, and beds edged in stone, filled with unstaked herbaceous plants, giving generous informality to the ordered design of the layout. A physic garden, overlooked by an arcaded loggia, has a great clipped drum of silver pear at the centre, surrounded by beds edged in London pride or thrift. On the road side of the house the formal garden has topiary of yew and of box, and square box-edged beds brim with different varieties of dicentra. The important thing throughout the garden is the strength and simplicity of the design. The nursery sells only herbaceous perennials and although the stock is not large the choice is fastidious.

HEXHAM HERBS
Northumberland

Chollerford, nr Hexham
NE46 4BQ
On the W edge of
Chollerford, 4m NW of
Hexham by A6079
Tel: 01434 681 483

Open: Easter to Oct, daily
10–5; phone for winter
opening hours

IN LOVELY COUNTRY hard by Hadrian's Wall Hexham Herbs has found a happy home in a 2-acre walled former kitchen garden. Here are gravel paths, ebullient box-edged borders and, beautifully displayed on a sloping gravel bed, the National Collection of thymes – over 120 species and cultivars. The nursery sells herbs, herbaceous plants and native species of wildflowers. There is no mail order but a catalogue is available (£1.50).

HOLDEN CLOUGH NURSERY
Lancashire

Illustration: Gentiana saxosa

Holden,
Bolton-by-Bowland,
Clitheroe BB7 4PF
7m NE of Clitheroe by
A671, A59 and minor roads
(turn off at Sawley)
Tel: 01200 447615

Open: All the year, Mon to
Thur 1–5, Sat 9–5; Apr to
May, also Sun 2–5. Bank
Hol Mon 9–5; closed
Christmas to New Year

THIS IS an outstandingly good nursery, specialising in alpines above all but with many other worthwhile plants. The alpine department will excite even veteran fans with its splendid collections of, for example, gentians (over 20 species and cultivars), very many saxifrages, dozens of sedums and so on. Apart from these there are some excellent ornamental grasses and a connoisseur's selection of ferns, heaths, herbaceous perennials, shrubs and climbers. The elegant, very informative catalogue (£1.20) is a model of such things. A mail order service is provided.

HOLEHIRD GARDENS
Cumbria

Patterdale Road,
Windermere LA23 3JA
2m N of Windermere by
A592
Tel: 015394 46238

Owner: The Lakeland
Horticultural Society

Open: Daily, dawn to
dusk. 13 1/2 acres

IN A WELL WOODED position on slopes above the eastern shore of Lake Windermere, Holehird has a marvellous site. The garden owes much of its present interest to William Groves who, in the early years of the 20th century, sponsored the plant-hunting expeditions of Reginald Farrer and William Purdom to north-west China. The Lakeland Horticultural Society took over in 1969 and is responsible for the impeccable upkeep and high level of plant interest that visitors may enjoy today. The soil is acid, and rainfall is famously high, giving excellent conditions for azaleas, ferns, heathers, Himalayan poppies, maples and rhododendrons. These are decoratively disposed on slopes intricately laced with winding walks. A fine walled garden, recently restored, gives protection to many surprisingly tender plants – callistemon, carpenteria, diascia and *Eucryphia*

Illustration opposite:
Holehird Gardens

glutinosa. Holehird has National Collections of astilbes – probably the largest in the world – hydrangeas and polystichum ferns. The plants are handsomely displayed in well planned borders.

HOLKER HALL
Cumbria

Cark-in-Cartmel, nr
Grange-over-Sands
LA11 7PL
4m W of
Grange-over-Sands
Tel: 0153 95 58328

Owner: The Lord
Cavendish of Furness and
Lady Cavendish

Open: Apr to Oct, daily
except Sat 10.30–6.
25 acres. House open

SOME OF THE most worthwhile gardens manage to juggle very different ingredients with complete success, and Holker Hall is a prime example. The late 16th-century house has a splendid neo-Elizabethan wing built in 1871 after a disastrous fire. Inventive formal gardens near the house provide secluded sitting places and much to admire: an alley of glistening Portugal laurels, herbaceous borders with well judged colour harmonies, stately gravel walks, yew hedges and elegant thorns (*Crataegus orientalis*) set in squares of box hedging. A gate pierces the wall and leads to a newly made meadow garden, a brilliant contrast to the formal enclosures by the house. To one side gardens of a woodland character spread out; eucryphias, hoherias, magnolias, rhododendrons and stewartias ornament a background of venerable beeches and oaks. Among the trees an ornamental staircase, with cascades of water on either side, leads to a 17th-century Italian figure of Neptune. Everywhere there are distinguished plants and the garden will give pleasure in any season, not least for the inspiringly high standard of upkeep. The garden holds the National Collection of *Styracaceae.*

HOWICK HALL
Northumberland

Alnwick NE66 3LB
6m NE of Alnwick by
B1340 and minor roads
Tel: 01665 577285

Owner:
Howick Trustees Ltd

Open: Apr to Sept, daily
1–6. 14 acres

HOWICK, very near the wild Northumbrian coast, has a secluded and romantic air. The grand late 18th-century house overlooks a series of balustraded terraces linked with steps. Thickets of *Choisya ternata* and *Carpenteria californica* flank the steps leading down from the uppermost terrace to a pool and to mixed borders rich with roses and lavender with, in late summer, great waves of blue agapanthus. Beyond the last terrace a meadow, brilliant in spring with narcissi and tulips, is planted with maples, birches and shrub roses. Although this is limestone country, part of the garden at Howick has acid soil and here, between the wars, an excellent woodland garden was made with azaleas, camellias, outstanding magnolias and rhododendrons under a canopy of old oaks, beeches and sweet chestnuts. Later in the season eucryphias, hydrangeas and viburnums continue interest, and in the autumn there is brilliant colour from cercidiphyllums and maples.

REGINALD KAYE LTD
Lancashire

PRACTICALLY ON THE SANDS overlooking Morecambe Bay, Reginald Kaye is in a fairly remote position but is well worth tracking down. At first appearance it seems a pretty chaotic jumble – beards of moss grow on crumbling cold-frames. But

Waithman Nurseries,
Silverdale,
Carnforth LA5 0TY
7m NW of Carnforth by
minor roads
Tel: 01524 701252

Open: Mar to Oct, Mon to
Sat 8–12.30, 2–5, Sun 10–5

persevere, for there are marvellous plants here. The speciality of the nursery is rock and alpine plants; it has specially strong selections of campanulas, dianthus, primulas, saxifrages and sedums. There is also an excellent range of hardy ferns, including some very rare cultivars, and of ericaceous plants. A well produced catalogue (60p) has valuable lists of plants for specific situations. There is no mail order service except for ferns, thus a visit is essential; also, what appear in the catalogue merely as *Helleborus orientalis* 'Mixed shades' may, on inspection, turn out to be something absolutely wonderful.

LEVENS HALL
Cumbria

Kendal LA8 0PD
5m S of Kendal by A591
and A6
Tel: 01539 560321

Owner: C.H. Bagot

Open: Apr to Sept, daily
except Fri and Sat 11–5.
House open

A MYSTERIOUS FRENCHMAN, Guillaume Beaumont, came to Levens Hall in 1690 and by 1694 had laid out an exotic formal garden – a forest of topiary and cool beech alleys – which still survives in splendid old age. Fanciful shapes of yew, both golden and common, and of box, many billowing and misshapen with age, are scattered about. Among them, bedding plants make blocks of colours, their brilliance going well with the monumental topiary.

Rising above all this is the grey stone house with its great square pele tower. On one side, behind castellated yew hedges, are excellent new borders, a herb garden and an ornamental *potager*. Beaumont's extraordinary beech alley opens out into a giant circle and a path leads to a field with a ha-ha – the first in England – and an avenue of sycamores. To celebrate the tercentenary of the garden in 1994 a splendid new fountain has been made.

LINDISFARNE CASTLE

Northumberland

Holy Island,
Berwick-upon-Tweed
TD15 2SH
11 1/2m SE of
Berwick-upon-Tweed by
A1 and causeway at low
tide; it is essential to phone
the number below to check
tide times, which are also
posted at each end of the
causeway
Tel: 01289 89244

Owner: The National Trust

Open: Apr to Oct, daily
except Fri (but open Good
Fri) 1–5.30

EDWIN LUTYENS RESTORED the castle as a holiday home for Edward Hudson, the famous editor of *Country Life*; Lytton Strachey thought it 'very dark, and nowhere to sit'. A garden by Gertrude Jekyll was an essential accompaniment, and she laid out a little walled enclosure, at some distance from the castle across sheep pastures. It survives today; aquilegias, irises, Jacob's ladder, lady's mantle and lamb's ears spread among stone flags, and roses are trained on walls and wooden frames. It is so surprising, and such an appropriately simple layout, that any gardener will enjoy seeing it in this remote and wonderfully beautiful setting.

J. & D. MARSTON

North Yorkshire

THE MARSTONS RUN the kind of specialist nursery that is one of the great glories of British horticulture. They specialise in ferns – hardy and tender – of which they sell a remarkable collection.

Culag, Green Lane,
Nafferton, nr Driffield
YO25 0LF
2m NE of Great Driffield
off A166
Tel: 01377 254487

Open: Easter to mid Sept,
Sat and Sun 1.30–5

These valuable garden plants, immensely fashionable
in the 19th century, are now deservedly coming back
into fashion, and this is one of the best places to
learn about them. Mrs J. K. Marston is an expert on
the subject, about which she has written a very useful
booklet. There is an excellent catalogue (£1.00) and
orders will be fulfilled by post. D. Marston makes
beautiful containers and ornaments of lead.

MUNCASTER CASTLE
Cumbria

Ravenglass CA18 1RQ
1m SE of Ravenglass by
A595
Tel: 01229 717614

Owner: Mrs P.
Gordon-Duff-Pennington

Open: Daily 11–5. 77 acres.
Castle open

MUNCASTER IS a wonderfully romantic place.
Rising over ravines near the wild Cumbrian
coast is a medieval granite castle, rebuilt by Anthony
Salvin in 1862. From the entrance lodge the drive
plunges down towards the castle, and marvellous old
rhododendrons line the way. Many of these were
planted by Sir John Ramsden who financed some of
Frank Kingdon-Ward's plant-hunting expeditions in
the 1920s. Near the castle a grassy terrace walk
snakes along the valley, giving unforgettable views of
the Esk and the mountains beyond. The slopes above
the terrace are richly planted with cherries,
magnolias, maples, rhododendrons and other
ornamental trees and shrubs. Along the other side of
the walk a box hedge has regularly spaced topiary
piers of golden and common yew; on the precipitous
slopes below, are marvellous trees, including
probably the biggest sweet chestnut you will ever
look down on.

NEWBY HALL GARDENS
North Yorkshire

Ripon HG4 5AE
4m SE of Ripon by B6265
Tel: 01423 322583

Owner: R.E.J. Compton

Open: Apr to Sept, daily
except Mon (but open
Bank Hol Mon) 11–5.30.
25 acres. House open

NEWBY HALL has one of the best private gardens in
England, with outstanding collections of plants
beautifully arranged and cared for. The gardens lie to
the south of the house on a magnificent site that
slopes gently down to the River Ure. Giant double
herbaceous borders, hedged on either side in yew,
sweep down to the river edge, and paths lead off
enticingly to other formal enclosures or into the
surrounding woodland. Among the formal parts are a
dramatic 19th-century statue walk; striking seasonal

gardens designed specifically for spring and autumn; an excellent garden of old roses; and Sylvia's Garden in which herbs and grey-leafed plants flourish round paved paths. In the woodland are many excellent trees, especially maples, birch and dogwoods (a National Collection). Although full of rarities, this is a garden that can be relished even by those who cannot tell a dandelion from a daffodil. Intensely visited in the summer months, it is big enough to absorb the numbers and provide all kinds of intimate corners where the visitor may be virtually alone.

NORDEN ALPINES
Humberside

Hirst Road, Carlton, nr Goole DN14 9PX
8m W of Goole by A614 and A1041
Tel: 01405 861348

Open: Mar to Sept, Sat, Sun and Bank Hol Mon 10–5

THIS NURSERY is, in the words of the owners, the result of a hobby that got out of hand. It sells only alpines of which it has a dazzling selection: over 2,500 varieties, with marvellous groups of campanulas, dianthus, gentians, irises, primulas, saxifrages (well over 70 varieties), sedums and violas, all propagated on the premises, often in quite small quantities. A catalogue is produced (four 2nd-class stamps) and there is a mail order service. Unusually, the nursery offers bed and breakfast for visitors.

PERRY'S PLANTS
North Yorkshire

River Gardens, Sleights,
Whitby YO21 1RR
2 1/2m SW of Whitby on
B1410
Tel: 01947 810329

Open: Easter to Oct,
daily 10–5

PATRICIA PERRY specialises in herbaceous perennials with a few woody plants, and has charming gardens on the River Esk – Victorian tea-gardens with all sorts of amusements of the time: croquet, boating and, of course, tea. The nursery has some very good things: a fine selection of anthemis, good hebes, excellent lavateras, mallows, and a very choice range of perennial wallflowers (erysimums). There is an intriguing group of euphorbias including the splendidly named *E. characias* 'Winter Blusher' which sounds like an essential plant . A list is issued (large s.a.e.) but there is no mail order service; it is a charming place and a visit is a pleasure.

RIEVAULX TERRACE
North Yorkshire

Rievaulx, Helmsley
YO6 5LJ
2 1/2m NW of Helmsley by
B1257
Tel: 0143 96 340

Owner:
The National Trust

Open: Apr to Oct, daily
10.30–6 or dusk if earlier.
15 acres

IT WAS ONE of the new ideas of 18th-century landscape gardening to make a terrace from which to admire fine views of the countryside and other beauties. At Rievaulx, high above the exquisite remains of the 12th-century abbey, a grassy terrace curves through woodland, giving wonderful views of the abbey, the valley and distant countryside. At each end of the terrace a little temple provides a punctuation mark;: the plain round Tuscan temple has a simple interior but the Ionic temple is sumptuously furnished, with a table laid for a feast, and decorated with a noble painted ceiling. All this was made in the late 1750s by Thomas Duncombe, an early exercise in picturesque landscape design that still has the power of enchantment. Modest in scale, it is the perfect place to grasp the genius of the 18th-century landscape revolution.

ROOKHOPE NURSERIES
County Durham

Rookhope, Upper
Weardale DL13 2DD
22 1/2m NW of Bishop
Auckland by A68 and A689
Tel: 01388 517272

Open: Apr to Oct, daily
9–5; Nov to Mar, times
vary, please phone

KAREN AND ALAN Blackburn's nursery on the Upper Pennine moors is over 1,000 feet up, and, among other things, provides a tough hardiness test-ground for garden plants. The most extensive part of the list is a representative collection of alpines, with many good campanulas, erodiums, gentians, the smaller geraniums, helianthemums, saxifrages, thymes and violas. In addition, there are dwarf conifers and heathers, and a good range of herbaceous perennials and of shrubs. The adjacent garden shows what may be done in this cold, windy place which has regular heavy snowfalls. A catalogue (three 1st-class stamps) is issued and there is a limited mail order service.

SEATON DELAVAL HALL
Northumberland

THE HOUSE AT Seaton Delaval is one of Vanbrugh's ripest confections, with a memorably dramatic position on the Northumberland coast, frequently veiled in sea mist. A few traces survive of the original garden but the present scheme has been almost

Seaton Delaval, Whitley
Bay, NE26 4QR
9m NE of
Newcastle-upon-Tyne on
the A190
Tel: 0191 2373040/2371493

Owner: Lord Hastings

Open: May to Sept, Wed,
Sun and Bank Hol Mon 2–6

entirely made by the present Lord Hastings who, in 1947, commissioned from James Russell a new formal garden to the west of the house. He laid out a splendidly theatrical arrangement of yew hedges and topiary, with lively patterns of box hedges, to which fine urns and a fountain were later added. Near the house a box parterre is planted with roses, and a pair of mixed borders sweeps round a wonderful old weeping ash. Behind yew hedges Lady Hastings has added a lily pond and a laburnum tunnel leading towards the Norman church. Everywhere the eye is caught by Vanbrugh's lovely swaggering house.

SELLET HALL GARDENS
Lancashire

near Kirkby Lonsdale LA6
2QF
1m SW of Kirkby Lonsdale
on the Low Biggins road
Tel: 015242 71865

Open: Mar to Oct, daily
10–5

THE LUNE VALLEY is one of the most beautiful parts of England, and Sellet Hall takes full advantage of its setting. It is a nursery, specialising in herbs, and a very attractive garden disposed in rooms linked by enticing vistas. Yew hedges and walls of the fine local stone divide the spaces, some of which are laid out as flowery parterres. Apart from a wide range of herbs, the nursery also sells trees (especially maples), shrubs, bamboos, many herbaceous perennials and a choice selection of auriculas.

SIZERGH CASTLE
Cumbria

THE GREAT THING at Sizergh, in the shadow of the late medieval stone castle, is one of the best rock gardens in England. It was laid out in 1926 by a local firm, T.R. Hayes & Son of Ambleside, and is now a

nr Kendal LA8 8AE
3 1/2m S of Kendal by A591
Tel: 015395 60070

Owner:
The National Trust

Open: 2 Apr to 31 Oct, Sun
to Thur 12.30–5.30.
14 acres. House open

densely planted jungle of conifers and Japanese
maples, laced with winding walks and a splashing
stream and underplanted with a marvellous collection
of hardy ferns – over 100 species and varieties. South
of the castle steps lead down to an ornamental lake
and to the west an avenue of rowans leads through a
rose garden with species and shrub roses.

STILLINGFLEET LODGE NURSERIES
North Yorkshire

Stillingfleet, York
YO4 6HW
7m S of York by A19 and
B1222; in the village, turn
opposite the church
Tel: 01904 728506

Open: Apr to mid Oct,
daily except Mon, Thur
and Sun 10–4

VANESSA COOK specialises in herbaceous perennials,
although she also sells some of the more versatile
of the woody plants such as artemisias, cistus,
daphnes, hebes, and lavenders. Mrs Cook's selection
of herbaceous plants is particularly attractive, with
good euphorbias, a long list of hardy geraniums, a
superb selection of irises, penstemons, primulas,
pulmonarias (of which she holds a National
Collection) and veronicas. There are also several
interesting grasses, or grass-like plants. Vanessa
Cook's list is specially rich in those smaller
ornamental items which find a decorative home in
odd corners of the garden and immensely add to its
character. A catalogue is issued (five 1st-class
stamps), from which plants may be supplied by post.

STUDLEY ROYAL
North Yorkshire

Fountains, Ripon
HG4 3DZ
4m W of Ripon by B6265
Tel: 01765 608888/601005

Owner:
The National Trust

Open: Daily except Fri in
Nov, Dec and Jan and 24
and 25 Dec; Apr to Sept
10–7 (closes at 5 on 10 and
11 Jun and 8 and 9 Jul);
Oct to Mar 10–5 or dusk if
earlier.

JOHN AISLABIE was Chancellor of the Exchequer in
1720 when the South Sea Bubble collapsed, and
subsequently he retired to his Yorkshire estate to lick
his wounds and make a garden. In the wooded valley
of the River Skell he laid out a great water garden
ornamented with statues of lead and stone, and, in
the woods above, built a banqueting house, an
octagonal tower, a Temple of Piety and a Temple of
Fame. John Aislabie's son William later acquired the
ruins of the nearby Cistercian Fountains Abbey, and
these were incorporated into the landscape scheme –
suddenly revealed round a curve of the river, like a
gigantic and exquisite garden ornament.

SUTTON PARK
North Yorkshire

Sutton-on-the-Forest, York
YO6 1DP
8m N of York by B1363
Tel: 01347 810249

Owner:
Mrs N.M.D Sheffield

Open: Easter to Oct, daily
11–5.30. 8 acres

THE APPROACH TO the garden at Sutton Park is
oblique, through groves of ornamental trees, with
the very pretty garden façade of the 18th-century
brick and stone house gradually revealed. A series of
terraces, filled with decorative planting, leads down
from the house. The second terrace has a geometric
pattern of beds, with standard roses underplanted
with *Alchemilla mollis*, artemisia, catmint and rue,
with a weeping silver pear in each corner. Vertical
emphasis is given by a series of soaring cypresses and
the last terrace has a long, calm lily pond. Across a
lawn a beech hedge dips down in the middle to
reveal the peaceful countryside beyond.

THORP PERROW ARBORETUM
North Yorkshire

Bedale DL8 2PR
2m S of Bedale off B6268
Tel: 01677 425323

Owner: Sir John Ropner Bt

Open: Daily dawn–dusk.
85 acres

THIS WAS STARTED by Colonel Sir Leonard Ropner
in 1931 as a private plant collection. Old trees,
especially conifers planted in the 1840s, provided
both protection and a fine sombre background to the
more colourful ornamental trees. Only a complete list
would give a full idea of the range and depth of the
woody plants represented here; it is a vast collection,
with great rarities and excellent specimens of
individual trees. From the gardener's point of view
there are excellent collections of flowering shrubs –
well over 50 cultivars of the common lilac, for
example – and very large collections of the smaller
ornamental trees such as cherries and crab-apples.

WALLINGTON
Northumberland

*Illustration opposite: The
Portico House at
Wallington*

THE HOUSE at Wallington looks out over a ha-ha
and parkland, with calm lawns and good trees on
either side. This is thoroughly correct but the real
garden lies at some distance from the house, across
the road, hidden in woodland that sparkles with lakes
– the remains of an early 18th-century garden.
Overlooking one of the ponds there remains the

Cambo, Morpeth
NE61 4AR
12m W of Morpeth
Tel: 0167 074 283

Owner:
The National Trust

Open: Apr to Sept, daily
10.30–7; Oct, daily 10.30–6;
Nov to Mar, daily 10.30–4
(or dusk if earlier).
100 acres. House open

handsome Portico House, a classical gardener's cottage, and one of the lakes is named the China Pond and was in the 18th century ornamented with 'a very expensive Chinese building'. In the heart of these woods an immense and eccentrically shaped walled garden bursts into view – long and narrow, irregularly shaped and built on a slope. Along one side a high terrace is planted with a long white and silver border, and its retaining wall is crested with lead statues. From the gravelled terrace walk there are views over grassy paths sweeping between mixed borders in the lavishly planted gardens spread out like an intricate patchwork quilt below.

ZEPHYRWUDE IRISES

West Yorkshire

48 Blacker Lane,
Crigglestone,
Wakefield WF4 3EW
4m SW of Wakefield and
1m SW of M1 Jnbct 39 by
A636
Tel: 01924 252101 (to
11pm)

Open: For viewing only
May to Jun, daily 9–dusk.
1/2 acre

RICHARD BROOK sells only bearded irises, mainly dwarf and intermediate varieties, of which he has one of the best collections in the country. He offers for sale by mail order over 300 carefully selected varieties, very many of which may be bought in this country only from him. He produces a plain catalogue (one 1st-class stamp) that is full of detail; it has exceptionally good notes on the planting and cultivation of irises – an excellent guide to the subject. In addition to those for sale there are many more irises on trial, and these may be seen when the display garden is open. It is usually at its peak of floriferous perfection in the second half of May – but as each year will vary a little, it is best to telephone before a visit.

SCOTLAND

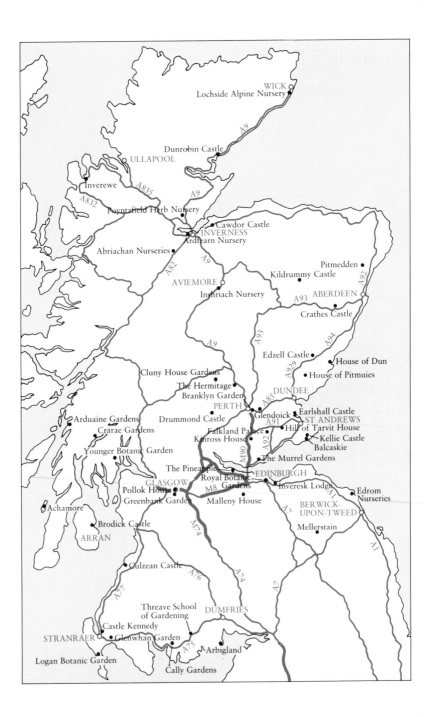

ABRIACHAN NURSERIES
Highland

Loch Ness Side IV3 6LA
9m SW of Inverness
on A82
Tel: 0146 386 232

Open: Daily 9–7

ON THE VERY BANKS of Loch Ness, Abriachan Nurseries has an enviable south-facing sloping site. Here are grown a good range of plants of which herbaceous perennials and alpines are the strongest suits. Among the herbaceous plants there are excellent aquilegias, with an emphasis on the species, a very good range of hardy geraniums and an immense collection of primulas. In the alpine department are gentians, helianthemums, lewisias, the smaller phlox and a large number of saxifrages. Well planted beds surround the nursery, and paths entice the visitor uphill to a further garden area. An attractive catalogue is produced (three 1st-class stamps) and plants are supplied by mail order.

ACHAMORE GARDENS
Strathclyde

Isle of Gigha PA41 7AD
Off west coast of Kintyre;
ferry from Tayinloan
Tel: 01583 505267/505254

Owner: Derek Holt

Open: Daily dawn–dusk.
50 acres

GIGHA IS a small island in the Inner Hebrides. Here Sir James Horlick came in 1944 and started to make a woodland garden, his new plantings protected by evergreens and old broad-leafed trees. Rhododendrons now reign supreme, constituting one of the best collections in Scotland, with the aristocratic, large-leafed species such as *R. falconeri* and *R. macabeanum* growing to exceptional size and beauty in this mild climate of high rainfall. Apart from the rhododendrons there is much else to admire, not least the rich underplanting of herbaceous and bulbous plants and the very wide range of ornamental trees and shrubs with excellent camellias, magnolias, mahonias, many shrub roses, viburnums and rare, tender trees such as the New Zealand Christmas tree, *Metrosideros umbellata*, and other very unusual things from the southern hemisphere. The wide range of plants growing in such a climate means that something interesting is happening in the garden on any day of the year.

ARBIGLAND
Dumfries and Galloway

Kirkbean DG2 8BQ
14m SW of Dumfries by
A710
Tel: 0138 788 283

Owner: Captain and Mrs
J.B. Blackett

Open: May to Sept, daily
except Mon (open Bank
Hol Mon) 2–6. 20 acres

SOME GARDENS provide the thrill of exploration and discovery, gradually unlocking their charms to the visitor. Arbigland, with its elegant mid-Georgian house handsomely framed in fine trees, does not at first reveal signs of any particular garden interest. But behind the house the Broad Walk plunges down through woodland towards the hidden sea. From this central axis enticing paths lead to Japan – a bosky water garden; to a hidden rose garden built on the site of old Arbigland Hall; and to glades planted with ornamental trees and shrubs that flourish in this climate of high rainfall and mild winters. There are wonderful rhododendrons such as the tender, giant *R. sino-grande*; beautiful old maples; eucryphias grown to great size; and very fine conifers giving shelter from the coastal winds. The cry of seagulls and the sound of unseen waves provide a curious further dimension to the delights of this rare garden.

ARDFEARN NURSERY
Highland

Bunchrew IV3 6RH
4m W of Inverness by A862
Tel: 01463 223607
Open: Daily, Mon to Sat
9–5, Sun 1–5

JAMES SUTHERLAND and his son Alasdair have established this relatively new nursery as one of the best sources of alpine plants. A courtyard of old cow byres makes an attractive setting for the plants, many of which are displayed in beautifully planted raised beds and troughs. Over 1,000 species and varieties are available, and there is a constant stream of new introductions – some from the wild by plant-hunting expeditions to which the nursery subscribes – and even expert alpinists will find unfamiliar things. For the non-alpinist there is a good range of herbaceous perennials and shrubs. An alpine catalogue is produced (four 2nd-class stamps) in September and orders are fulfilled by post between October and March. There remains plenty for visitors to buy – but rarities are snapped up quickly.

ARDUAINE GARDENS
Strathclyde

Kilmelford PA34 4XG
20m S of Oban by A816
Tel: 018522 287

Owner: The National
Trust for Scotland

Open: Daily 9.30–sunset.
18 acres

THE GARDEN AT ARDUAINE was started in 1897 by James Arthur Campbell, a tea planter, and friend of Osgood Mackenzie the maker of Inverewe. It is a splendid site which slopes gently down towards the shores of Loch Melfort. At first the garden is fairly open, with many smaller azaleas and rhododendrons planted in island beds, and enlivened by a stream and pools. There is rich underplanting of superb Himalayan poppies, groves of gunnera, hostas and trilliums. Paths lead up the hill and the visitor soon experiences the full Himalayan effect. Immense rhododendrons are at their most impressive against a backdrop of coniferous planting. The very rare *Rhododendron arboreum* ssp. *zeylanicum*, raised from seed brought from Ceylon in 1898, is now the largest specimen in Britain. It is essential to keep going to the top of the hill where a viewpoint gives an exquisite panorama of the calm waters of Loch Melfort below.

BALCASKIE GARDENS
Fife

nr Pittenweem KY10 2RD
2m W of Anstruther by
A917
Tel: 01333 311202/330585

Owner: Sir Ralph
Anstruther of that Ilk Bt

Open: By appointment for
groups only. 3 acres

THE CLASSICAL MANSION was built in the 1660s by
the architect and garden designer Sir William
Bruce, who laid out the garden in a series of great
terraces descending towards the Firth of Forth.
Beyond the final terrace an avenue continues an axis
centred on the house with, 13 miles away to the
south, the hump of the Bass Rock forming an
eye-catcher. William Sawrey Gilpin advised on the
garden in the early 19th century, and W.A. Nesfield
made new parterres in 1848. Today it is a marvellous
period piece with its spectacular views, old plantings
of cedars and many tender plants such as a datura,
hoherias, myrtles and sophoras flourishing in the
protection of the old terrace walls.

BRANKLYN GARDEN
Tayside

Dundee Road,
Perth PH2 7BB
On the eastern edge of
Perth by A85
Tel: 01738 25535

Owner: The National
Trust for Scotland

Open: Mar to 23 Oct, daily
9.30–sunset. 1 3/4 acres

JOHN AND DOROTHY Renton started to make this
garden in 1922. On a south-facing slope with acid
soil they built up a wonderful collection of
appropriate plants – smaller rhododendrons, maples,
daphnes, magnolias and many alpine plants such as
meconopsis, primulas and saxifrages. Narrow paths
of turf wind along the contours of the land, bringing
the visitor nose-to-nose with all kinds of
distinguished plants beautifully grown. The
combination of woody plants underplanted with
spring bulbs and later herbaceous plants is executed
with brilliant aplomb. There are good plants for sale,
especially alpines, at modest prices.

BRODICK CASTLE
Strathclyde

BRODICK CASTLE occupies a splendid position, well
protected from westerly winds and looking east
across the Firth of Clyde. The castle with its
castellated towers is partly medieval but rebuilt in the
early 17th century and in 1844. The present garden
dates from 1923 when the Duchess of Montrose

Isle of Arran KA27 8HY
2m from Brodick Ferry
Tel: 01770 2202

Owner: The National
Trust for Scotland

Open: Daily 9.30–sunset.
80 acres. Castle open

started an ambitious woodland garden with a
collection of rhododendrons, many of them recent
introductions from the great plant hunters, in
particular George Forrest; among them the
huge-leafed *R. macabeanum* and *R. sino-grande*.
From the castle paths wind downhill towards the
seashore, and in a shady place there is a fernery and
a delightful Bavarian summer house embellished with
rustic work and lovely inlaid panels of pinecones. In
spring the woodland, with meconopsis and primulas
flourishing about the ornamental shrubs, is a brilliant
sight. A walled garden, dated 1710, has been restored
with Victorian-style carpet-bedding, and mixed
borders on three sides prolong the flowering interest
to the very end of the summer.

CALLY GARDENS
Dumfries and Galloway

Gatehouse-of-Fleet,
Castle Douglas
DG7 2DJ
E of Gatehouse on
Dumfries Road
Tel: None

Open: Apr to Sept, Sat
and Sun 10–5.30

A 3-ACRE WALLED GARDEN is the setting for this
treasure trove of plants. Michael Wickenden has
around 3,000 different species and varieties, of which
about 500 are in stock at any one time. His sources
are exchanges with other collectors, seeds from
botanic gardens, and his own finds on
plant-collecting trips. The catalogue (three 1st-class
stamps) is therefore a moveable feast, but a feast
nonetheless, and you may always find something
unfamiliar and extremely desirable. He also sells
some beautiful terracotta pots from Crete. A mail
order service is provided but a visit is essential, to
inspect the stock, much of which is handsomely
displayed in deep, well filled borders against the walls.

CASTLE KENNEDY
Dumfries and Galloway

Rephad, Stranraer
DG9 8BX
5m E of Stranraer by A75
Tel: 01776 702024

Owner: The Earl and
Countess of Stair

Open: Easter to Sept,
daily 10–5

MANY GARDENS seem interesting enough at the time but later fade in the memory to a blur of borders. Castle Kennedy is a vast place, a piece of heroic landscaping with intimate moments, that would be hard to forget. The garden lies between two castles – 15th-century Castle Kennedy and the 19th-century Lochinch Castle which make splendid eye-catchers to vistas through woods and up hills. North of the old castle are the rare remains of the early 18th-century formal gardens – extraordinary terraces and turf mounds sculpted in the ground. Woodland is embellished with an immense collection of distinguished trees and shrubs: many very large conifers, exceptional rhododendrons and eucryphias which grow to vast size. By the old castle a walled garden has excellent borders and, to its south, an avenue of eucryphias and embothriums plummets down to the shores of the loch.

CAWDOR CASTLE
Highland

CAWDOR, with its outlook towers, crow-steps, drawbridge, dungeons and courtyards, is exactly what a Highland castle should be. To one side of the castle ancient stone walls enclose a flower garden; here a broad grass path runs down the middle between a pair of excellent herbaceous borders with old apple trees rising behind. A rose garden, its oval

Cawdor IV12 5RD
11m NE of Inverness by
A96 and B9090
Tel: 01667 404615

Owner: Countess Cawdor

Open: May to Sept,
daily 10–5.30

beds edged in lavender, is given height by soaring
columns of common and golden yew. There are some
beautiful pieces of formal planting: a long rose
tunnel, a peony walk and, in late summer, a virtuoso
pair of beds brimming with *Galtonia candicans* and
pale orange lilies. On one side of the walled garden a
gate leads to a wild woodland garden on the slopes
below, and, on the other side of the castle, a large
holly maze and herbaceous borders are laid out in the
old walled kitchen garden.

CLUNY HOUSE GARDENS
Tayside

by Aberfeldy PH15 2JT
3 1/2m NE of Aberfeldy.
From Aberfeldy go W to
bridge over Tay and turn
right at Weem–Strathtay
road
Tel: 01887 820795

Owner: Mr J. and Mrs W.
Mattingley

Open: Mar to Oct, daily
10–6

THIS PART of Perthshire, 600ft above the River Tay,
has an alpine character, and the name Cluny
means in Gaelic 'meadow place'. The house is a
pretty, early 19th-century mansion with gothic
touches, and the garden is disposed on the slopes
below it. Here are many shrubs and trees relishing
the acid soil and high rainfall, but its greatest glory is
the range of herbaceous plants. The National
Collection of Asiatic primulas, well over 100 species,
is kept here, and many of these exquisitely delicate
plants line the paths that thread their way through
the woods. Apart from these there are lovely
crocuses, fritillaries, gentians, spectacular examples of
the giant lily *Cardiocrinum giganteum*, narcissi and
trilliums. This is very much a garden to explore, and
gradually, as you get your eye in, you will discover
more and more – many of the best things are tucked
away in odd corners. A small nursery has some
admirable, and often rare, plants for sale.

CRARAE GARDENS
Strathclyde

CRARAE GARDENS have a marvellous site in a
precipitous glen on the north-west bank of Loch
Fyne. The garden was given to the trust that now
owns it by Sir Ilay Campbell Bt, whose grandparents
had come to live here in 1904. It was his father, Sir
George, a cousin of the great plant-hunter Reginald
Farrer, who had the greatest influence on the garden.
At the very centre of it lies the glen, a romantic

Crarae, by Inveraray
PA32 8YA
10m S of Inveraray by A83
Tel: 01546 86614

Owner: The Crarae Garden
Charitable Trust

Open: Summer, daily 9–6;
winter, daily dawn–dusk.
50 acres

wooded ravine, stuffed like a good plum pudding
with plenty of rich fruit: the great Asiatic flowering
shrubs – azaleas, camellias, magnolias and
rhododendrons – are well represented but there are
choice collections of many other groups: several
species of the southern beech, Nothofagus, excellent
rowans, some lovely examples of styrax and much
else. Paths girdle the glen which is occasionally
traversed by wooden bridges giving exquisite views of
the magnificent plants and rocky burn below. Crarae
is worth visiting in any season, and there is always
the piquant contrast of exotic introductions in a
natural Scottish setting of special beauty.

CRATHES CASTLE

Grampian

nr Banchory AB31 3QJ
3m E of Banchory and 15m
SW of Aberdeen by the
A93
Tel: 0133 044 525

Owner: The National
Trust for Scotland

Open: Daily 9.30–sunset.
92 acres. Castle open

ALTHOUGH THE BONES of this garden are old – the
superb yew hedges were planted in about 1700
and the romantic tower house dates from the 16th
century – the garden is almost entirely of the 20th
century. Sir James Burnett of Leys inherited the estate
in 1926, and he and his wife started a new garden
much influenced by the Hidcote tradition of lavish
plantings of often unusual plants within a firmly
disciplined plan of enclosed areas. The Burnetts made
a series of magnificent borders, some with single
colour schemes, and one of the finest herbaceous
borders in Britain. Gardeners from farther south will
note that herbaceous plants, because of the much
longer daylight hours at this northern latitude, grow

exceptionally well. All this is maintained impeccably, and visitors will learn much about practical gardening as well as enjoying an exceptionally beautiful garden.

CULZEAN CASTLE
Strathclyde

Maybole KA19 8LE
4m SW of Maybole and
12m S of Ayr by A719
Tel: 0165 56 274

Owner: The National
Trust for Scotland

Open: Daily 9.30–sunset.
120 acres. Castle open

ROBERT ADAM'S gothic castle – towered, turreted and irresistible – occupies a suitably dramatic site on the very brink of cliffs, looking north-west across the sea to the Isle of Arran. To the south of the castle, terraces with fine borders overlook a pool and fountain, and, in the walled former kitchen garden at some distance from the castle, are glasshouses and a peach-house . Fruit is still grown here and there are excellent borders of old roses and herbaceous perennials. The benign coastal climate allows many tender plants to flourish – cabbage palms, mimosa, myrtles, olearias and pittosporums. But the real excitement is the woodland with its marvellous 19th-century conifers and, in spring, immense numbers of bluebells, narcissi and snowdrops.

DRUMMOND CASTLE GARDENS
Tayside

Muthill, nr Crieff
PH7 4HZ
2m S of Crieff by A822
Tel: 01764 681257

Owner: Grimsthorpe and
Drummond Castle Trust

Open: May to Oct, daily
2–6. 15 acres

THE CASTLE is of different periods – chiefly a late medieval keep and a fine 17th-century house. Backed by old woodland, it sits at the top of a slope below which spreads one of the most extraordinary formal gardens in Britain. Inspired by 17th-century garden taste, it was laid out in the 1830s when garden makers looked to the past for inspiration. A huge rectangle is divided by paths forming a St Andrews cross, with a magnificent multi-facetted sundial at the centre, and within the areas formed by this division an intricate symmetrical pattern of ornament and planting is laid out. Box-edged parterres are filled with roses, bedding schemes or gravel, and height is given by a profusion of clipped cones of yew, Portugal laurels and purple Japanese maples. These varied ingredients are given order by the firm underlying pattern of the design, and the place has an exuberant and festive air.

DUNROBIN CASTLE GARDENS
Highland

Golspie KW10 6RR
1m N of Golspie by A9
Tel: 01408 633177/633268

Owner:
The Sutherland Trust

Open: 14–17 Apr, May to 15 Oct, Mon to Sat 10.30–5.30, Sun 1–5.30 (closes 4.30 14–17 Apr, May and Oct). Castle open

DUNROBIN is the ancient estate of the earls and dukes of Sutherland, and at its centre is a wonderful early 19th-century fantasy castle with a touch of the Loire and a dash of Bavaria, rising cheerfully on the slopes above the Dornoch Firth. Sir Charles Barry rebuilt the house in its present form, and almost certainly laid out the formal gardens on terraces that descend to the sea. The first terrace wall gives shelter to a long border with bold mixed plantings. Below this, a circular parterre in Barry's full-blown formal style has box-edged compartments planted with echiums, geraniums and potentillas, and clipped domes of yew rising above them.

EARLSHALL CASTLE
Fife

ROBERT LORIMER, who restored the castle and designed its garden at the turn of the century, wanted a 'garden that is in tune with the house'. Lorimer was an architect with a spritely interest in traditional styles of building and the gardens associated with them. Here at Earlshall he laid out between 1899 and 1901 a series of magical enclosures of stone walls and hedges of yew or holly at the foot of the romantic 16th-century towered and crow-stepped castle. These enclosures contain many different ingredients: a parade of giant yew topiary

Leuchars, by St Andrews
KY16 0DP
1m E of the village of
Leuchars by minor road
Tel: 01334 839205

Owner: The Baron and
Baroness of Earlshall

Open: By appointment only

shapes; a sunken garden with lavish borders surrounding a bowling green; a formal orchard; a kitchen garden in which old espaliered fruit trees and vegetables mingle with flowering borders; and a secret garden of alpines and herbs scattered among paving stones. Everywhere there is the beautiful craftsmanship that one associates with the Arts and Crafts movement – fine ironwork, masonry and witty decoration: a row of cheeky monkeys carved in stone frolic along the gable of an outhouse. Lorimer was a brilliant designer of gardens and houses, and this is one of his most delightful works.

EDROM NURSERIES

Borders

Coldingham, Eyemouth
TD14 5TZ
12m NW of
Berwick-upon-Tweed by
A1 and A1107
Tel: 01890 771386

Open: Mar to Sept, Mon
to Fri 10–4.30, Sat and Sun
2–5

THIS IS NOT a large nursery but it has a very carefully chosen list of excellent plants, some of which are rarely found for sale. The great speciality is alpines, but there are a few rhododendrons and various oddities that have caught the nursery's fancy (like *Zaluzianskya ovata* from Lesotho). In the alpine department there are androsaces, marvellous gentians, lewisias, several meconopsis and one of the most fastidiously selected collections of primulas you will find anywhere. The owners' woodland garden adjacent to the nursery is also open to visitors. The plants are described in valuable detail in the excellent catalogue from which mail orders are fulfilled. Occasional seasonal supplements, for example of spring bulbs, are also produced.

EDZELL CASTLE

Tayside

Edzell, nr Brechin
DD9 7TG
7m N of Brechin by A94
and B966
Tel: 01356 648631

Owner: Historic Scotland

Open: Apr to Sept, Mon to
Sat 9.30–6, Sun 2–6; Oct to
Mar, Mon to Sat 9.30–4,
Sun 2–4. 1 acre

IN THE EARLY 17th century the now ruined castle of the Lindsays had a fine ornamental garden, or 'pleasaunce', enclosed in walls carved with the Lindsay arms and all kinds of symbolic motifs representing virtues, the arts and planetary deities. To this rare and beautiful survival was added in the 1930s a box-edged parterre, of vaguely 17th-century character, and it is a pretty sight viewed from the upper rooms of the castle and corner towers of the garden walls.

FALKLAND PALACE

Fife

Falkland KY7 7BU
11m N of Kircaldy by A912
Tel: 01337 57397

Owner: The National
Trust for Scotland

Open: Apr to 23 Oct, Mon
to Sat 11–5.30, Sun 1–5.30.
7 acres. Palace open

HIDDEN BEHIND stone walls in the centre of Falkland, the gardens still have the feeling of a royal 'privy' garden. The 16th-century palace of the Kings of Scotland, formerly a Stewart hunting lodge, gives immense character to what is an almost entirely 20th-century garden. Large areas of lawn are broken by island beds lavishly planted with shrubs and ornamental trees – a scheme designed by Percy Cane in the 1950s. These beds are straight where they run along the perimeter walls but curved where they face each other across the lawn, giving a lively, sinuous walk between them. A giant mixed border almost 500 feet long faces west across the lawn to a blue and

white herbaceous border and a dazzling new border of delphiniums. At the southern extremity of the lawn, monumental yew hedges shelter a lily pond, and at an upper level there is a formal arrangement of yellow ('Allgold') and scarlet ('Frensham') roses – the heraldic colours of the Stewarts – underplanted with lavender and silver *Brachyglottis greyi* and given emphasis with pyramids of golden yew.

GLENDOICK GARDENS
Tayside

Glendoick, nr Perth
PH2 7NS
7m E of Perth by A90
Tel: 01738 8860260

Open: Garden Centre, daily
9–6 (5 in winter); garden,
Suns in May, 2–6

AT FIRST GLANCE this looks like just another a big garden centre, but although it carries a wide stock of plants and garden sundries, its overwhelming interest to gardeners lies in its outstanding collection of rhododendrons, one of the largest and most comprehensive stocks commercially available in Britain. Glendoick's proprietor, Peter Cox, is an authority on rhododendrons, of which he has introduced many new species and hybrids. In the private garden adjoining the nursery the great collection, started by Peter Cox's father, may be visited at flowering time, and it is well worth making a special visit to see it. But visitors to the garden centre throughout the year will find much to interest and tempt them. Glendoick runs a mail order service for rhododendrons only, and its catalogue (£1.50) is an amazing treasure trove. The garden holds National Collections of enkianthus and kalmia.

GLENWHAN GARDEN
Dumfries and Galloway

Dunragit, by Stranraer
DG9 8PH
7m E of Stanraer by A75
Tel: 01581400222

Owner: Mr and Mrs
William Knott

Open: Easter to Sept, daily
10–5. 12 acres

HIGH ABOVE the main road to Stranraer, Glenwhan Garden spreads out over a windy hilltop with marvellous views of Luce bay and the Mull of Galloway. Since 1979 the Knotts have made a very large, interesting and individual garden that is filled with good plants. At its heart is an extensive pool, divided by a grassy causeway and fed by a tumbling stream. The slopes above are lavishly planted with trees and shrubs. Several different habitats are provided by the lie of the land, and the wet, mild climate promotes luxuriant growth. There is no point in beginning to list plants – almost any gardener will find something unfamiliar here. But this is not just a plant collection for there are all sorts of well planned ornamental schemes and wonderful views over water and hills. A nursery attached to the garden sells a wide range of herbaceous and woody plants of the kind seen growing in the garden.

GREENBANK GARDEN
Strathclyde

Flenders Road, Clarkston,
Glasgow G76 8RB
6m S of city centre
Tel: 0141 639 3281

Owner: The National
Trust for Scotland

Open: Daily 9.30–sunset
(closed 25 and 26 Dec and
1 and 2 Jan). 16 acres

GREENBANK is a very decorative 18th-century house of stucco and stone with a pediment capped with urns. South of the house an old walled kitchen garden, of the same date as the house, is divided into several enclosures with, at its heart, a rondel of clipped yew hedges and a sundial. In other enclosed areas there is that beguiling mixture, so often found in Scottish gardens, of ornamental planting and fruit and vegetables. Old espaliered apple trees rise out of mixed borders which are particularly rich in shrub roses, and orderly vegetable beds spread beneath the walls. Beyond, a surrounding woodland garden threaded with shady walks provides further seclusion. Although the Glasgow suburbs press all around, Greenbank preserves a delicious rural character.

THE HERMITAGE
Tayside

16m N of Perth, 1m W of
Dunkeld, signposted off the
A9

Owner: The National
Trust for Scotland

Open: Daily, dawn–dusk.
37 acres

THERE IS NOT MUCH here for lovers of flower power, but for connoisseurs of dramatic atmosphere few places can beat it. A path winds along the banks of the fast-flowing River Braan through cool coniferous woods; all about are Douglas firs (*Pseudotsuga menziesii*), some of immense size. Soon a vast placid pool is seen, with a mossy stone bridge arching over a narrow ravine, and, on one side, the Hermitage itself. A tremendous roar increases as the visitor enters the building. An open

platform reveals the source of the noise – a spectacular broad waterfall whose waters lunge between great boulders lies below the Hermitage on its far side. The Hermitage was built in 1758 by the heir to the 2nd Duke of Atholl, who named it Ossian's Hall; deeper in the woods lies a rustic grotto, Ossian's Cave.

HILL OF TARVIT HOUSE
Fife

nr Cupar KY15 5PD
2 1/2m S of Cupar by A916
Tel: 01334 53127

Owner: The National
Trust for Scotland

Open: Daily 9.30–sunset.
10 acres. House open

ROBERT LORIMER rebuilt the 17th-century mansion at Hill of Tarvit in 1906, and gave it a new formal garden on the slopes below. Here an avenue of sentinel yews, blown sideways by the wind, links yew-hedged terraces which descend to the pastures below. A long border under the first terrace is planted with perennials and annuals and, specially planned for the blind and those with poor sight, has a section of aromatic plants with labels in braille. On one side a lead satyr pipes at the centre of a formal rose garden, and, by the house, a well-head is decorated with a beautiful wrought-iron overthrow designed by Lorimer. Above the house, sweeping along a high wall interrupted by a grand iron gate, a deep border has repeated plantings of kolkwitzia, purple cotinus, philadelphus and *Rosa moyesii* underplanted with anemones, campanulas, geraniums and potentillas. The Edwardian potting shed, heady with compost, is also on view.

HOUSE OF DUN
Tayside

Angus DD10 9LQ
4m NW of Montrose by
A935
Tel: 0167 481 264

Owner: The National
Trust for Scotland

Open: Daily, 10–sunset.
45 acres

ON GENTLY SLOPING LAND with views of Montrose Basin the House of Dun, a very pretty villa by William Adam, started in 1730, has an enviable position embowered in woodland on the northern slopes. To one side of the house Lady Augusta's Walk follows a tumbling burn through woodland and has an air of agreeable melancholy. In front of the house a long gravel walk, hedged in yew on one side, runs along a wall on which are trained many old varieties of apple and pear, some of which are old Scottish varieties for which these parts were particularly noted. At the end of the walk a restored formal rose garden is sheltered by old stone walls.

HOUSE OF PITMUIES
Tayside

TO THE FRONT of the early Georgian house a gentlemanly atmosphere prevails – fine parkland beyond a ha-ha is framed by old trees, including an exceptional sweet chestnut. The flower garden is behind the house where, in an old walled garden, lavishly planted borders are planned to maintain their flowering interest over a very long season. Colour

Guthrie, by Forfar
DD8 2SN
7m E of Forfar by A932
Tel: 01241 828245

Owner: Mrs Farquhar
Ogilvie

Open: Apr to Oct, daily
10–5. 25 acres

schemes are fastidiously chosen; a double border, for example, seen from the drawing-room window, has a scheme of blue, cream, white and yellow to go with the colours of the room. Throughout this part of the garden use is made of shrub roses, but abundant other planting, woody and herbaceous, extends the flowering period. The busy-ness of borders is alleviated by occasional simpler schemes – a collection of old delphinium cultivars, a stately walk of *Prunus serrula* with its glistening, peeling bark, hedges of coppiced *Prunus pissardii*, and an airy arch of clipped silver pear. Beyond the walled gardens a riverside walk leads past a castellated dovecote through old woodland of marvellous beeches and oaks underplanted with ornamental shrubs.

INSHRIACH NURSERY
Highland

Illustration: Lewisia cotyledon '*Sunset Strain*'

Aviemore PH22 1QS
4m SW of Aviemore by
B970
Tel: 01540 651 287

Open: Mon to Fri 9–5, Sat
9–4

AMONG ALPINE plant enthusiasts this is one of the best-known nurseries in Britain. It was founded before World War II by Jack Drake, a former colleague of Will Ingwersen's. A very wide range is carried, and rarities pop up all the time. A brief list, in addition to the exceptionally informative main catalogue, describes rare and unusual plants in short supply. The main list (£1.00), apart from plants for the rock garden, also includes plants suitable for wild and bog gardens. A mail order service is provided and, in addition to the two lists mentioned above, a special list of seeds of alpine plants is available every winter. The nursery lies in fine birch and juniper woodland, and parts have been beautifully arranged to show the plants in action.

INVERESK LODGE GARDEN
Lothian

nr Musselburgh EH21 6BQ
6m E of Edinburgh
Tel: 0131 665 7181

Owner: The National
Trust for Scotland

Open: Apr to Sept, Mon to
Fri 10–4.30, Sat and Sun
2–5; 2 Oct to Mar, Mon to
Fri 10–4.30, Sun 2–5.
13 acres

INVERESK is a charming village rich in distinguished houses of the 17th and 18th centuries. Inveresk Lodge belongs to the earlier period, and the unpretentious walled garden with its decorative central sundial complements it well. An excellent rose border was designed by Graham Stuart Thomas; a raised alpine bed is filled with ericaceous plants; good use is made of smaller flowering trees like cherries; and the garden is a model of appropriate and floriferous planting in a modest space.

INVEREWE
Highland

Poolewe IV22 2LQ
6m NE of Gairloch by
A832
Tel: 0144 586 200

Owner: National Trust for
Scotland

Open: Daily 9.30–sunset.
62 acres

FAMOUS GARDENS do not always live up to their reputations but it would be hard to imagine any gardener failing to be excited by Inverewe. In 1862 Osgood Mackenzie came to this very remote corner of the western Highlands – a windswept, bare rocky site at the very edge of a sea-loch. It was 15 years before he got much to grow, but once windbreaks began to be established, the high rainfall and balmy Gulf Stream Drift climate promoted luxuriant growth. Today it is a jungle of mature exotic trees and shrubs laced with winding walks, rising and falling, which give sudden glimpses of shimmering water through foliage. Spring is obviously the showiest season but flowering interest continues throughout the year; in any case, there is immense pleasure to be had at any time in admiring the exotic bark of giant eucalyptus, myrtles and rhododendrons, and much strange and beautiful foliage.

KELLIE CASTLE
Fife

nr Pittenweem KY10 2RF
3m NW of Pittenweem by B9171
Tel: 01333 8271

Owner: The National Trust for Scotland

Open: Daily 9.30–sunset.
1 1/3 acre. Castle open

O N SOUTH-FACING SLOPES to the sea, Kellie Castle, with its crow-steps and turrets, is the perfect Scottish castle. It dates from the 16th to the 17th century but the little walled garden nestling against the castle walls was laid out in 1880 by Robert Lorimer, a great architect in the Arts and Crafts tradition, who was then a boy of 16. Here at Kellie, his family home, he made an appropriately romantic garden of gravel paths, box-edged beds and rose arbours. His, too, is the gardener's house in the north-west corner with a jaunty carved stone bird on the ridge. Much replanting has recently been done, keeping to plants available when the garden was first laid out, and a recently appointed head gardener has introduced organic methods throughout the garden, which looks in the pink of good health.

KILDRUMMY CASTLE

Grampian

nr Alford AB33 8RA
10m from Alford by A944
Tel: 019755 71264/71203

Owner: Kildrummy Castle
Garden Trust

Open: Apr to Oct, daily
10–5

KILDRUMMY is in the tradition of romantic Victorian gardens where the most important ingredient is the response to the site. Here, in a glen through which flows the burn of Backden, sandstone was quarried in the late middle ages to make Kildrummy Castle whose ruins rise above the old silver firs and beeches that clothe the glen. The estate was bought in 1898 by Colonel James Ogston, a soap tycoon, who developed the garden, making excellent use of the old quarry, the linked pools of the burn, and its wooded banks. He commissioned a rock garden from the famous Yorkshire firm of Backhouse, and this today has a good collection of alpine plants, in particular heathers. A copy of a bridge in Aberdeen – the Brig o' Balgownie – spans the burn, and paths wind along its banks giving views of rhododendrons and other flowering shrubs.

KINROSS HOUSE

Tayside

Kinross KY13 7ET
In the centre of Kinross

Owner: Sir David
Montgomery

Open: May to Sept, daily
10–7. 4 acres

DECORATIVE GATE-PIERS mark the entrance to Kinross House, and an avenue of limes leads straight as an arrow to the house itself – long, low and with a distinct whiff of something French. It was designed in the 1680s by Sir William Bruce for his own use and he also designed the garden that goes with it. The entrance avenue forms a central axis which continues on the far side of the house to a gate with a beautifully carved stone surround through which are glimpsed the ruins of Loch Leven castle. Romantically sited on an island, this is where Mary Queen of Scots was imprisoned in 1567. The garden between the house and the loch descends in gentle terraces with grassy walks and herbaceous borders. A deep border runs along the far wall which is finely decorated with piers and heraldic animals.

LOCHSIDE ALPINE NURSERY
Highland

Illustration:
Campanula carpatica

Ulbster KW2 6AA
7m S of Wick by A9
Tel: 0195 585 320

Open: Mar to Oct, daily
10–6; also by appointment

TERRY AND JANE Clarke's nursery is almost certainly the northernmost supplier of good plants in Britain – and possibly in Europe; it is about the same latitude as Stockholm. It is so remote that the Clarkes offer its visitors bed and breakfast hospitality which is an arrangement that makes even more sense now that they no longer provide a mail order service. The list, brief but pithy, is full of good things at exceptionally reasonable prices: campanulas in variety, cyclamen, outstanding gentians, many phlox, a long list of primulas and wonderful saxifrages. It is never possible for them to list everything that is for sale at the nursery, so a visit is to be recommended.

LOGAN BOTANIC GARDEN
Dumfries and Galloway

PORT LOGAN lies in the middle of a narrow spit of land, the Mull of Galloway, which juts out into the sea in the extreme south-west of Scotland. A grove of Chusan palms immediately announces the

Port Logan, Stranraer
DG9 9ND
14m S of Stranraer by A716
Tel: 01776 860231

Owner: Royal Botanic
Garden Edinburgh

Open: 15 Mar to 31 Oct,
daily 10–6. 10 1/2 acres

character of this place – sub-tropical plants flourish
here and provide some rare and beautiful sights. The
garden was started by the McDouall family who
lived here for 800 years, and since 1969 it has been in
the care of the Royal Botanic Garden at Edinburgh.
But this is not just a botanic garden, for it is
beautifully laid out, particularly in the walled garden
which has fine terraces and well planned borders
under an avenue of cabbage palms (*Cordyline
australis*). The climate is exceptionally mild, and
several different habitats provide conditions for a
huge range of tender plants. A small selection of
plants is offered for sale.

MALLENY HOUSE GARDEN
Lothian

Balerno EH14 7AF
In Balerno, 7m SW of
Edinburgh by A70
Tel: 0131 449 2283

Owner: The National
Trust for Scotland

Open: Daily 9.30–dusk.
2 acres

THE HOUSE at Malleny is an ornamental riddle,
with features of the 17th and 18th centuries and
hints of something much older. Its tower and conical
roof on the garden side contribute much to the
atmosphere of the place. A walled enclosure divided
by a yew hedge lies at the heart of the garden, with a
splendid quartet of ancient yew trees clipped into the
shape of pointed mushrooms. Roses are everywhere,
and Malleny has a National Collection of
19th-century shrub roses which are mingled with
other plants in handsome mixed borders on two sides
of the walled garden. There is, in addition, a separate
collection of modern roses. In a corner of the garden

behind the greenhouse is displayed a collection of bonsai arranged by the Scottish Bonsai Society. Despite being in the suburbs of Edinburgh, Malleny has a rare quality – the remote and soothing atmosphere of an old-fashioned garden in the depths of the country.

MELLERSTAIN

Borders

nr Gordon TD3 6LG
7m NW of Kelso by A6089
Tel: 01573 410225

Owner: The Earl of Haddington

Open: Easter weekend 12.30–5; May, Jun and Sept, Wed, Thur and Sun 12.30–5; Jul and Aug, daily except Sat 12.30–5

THE GREAT EARLY 18TH-CENTURY house at Mellerstain, designed by William Adam and later added to by his son Robert, originally had a formal garden that was removed in the 18th-century landscape gardening craze. In the early 20th century, however, a version of it was reinstated by the architect Sir Reginald Blomfield. A row of clipped cones of yew runs across the back of the house, and terraces descend in stately progression – starting with a splendid double staircase – ornamented with parterres of modern roses, lavender, clipped shapes of box and generous lawns. All this provides a decorative foreground for the curvaceous lake set in woodland below – with idyllic views of the Cheviot Hills in the distance.

THE MURREL GARDENS
Fife

Aberdour KY3 0RN
1m N of Aberdour on B157

Owner: Mr John Milne

Open: Apr to Oct, Mon to
Fri 10–5. 7 1/2 acres

HIDDEN IN A FOLD of land facing south towards the
Firth of Forth, The Murrel has a rare site.
Designed in 1908 by Frank Deas in the Arts and
Crafts style the house and garden have been
excellently restored since 1984 by a new owner. To
one side of the house, on south-facing slopes, a
walled garden gives protection to many tender plants,
such as *Buddleja crispa* and *Pittosporum tobira,* rarely
seen out-of-doors in these parts. Below the walled
garden a formal sunken garden with rose beds leads
to a water garden overhung with old rhododendrons
and ornamental trees. A ravine-like wild garden, still
being replanted but already exquisitely beautiful,
leads back up the hill where, to the west of the
house, a large rock garden is laid out with scree beds.
An excellent range of plants, some unusual and
propagated in the garden, is for sale.

THE PINEAPPLE
Central

Dunmore, nr Stirling
On the Dunmore Estate
(enter by East Lodge) 6m
SE of Stirling by A905
Tel: 01628 825925

Owner: The National
Trust for Scotland

Open: Daily, 10–sunset

THE PINEAPPLE IS a wonderful survival, a
banqueting house of lovely eccentricity. Built in
1761 in the south-facing wall of the great kitchen
garden of Dunmore Castle, it was given to the
National Trust for Scotland who leased it to The
Landmark Trust who have beautifully restored it. No
architect is known but the craftsmanship is superb –
the pineapple leaves are exquisitely carved in stone,

and curvaceous gothic windows ornament the second floor. The former kitchen garden has been replanted as a formal orchard with rows of fruit-trees planted in turf. The garden walls were heated with water-pipes and the elegant urns flanking The Pineapple are chimneys. Visitors may not enter the interior; it may, however, be rented as a holiday house from The Landmark Trust (Shottesbrooke, Maidenhead, Berkshire SL6 3SW. Tel: 01628 825925).

PITMEDDEN
Grampian

nr Pitmedden, Ellon
AB4 0PD
14m N of Aberdeen by
A920 and B999
Tel: 01651 842352

Owner: The National
Trust for Scotland

Open: May to Sept, daily
10–5.30. 4 3/4 acres

IN THIS REMOTE CORNER of Aberdeenshire is one of the most beguiling gardens you could hope to see. There was a garden here in the 17th century but in 1818 the house was burnt down, the estate changed hands and the original garden disappeared. However, the garden walls, elegant pavilions, garden steps and gate-piers all survive, and in 1954 the National Trust planted immense formal parterres with a central avenue of clipped yew pyramids and a fountain. The parterres are edged in intricately shaped box hedges with compartments filled with coloured chippings and arrangements of annuals, blocks of a single colour, different every year. Looking down from the surrounding terraces with their beautiful gazebos, the effect is marvellous and unforgettable. Running along the south- and east-facing walls are a pair of excellent borders designed by Lady Burnett of Leys who lived nearby at Crathes Castle. Up above the walled garden a tunnel of old varieties of apples leads to a formal herb garden. Pitmedden has an enchanting atmosphere, unlike any other garden.

POLLOK HOUSE
Glasgow

ALTHOUGH NOW ENGULFED by urban sprawl the Pollok House estate, for 800 years the property of the Maxwell family, preserves the beautiful character of old parkland. The dashing grey stone house was built in the mid 18th century and has pretty formal gardens spreading out below the house. From box-edged parterres and a gravel walk a double

2060 Pollokshaws Road,
G43 1AT
3m SW of the city centre
by A77 and B762
Tel: 0141 632 0274

Owner: City of Glasgow
District Council

Open: Daily except
Christmas and New Year's
Day, Mon to Sat 10–5, Sun
11–5. 361 acres

staircase leads to a lower terrace with lovely views of
the parkland on the far side of the river. Elegant
ogee-roofed pavilions overlook the terrace, and to one
side a path leads up to grassy walk between beds
planted with Himalayan birches underplanted with
hostas and backed by rhododendrons. Nearby,
through the woods, is the famous Burrell Collection.

POYNTZFIELD HERB NURSERY
Highland

Poyntzfield, Black Isle, by
Dingwall IV7 8LX
5m W of Cromarty on
B9163
Tel: 01381 610352

Open: Mar to Oct, Mon to
Sat 1–5

THIS IS ONE of the northernmost nurseries in
Britain, which gives it a special interest. It
specialises in herbs and, over the years, a collection
of clones has been built up that are hardy in this
severe climate. Thus, anyone buying plants here may
be confident that they are acquiring pretty tough
customers. Over 300 varieties are stocked, all
organically grown, and there is a particularly
attractive collection of culinary and medicinal plants
native to Scotland. An excellent catalogue (three
1st-class stamps and s.a.e.) is produced, the only one
I know of that gives common names in Gaelic, where
they exist. A mail order service is provided.

ROYAL BOTANIC GARDEN
Edinburgh

ONE OF THE OLDEST botanic gardens in Britain, it
was founded in 1670 and moved to its present
site in 1820. Today, from the gardener's point of
view, it is an exciting place. There are areas of
specific habitats – an unforgettable rock garden, a

Inverleith Row, EH3 5LR
1m N of the centre of
Edinburgh
Tel: 0131 552 7171/0382

Owner: Trustees of the
Royal Botanic Garden
Edinburgh

Open: Nov to Feb, daily
10–4 (closed 25 Dec and 1
Jan); Mar to April, daily
10–6; May to August, daily
10–8; Sept to Oct, daily
10–6. 67 acres

woodland garden and a peat garden; collections of rhododendrons, heaths and alpines; several magnificent glasshouses; marvellous trees everywhere; and excellent demonstration gardens. These are ingredients found in dozens of botanic gardens, but at Edinburgh the beauty of the setting – high, undulating land with sweeping views of the city to the south and the hills beyond the Firth of Forth to the north – the exemplary standards of upkeep, and the liveliness of it all make it exceptional. Also, unlike other botanic gardens, Edinburgh seems to have the interests of the ordinary gardener close to heart. For its size it has a remarkably diverse collection, so one plant or another will be flowering at any time of the year. Places like this set standards from which all gardeners may learn.

THREAVE SCHOOL OF HORTICULTURE

Dumfries and Galloway

Stewartry, Castle Douglas
DG7 1RX
1m W of Castle Douglas by
A75
Tel: 01556 2575

Owner: The National
Trust for Scotland

Open: Daily 9.30–sunset.
65 acres

THE NATIONAL TRUST FOR SCOTLAND has its own school of horticulture here, and the gardens, largely created by the students since the school started in 1960, are of great interest. Mature woodland of beech, conifers and oak forms the background to a large collection of shrub roses, sweeping mixed borders, many dwarf heathers and conifers, peat and rock gardens, a collection of over 200 narcissi and a youthful arboretum that is already showing its paces. A walled kitchen garden has splendidly blowsy borders and superbly maintained glasshouses. Threave holds a National Collection of penstemons.

YOUNGER BOTANIC GARDEN BENMORE
Strathclyde

Illustration:
Rhododendron morii

Benmore, Dunoon
PA23 8QU
7m N of Dunoon by A815
Tel: 01369 6261

Owner: Trustees of the Royal Botanic Garden Edinburgh

Open: 15 Mar to 31 Oct, daily 10–6. 120 acres

THE YOUNGER BOTANIC GARDEN BENMORE is a country annexe of the Royal Botanic Garden in Edinburgh. Its history starts in the 1820s with the first plantings of conifers, and today, superb old specimens of Douglas firs, larch, Scots pine and a splendid avenue of Wellingtonias (*Sequioadendron giganteum*) make a wonderful background to later collections of ornamental shrubs and trees. The mild climate and very high rainfall promotes spectacular growth in conifers, and some of the specimens here are among the largest in the British Isles. The climate also makes this an ideal place for rhododendrons and today there are about 250 different species, 100 subspecies and forms and a further 300 hybrids and cultivars. There are excellent specimens, too, of deciduous trees such as southern beeches (*Nothofagus* species) and *Davidia involucrata*, and autumn is brilliant with the foliage of azaleas, cercidiphyllums, enkianthus and maples.

NORTHERN IRELAND

CASTLEWELLAN NATIONAL ARBORETUM

County Down

Castlewellan BT31 9BW
30m S of Belfast by A24
and minor roads
Tel: 013967 78664

Owner: Department of
Agriculture (Northern
Ireland)

Open: Daily, 10–dusk. 108
acres

THE ANNESLEY FAMILY started this great arboretum and plant collection in the 1870s. It benefits from a fine site, with a curving lake, in the foothills of the Mourne Mountains near the coast of southern County Down. The original 12 1/2-acre walled arboretum, now called the Annesley Garden, has fine borders, and exceptional flowering shrubs and ornamental trees, many of them rare and tender species from the southern hemisphere such as the evergreen *Carpodetus serratus* from New Zealand and *Pilgerodendron uviferum* from the Andes. North of the walled garden, azaleas, camellias and rhododendrons thrive under the canopy of beech and oak. An area of woodland by the lake is planted with deciduous trees chosen for especially brilliant autumn colouring. Throughout the arboretum there are outstanding specimens of trees, several of which date from the original 19th-century plantings, giving great character to the place.

MOUNT STEWART
County Down

Newtownards BT22 2AD
15m E of Belfast by A20
Tel: 012477 88387/88487

Owner:
The National Trust

Open: Mar, Sun 1–5; Apr
to Sept, daily 10.30–6; Oct,
Sat and Sun 10.30–6. 78
acres. House open

GOOD GARDENS often bear the stamp of one exceptional creator, but few so firmly as Mount Stewart. Edith, Marchioness of Londonderry came to Mount Stewart as a young wife in 1921 and plunged into the making of the garden; today, restored by the National Trust, it is still very much as she made it. The climate at Mount Stewart is exceptionally mild, with high humidity from the sea. This allows an exceptional range of tender plants: huge eucalyptus, an avenue of the New Zealand cabbage palm (*Cordyline australis*) and tender conifers such as *Cupressus cashmiriana*. To the west of the house a sunken garden is surrounded on three sides by a pergola with roses, vines and the rare *Billardiera longiflora* with brilliant blue berries in autumn. Beds in the centre are brilliant in spring with orange azaleas, and in summer with a rich mixture of herbaceous plants. Behind the house the Italian garden is a giant parterre in which the beds – edged with purple berberis or golden thuya – have artful but ebullient colour schemes: grey, white and blue to the west, and orange, yellow and scarlet to the east.

Curious statues of monkeys and other animals decorate the enclosing walls and a menagerie of creatures lurks in the undergrowth. On the far side of the house woodland, with many rhododendrons and ornamental trees, presses in on a lake whose banks are planted with drifts of iris, crocosmia or kniphofia. Mount Stewart is nothing if not bold, but Lady Londonderry's strong sense of design holds it brilliantly together and makes it one of the finest gardens in Britain.

ROWALLANE GARDEN
County Down

Illustration: Penstemon *'George Home'*

Saintfield, Ballynahinch
BT24 7LH
11m SE of Belfast by A7
Tel: 01238 510131

Owner:
The National Trust

Open: Apr to Oct daily 10.30–6 (weekends 2–6); Nov to Feb daily except Sat and Sun 10.30–5 (closed 25 and 26 Dec, 1 Jan). 20 acres

THE DRIVE leading up to Rowallane passes through dense woodland with mossy rocks pressing in on either side. The garden was chiefly made by Hugh Armytage Moore who came here in 1903. He was particularly interested in woody plants, especially rhododendrons which he planted in the handsomely undulating site in bold clumps and belts, as though they were the ingredients of a landscape garden. Many of his plantings were raised from seed collected by the great plant hunters of the early 20th century – such as Wilson, Forrest and Kingdon-Ward. The microclimate is very benign, as the many species from the southern hemisphere show – olearias from Australia, the orange-flowered *Desfontainea spinosa* from Chile and *Pseudowintera colorata*, with curiously variegated foliage, from New Zealand. The character of the garden is essentially informal but beds in the walled garden have excellent shrub roses and flowering shrubs, and the National Collection of large-flowered penstemons.

Arboreta
Batsford Arboretum
Bedgebury National
  Pinetum
Borde Hill
Castlewellan National
  Arboretum
Exbury Gardens
Hergest Croft
The Hillier Garden and
  Arboretum
Milton Lodge
Ness Garden
Royal Botanic Garden,
  Edinburgh
Royal Botanic Garden,
  Kew
Saling Hall
Savill Garden
Thorp Perrow
Valley Garden
Wakehurst Place
Westonbirt
Winkworth

Especially Good Borders
Anglesey Abbey
Arley Hall
Barnsley House
Benington Lordship
Blickling Hall
Clare College
Cottesbrooke Hall
Crathes Castle
Falkland Palace
Great Dixter
Hardwick Hall
Helmingham Hall
House of Pitmuies
Kellie Castle
Knightshayes Court
Manor House, Upton Grey
Mount Stewart
Newby Hall

Oxburgh Hall
Parham House
Powis Castle
The Priory
Tintinhull House
Upton House

Botanic Gardens
Cambridge Botanic Garden
Chelsea Physic Garden
Harlow Carr Botanical
  Gardens
Logan Botanic Garden
Oxford Botanic Garden
Royal Botanic Garden,
  Edinburgh
Royal Botanic Garden,
  Kew
Younger Botanic Garden
  Benmore

Demonstration Gardens
Capel Manor
Harlow Carr
Probus Gardens
Ryton Organic Gardens
Wisley Garden

Herb Gardens
Acorn Bank
Gunby Hall
Hardwick Hall
Herb and Heather Centre
Hexham Herbs
Holdenby Hall Gardens
Hollington Nurseries
Iden Croft
Lower Severalls Herb
  Nursery
Pitmedden
Poyntzfield Herb Nursery
Scotney Castle
Sissinghurst Castle

Japanese Gardens
Capel Manor
Compton Acres
Heale House
Kyoto Garden
Newstead Abbey
Saling Hall
Tatton Park

Kitchen Gardens
Barnsley House
Barrington Court
Calke Abbey
Clumber Park
Earlshall Castle
Edmondsham House
Felbrigg Hall
Greys Court
Gunby Hall
Harlow Carr
Helmingham Hall
Tintinhull House
Upton House
Wisley Garden

Landscape Gardens
Antony House
Audley End
Blenheim Palace
Boughton House Park
Bowood
Chatsworth
Claremont
Euston Hall
Farnborough Hall
Hackfall Wood
Hermitage, The
Mount Edgcumbe
Osterley Park
Painshill
Painswick Rococo Garden
Petworth
Rievaulx Terrace
Royal Botanic Garden,
  Kew
Scotney Castle
Sheffield Park
Sheringham Park
Shugborough
Stourhead
Stowe
Studley Royal
West Wycombe Park
Wolterton Park
Wrest Park
Wroxton Abbey

Rock Gardens
Cragside House
Killerton House
Luton Hoo
The Murrel

Newby Hall
Newstead Abbey
Royal Botanic Garden,
    Edinburgh
Sizergh Castle
Wisley Garden

Rose Gardens
Broughton Castle
Castle Howard
Cliveden
The Gardens of the Rose
Haddon Hall
Helmingham Hall
Hodges Barn
Hyde Hall
Kiftsgate Court
Malleny House
Mannington Hall
Mottisfont Abbey
Polesden Lacy
Queen Mary's Garden
Sissinghurst Castle
Sudeley Castle
Warwick Castle

Water and Bog Gardens
Buscot Park
Beth Chatto Gardens
Coleton Fishacre
Doctyn Mill
Forde Abbey
Hermitage, The
Hodnet Hall
Marwood Hill Gardens
Minterne
Sezincote
Stapeley Water Gardens
Westbury Court

Woodland Gardens
Abbotsbury Sub-tropical
    Gardens
Achamore
Antony Woodland Garden
Arbigland
Arduaine
Bodnant
Borde Hill
Brodick Castle
Caerhays Castle
The Dorothy Clive Garden
Castle Howard

Cotehele
Cragside House
Crarae Garden
Exbury Gardens
Fairhaven Garden Trust
Furzey Gardens
Glendurgan Garden
Gravetye Manor
Great Comp
Greencombe
Hare Hill
The High Beeches
Holker Hall
Howick Hall
Inverewe
Killerton House
Knightshayes Court
Leonardslee
Minterne
Muncaster Castle
Nymans
Penjerrick
Rowallane
Saltram House
Savill Garden
Scotney Castle
Sheffield Park
Thorp Perrow
Trebah
Trelissick
Trengwainton
Trewithen

N U R S E R I E S
F O R
S P E C I F I C
K I N D S   O F
P L A N T S

Alpines
Abriachan Nurseries
Ardfearn Nursery
Edrom Nursery
W. & L. Harley
Holden Clough Nursery
W.E.Th. Ingwersen
Inshriach Nursery
Reginald Kaye Ltd
Lochside Alpine Nursery
Norden Alpines
Old Court Nurseries
Padlock Croft
Perhill Nurseries
Potterton & Martin
Rookhope Nurseries

Aquatic Plants
Rowden Gardens
Stapeley Water Gardens
Washington Aquatic

Bulbs
Jacques Amand
Avon Bulbs
Broadleigh Gardens
Paradise Centre

Camellias
Burncoose & Southdown
Coghurst
Marwood Hill Garden
Starborough

Campanulas
Bernwode Plants
Padlock Croft
W. E. Th. Ingwersen
Reginald Kaye Ltd
Norden Alpines
Wootten's Plants

Citrus Fruit
Reads Nursery

Clematis
John Beach Ltd
Caddick's Clematis Nursery
Fisk's Clematis Nursery
Great Dixter
Treasures of Tenbury Ltd
Valley Clematis

Colchicums
Broadleigh Gardens
W.E.Th. Ingwersen

Conifers
Blooms of Bressingham
Hartshall Nursery Stock
Hilliers Nurseries Ltd
Kenwith Nursery

Cyclamen
Potterton & Martin
Tile Barn Nursery

Daylilies
Apple Court

Delphiniums
Blackmore & Langdon Ltd

Ferns
Fibrex Nurseries
J. & D. Marston
Spinners

Fruit Trees
Deacons Nursery
Hilliers Nurseries Ltd
Reads Nursery
Scott's Nurseries Ltd

Fuchsias
B. and H.M. Baker

Geraniums
Bernwode Plants
East Lambrook Manor
Glebe Cottage Plants
Rushfields of Ledbury

Grasses
Apple Court
Hoecroft Plants
Rushfields of Ledbury

Heathers
Herb and Heather Centre

Hellebores
Avon Bulbs
Blackthorn Nursery
Fibrex Nurseries Ltd
Reginald Kaye Ltd
Washfield Nursery

Herbaceous Perennials
Blackthorn Nursery
Blooms of Bressingham
Bosvigo House
Bernwode Plants
Cally Garden
Beth Chatto Garden
Church Hill Cottage
   Garden
East Lambrook Manor
Eastgrove Cottage Gardens
Foxgrove Plants
Gannocks Growers
Green Farm Plants
Hadspen Garden
The Hannays of Bath
W. & L. Harley
Merriments Nursery
Monksilver Nursery
Old Court Nurseries Ltd
Perhill Nurseries
Perry's Plants
Rowden Gardens
Rushfields of Ledbury
Stillingfleet Lodge Nursery
Washfield Nursery
Waterwheel Nursery
Wootten's Plants

Herbs
Herb and Heather Centre
Hollington Nurseries
Iden Croft
Lower Severalls Herb
   Nursery
Poyntzfield Herb Nursery

Hostas
Apple Court
Hadspen Garden
Park Green Nurseries

Irises
Zephyrwude Irises

Ivy
Fibrex Nurseries Ltd

Oaks
Mallet Court Nursery
Spinners

Magnolias
Burncoose & Southdown
   Nurseries
Pickards
Spinners
Starborough Nursery

Maples
Mallet Court Nursery
Spinners
Starborough Nursery

Pelargoniums
Fibrex Nurseries Ltd
Wootten's Plants

Peonies
Kelways Nurseries

Pinks
Bernwode Plants
Glebe Cottage Plants
Hayward's Carnations
W.E.Th. Ingwersen
Kingstone Cottages

Primulas
Abriachan Nurseries
Cluny House
Edrom Nurseries
Glebe Cottage
W.E.Th. Ingwersen
Inshriach Nursery
Monksilver Nursery
Norden Alpines
Paradise Centre
Rowden Gardens

Rhododendrons
Burncoose & Southdown
Glendoick Gardens
Lea Gardens
G. Reuthe

Spinners
Starborough
Wall Cottage Nursery

Roses
David Austin
Peter Beales Roses
Cottage Garden Roses
Cranborne Manor
R. Harkness & Co Ltd
Mattock's Roses
Perryhill Nurseries
Scott's Nurseries Ltd
Sudeley Castle

Shrubs
Burncoose & Southdown
Hillier's Nurseries Ltd
Hopley's Plants
Notcutt's Nurseries Ltd
Spinners
Waterwheel Nursery

Snowdrops
Avon Bulbs
Foxgrove Plants

Trees
Gardener's World
Hillier's Nurseries Ltd
Mallet Court Nursery
Notcutt's Nurseries Ltd
Pantiles Nurseries
Scott's Nurseries Ltd
Spinners

Tulips
Jacques Amand
Broadleigh Gardens
W.E.Th. Ingwersen

Violas and Pansies
Hazeldene
W.E.Th. Ingwersen
Norden Alpines

Water Lilies
Stapeley Water Gardens

GARDENS BY FAMOUS DESIGNERS

Sir Reginald Blomfield
(1856–1942)
Godinton Park
Mellerstain
Sulgrave Manor

Charles Bridgeman
(d.1738)
Claremont
Rousham Hall
Stowe
Wimpole Hall
Wolterton Park

Lancelot 'Capability' Brown
(1716–83)
Audley End
Berrington Hall
Blenheim Palace
Bowood
Castle Ashby
Chatsworth
Chilham Castle
Claremont
Clumber Park
Euston Hall
Harewood House
Ickworth
Luton Hoo
Petworth
Sheffield Park
Stowe
Warwick Castle
Wimpole Hall
Wrest Park

Percy Cane
(1881–1976)
Dartington Hall
Falkland Palace

Dame Sylvia Crowe
(1901–)
Cottesbrooke Hall
Oxford Botanic Garden

William Emes
(1730–1803)
Belton House
Erddig

Beatrix Farrand
(1872–1959)
Dartington Hall

W.S. Gilpin
(1762–1843)
Audley End
Balcaskie
Scotney Castle

Gertrude Jekyll
(1843–1932)
Broughton Castle
Hatchlands
Hestercombe
Knebworth
Lindisfarne Castle
Manor House, Upton Grey

Sir Geoffrey Jellicoe
(1900–)
Cliveden
Cottesbrooke Hall
Mottisfont Abbey

William Kent
(1685–1748)
Claremont
Euston Hall
Rousham House
Stowe

George London
(d. 1714)
Chatsworth
Petworth

Sir Robert Lorimer
(1864–1929)
Earlshall
Hill of Tarvit
Kellie Castle

Sir Edwin Lutyens
(1869–1944)
Castle Drogo
Hestercombe
Knebworth

Thomas Mawson
(1861–1933)
Wightwick Manor

W.A. Nesfield
(1793–1881)
Balcaskie
Castle Howard
Harewood House

Russell Page
(1906–85)
Leeds Castle
Port Lympne

Sir Joseph Paxton
(1803–65)
Chatsworth
Somerleyton
Tatton Park

Harold Peto
(1854–1933)
Buscot Park
Heale House
Iford Manor
West Dean Gardens

Humphry Repton
(1752–1818)
Antony House
Bowood
Hatchlands
Plas Newydd
Sheffield Park
Sheringham Park
Tatton Park
Wimpole Hall

William Robinson
(1838–1935)
Emmetts
Gravetye Manor
Killerton House
Nymans

Lanning Roper
(1912–83)
Claverton Manor
Penshurst Place
Scotney Castle

Edward Weir Schultz
(1860–1951)
Cottesbrooke Hall

F. Inigo Thomas
(1866–1950)
Athelhampton

Sir John Vanbrugh
(1644–1726)
Blenheim Palace
Claremont
Seaton Delaval Hall

Sir Clough Williams-Ellis
(1883-1978)
Plas Brodanw
Portmeirion

NATIONAL COLLECTIONS OF PLANTS

The National Council for the Protection of Plants and Gardens (NCCPG) has set up National Collections of groups of plants, most of which are not normally accessible to the public. However, some of particular interest to gardeners are held by gardens and nurseries described in this book. They are as follows:

agapanthus
    Bicton College
astilbes
    Holehird Gardens
    Marwood Hill Gardens
begonias
    Stapeley Water Gardens
bromeliads
    Stapeley Water Gardens
campanulas
    Padlock Croft
cistus
    Chelsea Physic Garden
clematis
    Burford House Gardens
colchicums
    Felbrigg Hall
crab-apples
    Hyde Hall
crocosmias
    Lanhydrock
daylilies
    Antony House
dodecatheon
    Manor House,
    Walton-in-Gordano
dogwoods
    Newby Hall
    Rosemoor
enkianthus
    Glendoick Gardens

euphorbias
Abbey Dore Court
Bernwode Plants
ferns (polystichum)
Greencombe
Holehird Gardens
figs
Reads Nursery
foxgloves
Botanic Nursery
geraniums
East Lambrook Manor
galeobdolon
Monksilver Nursery
hollies
Valley Garden
hydrangeas
Holehird Gardens
ivy
Erddig
junipers
Bedgebury National
Pinetum
kalmia
Glendoick Gardens
kniphofias
Barton Manor
lamium
Monksilver Nursery
lavender
Norfolk Lavender
Lawson cypresses
Bedgebury National
Pinetum
magnolias
Valley Garden
mahonias
Valley Garden
maples (excluding Acer
japonicum *cultivars)*
Hergest Croft
(Acer japonicum)
Westonbirt Arboretum
Michaelmas daisies
Old Court Nurseries
mints
Iden Croft
oaks
The Hillier Garden and
Arboretum
origanums
Iden Croft

*penstemons (large-
flowered)*
Rowallane
periwinkles
Monksilver Nursery
pieris
The High Beeches
Valley Garden
pinks (old garden varieties)
Kingstone Cottages
pittosporum
Bicton College
polygonums
Rowden Gardens
primulas (Asiatic species)
Cluny House
pulmonarias
Stillingfleet Lodge
Nurseries
rhododendrons (species)
Valley Garden
roses (pre 1900)
Mottisfont Abbey
roses (19th-century)
Malleny House
santolina
Herb and Heather Centre
*saxifrages (European
species)*
Cambridge Botanic
Gardens
saxifrages (porophyllum)
Waterperry Gardens
stewartias
The High Beeches
styracaceae
Holker Hall
thymes
Hexham Herbs
viburnums
Hyde Hall
willows (lowland species)
Westonbirt Arboretum

INDEX